Zoë Wilson's innovative study shows how recent critiques of mainstream development thinking have been incorporated into the programs and policies of UN agencies as what she terms "minor discourses," in a complex and uneasy jumble with the older, "top-down" models that continue to be dominant. Her analysis of the political effects of this apparent confusion sheds a powerful light on how and why UN interventions based on what seem to be the most benevolent principles so often turn out badly for the "ordinary people" they are intended to benefit.

James Ferguson

STUDIES IN
INTERNATIONAL RELATIONS

Edited by
Charles MacDonald
Florida International University

A ROUTLEDGE SERIES

STUDIES IN INTERNATIONAL RELATIONS
CHARLES MacDONALD, *General Editor*

THE UNITED NATIONS AND DEMOCRACY IN AFRICA
Labyrinths of Legitimacy

Zoë Wilson

Routledge
New York & London

Routledge
Taylor & Francis Group
270 Madison Ave,
New York NY 10016

Routledge
Taylor & Francis Group
2 Park Square,
Milton Park, Abingdon,
Oxon, OX14 4RN

© 2006 by Taylor & Francis Group, LLC
Routledge is an imprint of Taylor & Francis Group, an Informa business

Transferred to Digital Printing 2009

International Standard Book Number-10: 0-415-97987-0 (Hardcover)
International Standard Book Number-13: 978-0-415-97987-0 (Hardcover)

Library of Congress Cataloging-in-Publication Data

Wilson, Zoë.
    The United Nations and democracy in Africa : labyrinths of legitimacy / Zoe Wilson.
        p. cm. -- (Studies in international relations)
    Includes bibliographical references and index.
    ISBN 0-415-97987-0 (alk. paper)
    1. United Nations. 2. Peace-building--Africa. 3. Democracy--Africa. I. Title.
    II. Series: Studies in international relations (Routledge (Firm))

JZ4984.5.W55 2006
341.23'6--dc22   2006009431

ISBN10: 0-415-97987-0 (hbk)
ISBN10: 0-415-80579-1 (pbk)

ISBN13: 978-0-415-97987-0 (hbk)
ISBN13: 978-0-415-80579-7 (pbk)

Visit the Taylor & Francis Web site at
http://www.taylorandfrancis.com

and the Routledge Web site at
http://www.routledge-ny.com

Contents

List of Abbreviations

AGF-V—Fifth African Governance Forum

BACONGO—Botswana Council of Non-governmental Organisations

CCF—Common Country Framework

CCM—Chama Cha Mapinduzi

ESRF—Economic and Social Research Foundation

GDH—Good Governance, Democracy and Human Rights

GoA—Government of Angola

GoB—Government of Botswana

GRN—Government of the Republic of Namibia

HDR—Human Development Report

HRC—Human Rights Committee

HRW—Human Rights Watch

ICISS—International Commission on Intervention and State Sovereignty

IDEA—Institute for Democracy and Electoral Assistance

IDG—International Development Goals

IDP—Internally Displaced Person

IMF—International Monetary Fund

IO—International Organization

IPPR—Institute for Public Policy Research

MISA—Media Institute for Southern Africa

MONUA—United Nations Mission of Observers in Angola

MPLA—Movimento Popular da Libertação de Angola

NBC—Namibian Broadcasting Company

NGO—Non-governmental Organization

NSHR—Namibian Society for Human Rights

OCHA—Office for the Coordination of Humanitarian Affairs

ODI—Overseas Development Institute

PRA—Participatory Research Assessment

PSO—Peace Support Operation

REDET—Research and Education for Democracy in Tanzania

SWAPO—South West African Peoples Party

UN—United Nations

UNAVEM—United Nations Verification Mission in Angola

UNDAF—United Nations Development Assistance Framework

UNDP—United Nations Development Programme

UNESCO—United Nations Education, Scientific and Cultural Organisation

UNHCR—United Nations High Commission for Refugees

UNICEF—United Nations Children's Fund

UNITA—União Nacional para a Independência Total de Angola

UNOA—United Nations Observer Mission in Angola

USAID—United States Agency for International Development

WTO—World Trade Organisation

Preface and Acknowledgments

The book represents the complex working out of a number of troublesome questions and deep uneasy feelings. These chafed with persistence as I wrestled with my own commonsensical and deeply schooled beliefs about the intrinsic goodness of values such as human rights and democracy. The wellspring for this uneasiness came from my experience as a woman and an increasingly acute consciousness of the deep structures of knowledge that appropriate the category of woman towards consequence-laden social practices. Could these not also be used to appropriate such widely venerated concepts as human rights and democracy? And if so, by whom and to what end?

This is not a book about gender, but about rendering visible the structuring practices of taken-for-granted assumptions about the *way things are*. Specifically, the book challenges the idea of stateness, states themselves, and the state system—of which the United Nations is a key constituent. Social organization, to be sure, can be empowering, *but it isn't necessarily so*. States can be empowering (even if never wholly or straightforwardly), *but they are not necessarily so*. They can also limit freedom, constrain opportunities and render difficult certain ways of being and knowing. They are also the champions of myths upon which tangled clots of petty powers are based; inheritors of the self-perpetuating character of power, imagineers of democracy and rights as *necessarily* bounded by themselves.

After years in and out of Africa, assumptions about states as the underlying self-justified fundamental unit of development, and artful imagining that democracy and human rights were straightforward—and not easily rendered as the play things of politics— started to stand out as the core ordering assumption of a certain kind of failed development practice. Yet, unmooring the idea of the African state from its anchors in inevitability, nature, order, and civilization, proved a twisted and tangled descent into sticky webs of meaning and power. Paradigmatic of our era is that we cling to an artful amnesia. States are not now, nor have they ever been, the basic fundamental unit of security—at least not for women—however much they have evolved (paternalistic) mechanisms to mitigate the structural violence they, themselves, structure. To lay unearned and undiffused power on their alters like sacrifice to false Gods, is to do profound injustice to the future, and those who will inherit it.

It is worth noting, that when this project began, I was an ardent supporter of the United Nations and its attendant instruments and ideologies, only to find that its institutionalized and bureaucratized practices contained troubling streams from an ignoble past, which sought conformity over individuality, stultifying hierarchy over freedom, and myriad contrivances to mold people to be like one another and amenable to a well defined end-point; an end-point that those already skeptical of the influence of the centre on the distribution of shares (of goods, services, opportunities, networks, etc.) might find good reason to resist seeing replicated at a global scale in the global future. A global future which may (perhaps necessarily) see existing clots of state power transcended by the aggregate of human co-operation that (some) states have, to some extent, facilitated by way of an awkward dance between survival imperatives in service of hierarchy and conformity and competitive forces for innovation, change and renewal. By the end of this project, I found myself, as sometime optimistic imagineer of the future, concerned about what the UN will transfer into *Africa*'s future, and to whom? Up to now, states here, to be sure, have survived by way of the United Nations and the geopolitical machinations of the state system. Impudent individuality, manifold diversity and human flourishing have not fared as well.

This book is based on my Ph.D. dissertation entitled *Wishful thinking, Wilful blindness and Artful Amnesia: The United Nations and democracy, good governance and human rights in Africa*. The work's new title is more than simply concise. Throughout the book, I often refer to UN *stories* about development, about our common future, in maze-like terms, as messy and obfuscating. But UN stories are not unruly. They are not designed to confound or mislead. Rather they lead us into a construction of knowledge where certain things are commonsensical and others unthinkable; to a place where the underlying power relations could not be other. Their design is to conceal the labyrinth's core to which the stories inevitably lead.

I would like to thank friends, family and colleagues who supported me throughout the Ph.D. including Erin Baines, Mike Barnaby, Cameron Ells, Wanda Severns, Larry Swatuk, Susan Thomson, Thyme, Parsley and Bram, my mom and dad—Toni and Jim—as well as ultimate Frisbee and Shambhala meditation. I would also like to thank my committee members Jane Parpart and Timothy Shaw, and especially my supervisor David Black and external Peter Vale, whose intellectual provocativeness stealthily disbursed the long decay ideas sustaining the writing process. I would also like to thank the Social Sciences and Humanities Research Council, the Department of National Defence and the UNHCR in Angola for generous support. Turning this work into a book would not have been possible without the generous support of the Centre for Civil Society and School of Development Studies at the University of KwaZulu Natal, the Institute for Research and Innovation at York University (Canada) and new friends and colleagues in Durban and around the world, including Victoria Ayer, Vanessa Black, Chris Buckley, Mary Galvin, Mike Valente and David Wheeler. For support and encouragement in the final stages, I also thank my editor Benjamin Holtzman and series editor Charles MacDonald. Finally, I would like to thank my dear friend and counterpoint, Patrick Bond. Things arise together. Although a work such as this depends on a complex network of knowledge, there are nevertheless a few people whose work I acknowledge as having been particularly evocative, starting of course those who agreed to participate in interviews and otherwise share their valuable knowledge. Among the intellectuals without whom this work would not have been possible include, most notably, Foucault, but also classic radical liberal theorists, such as John Stewart Mill, Mary Wollstonecraft, de Tocqueville, and George Orwell. More recently, I'd like to acknowledge a great debt to James Ferguson, Rita Abramhamsen, Chris Brown, Cynthia Enloe, Spike Peterson, Ronnie Lipshutz, Catherine MacKinnon, Mahmood Mamdani, Michael Mann, Susan Marks, Rosemary Righter, James Scott, Charles Tilly, Martin van Creveld, Ernesto Laclau, among others from various intellectual traditions.

Rich are these thinkers, and among many other influences and inspirations, they continue to provide valuable insights into the deep structure of what we think and why, across new disciplinary and thematic divides. Yet, interesting times challenge us to cross boundaries, scan emergent scapes and refresh our eyes. New sources of inspiration range from Neil Gaiman and Hakim Bey to Vilfred Pareto and Mitchell Waldrop, from Saksia Sassen and Richard Florida to South Park and Wired, from Veronica Strang and Zoe Souflis to Ecosanres and Mozambican informal water sector entrepreneurs, from Jared Diamond and Manuel Castells to the Tao Te Ching and Octavia Butler. New projects revolve around what I perceive to be a groundswell of mindshift away from mainstream ways of conceptualizing solutions to the global water and sanitation crisis, towards alternative, sustainable and closed-loop solutions. The future continues to hang in the balance of the politics of change, and I look forward to exploring the issues further along with the transdisciplinary gang at the Pollution Research Group (UKZN) in the coming years.

Chapter One
Power, Politics and Doomed Projects

Africa makes us look stupid. It makes us realize that our assumptions require re-examination and reformulation.

—Robert H. Bates, Political Science, Harvard[1]

INTRODUCTION

If there is such thing as the development zeitgeist, it is characterized today by three concepts: good governance, democracy and human rights. This agenda is set, in large part, by the United Nations, the author of such core development texts as the *Human Development Report* (HDR) and the *Millennium Declaration*. In 2002, the HDR was subtitled: *Deepening Democracy in a Fragmented World*, and referred to one or all of these concepts on every page. Yet, even a cursory look at the history of successive UN development decades makes it hard to escape the observation that the turn to "good governance" does not crown a list of stunning development achievements.

Current fashion in the explanations of development failure has turned towards the lack of coordination, as Gerald Ruggie notes (2003[2]):

> The most distinctive institutional feature of the UN system . . . is that it is not designed as a matrix at all but as a set of deeply rooted columns connected only by thin and tenuous rows. Nothing that has transpired since 1945 has transformed that fundamental reality.

Pinpointing development failure as the result of *institutional* messiness seems to suggest that not only is the intellectual content more or less on target, that, indeed, it is more coherent than its institutional delivery mechanism. Ruggie goes on, in fact, to argue that the effects of the UN's institutional fragmentation are partially mitigated by a new conceptual clarity (*ibid*.):

> At the conceptual level, the consensus encompasses the centrality of governance, the rule of law, education, and health to economic success . . . and the need for governments and international institutions alike to forge partnerships with the private sector and a wide range of civil society actors.

In the forthcoming chapters, however, I synthesize the evidence that led to the conclusion that this "conceptual clarity" is a hall of mirrors—at least with respect to the political and institutional dimensions of the good governance agenda. If a reader vigilantly interrogates key documents such as the *Human Development Reports* for the meaning and the means of such good things as democracy or human rights, what she will find is a sum of fragments, reflecting tensions between structured totalities and splintered pieces, and which obfuscate rather than illuminate what is really at stake: the restoration of the failing state/state-system project. Sandwiched within a seemingly incoherent combination of fragmentary concepts is a "dominant discourse" of state-system restoration that is both internally consistent and deeply troubling—especially for its anti-democratic tendencies.

That is, Ruggie emphasizes the transformative potential of what he calls the Millennium Development Goals Network—"an unprecedented . . . unifying substantive framework"—and argues that we have entered something of a new era in country coordination with the *Common Country Assessments* and *Frameworks*. In related analyzes, both Thomas Weiss (2000: 9) and Jean-Phillippe Thérien (1999: 14) applaud evolutions in the UNDP's governance agenda, arguing respectively that it represents an "incipient heresy against conventional wisdom" and that "the UN paradigm seeks to take into account all the complexity of the social environment in which poverty exists." The forgoing evidence, however, suggests that if such a unifying conceptual framework exists, its most substantive elements are the privileging of UN expertise, top-down intervention, the enhancement of state power and the bracketing and disciplining of the ways in which people can participate in conversations about where their communities are going and how they want to get there. This argument is based on "thick description"[3] of the UN's good governance agenda—whose political features are typically championed by the United Nations Development Progamme.[4] The chapters that follow trace policy and praxis from global documents such as the *Human Development Reports* (2000; 2002), to African regional documents such as the *Causes of Conflict* Report to the Secretary General (UN General Assembly 1998), to country documents and interviews with UN country staff in four country case studies: Angola, Botswana, Namibia and Tanzania.

Thick description fleshes out a picture of a governance agenda that everywhere exhibits a commitment to top-down intervention at the level of a hypothetical apolitical and uncomplicated developmental state, but also everywhere and simultaneously, makes concessions to more progressive, even radical, democratic thinking. These two streams, top-down and state centric on the one hand, and democratic and participatory on the other, often conflict and contradict each other. The effect is a conceptual framework comprising an awkward and often incoherent sum of multiple ways of understanding the problematic of democracy and development.

The chapters that follow also explore the functions *served* by the ambiguities and contradictions embeded within the governance agenda. Does ambiguity and internal contradiction have a role to play in creating the illusion that the latest UN development thinking has answered its worst critics and redressed its most harmful tendencies? In mixing, even jumbling together, top-down and bottom up epistemologies, the governance agenda is all things to all people. It has something to please everyone, from state elites of various persuasions to grassroots movements clamouring for greater voice. In this light, evidence indicates that caution should also be exercised when assuming that the governance agenda will be more successful and participatory and less harmful than the social engineering experiments of the development past. The evidence considered later suggests a propensity for the governance agenda to create space for elitist and authoritarian regimes to flourish, while providing few substantive opportunities for the people whose poverty has become the *raison d'être* of the humanitarian machinery to participate in conversations—and political processes—concerning where their communities are going and how various members want to get there.

Before saying any more about this, however, I would first like to explain why and under what circumstances my research question, methodology and geographical focus changed substantively over the course of the research process. Research evolved from interrogating why UN Peace Support Operations in Angola floundered throughout the nineties, to a multi-levelled analysis tracing UN aspirations to foster good governance, democracy and human rights in four African countries. In the process of this explanation, I hope to illuminate, and to some extent justify, why the research project was ultimately transformed from a theory-*bounded* to a theory-*building* exercise. That is, in the interests of theory *building*, the remaining chapters describe the progressive integration and analysis of multiple perspectives on and dimensions of the governance agenda in an effort to see how the greatest number of pieces of the puzzle fit, or do not fit, together in heretofor unimagined ways.

BACK TO THE DRAWING BOARD

This book began its life as a doctoral thesis proposal promising to explore the reasons why United Nations (UN) Peace Support Operations (PSO), succeed, fail, or simply muddle along of their own accord. Primary field research was to be conducted in Angola in April 2001, where I hoped to observe intervening variables that could account for why things did not always work out as planned. Research proposed to identify where specific changes could be made at the operational level to help PSO strategies perform better.[5] To do this, I first identified the independent (causal) variable as the plan or strategy—in this case evidenced in the *2001 Consolidated Inter-Agency Appeal* and April 2000 *Report of the Secretary General on the United Nations Office in Angola*, and the UNHCR Angola statement, *Internally Displaced Persons (IDP) Protection Programme: July 2000-December 2001*. These documents were also situated within global UN strategies, including the *Millennium Declaration* and *Human Development Reports*, of which they were seen to be a part. In other words, from these documents I assumed I would be able to determine what it was that the UN wanted to accomplish in Angola. My thematic emphasis was on human rights promotion, often used interchangeably with the term "protection." Thus, the plans and strategies floated within the global emphasis on "human rights, democracy and good governance" and "protecting the vulnerable" (Secretary General 2001a: 4).

This simple plan was foiled mainly because it proved difficult to isolate a clear set of causal variables related to human rights. All official documents, including "*Road Maps*," tended to be relatively vague and inexact. For example, characteristically, the *Implementation Strategy* found in the *IDP Protection Programme: July 2000-December 2001* (3) asserted:

> The [IDP] programme uses community-based implementation. The capacity of communities to respond to urgent needs of IDPs is strengthened through public awareness campaigns, capacity building, and affirmative action to entrench an understanding of IDP rights, and to use that understanding as a launching pad for the recognition of other fundamental human rights.

It sounds good at first blush, although ideas such as "affirmative action to entrench an understanding of IDP rights" were never fully explained or linked to concrete practices. Nevertheless, I remained wedded to a realist notion of language as neutral and purely descriptive. I expected, then, that the content of the practices would become clear with first hand experience and observation in the field. Practices that were not described in the strategic plans would certainly speak for themselves on the ground.

Fieldwork began in 2001, with an internship at the UN High Commission for Refugees (UNHCR) in Luanda, and later the northern province of Uige. What I observed subverted my hope of identifying a clear and coherent set of strategies and practices. Both the documents and practices expressed multiple and often conflicting approaches to understanding and actualizing human rights objectives. Further, these processes were rendered yet more complex by operating procedures that were, *inter alia*, simultaneously decentralized, fragmented, and crosscut by rigid (and often resented) hierarchies emanating from New York and Geneva head offices. For example, Provincial Working Group meetings (including UN and non-governmental organization partners) in Luanda highlighted the interplay between the various institutional cultures and individual perspectives on a wide range of issues. In a particularly interesting exchange, the representative for the Office of the Coordinator for Humanitarian Affairs (OCHA)—the the newly appointed coordination agency—admitted that despite the fact that OCHA was not yet competent in many key areas,[6] approaches had shifted wildly over the past year, from consensus-based to "OCHA led and dominated." The *latest* approach was to be characterized by a focus on big picture constructive engagement, guided by Mary Anderson's "do no harm" guidelines for humanitarian intervention. According to OCHA, the new thinking was that protection goals were best viewed through the prism of medium- to long-term constructive engagement.

A number of paradoxes were in play. Concerns about accountability, corruption, authoritarian tendencies and human rights abuses were expressed, yet seemed to co-exist more or less discretely from fresh commitment to the idea of constructive engagement designed to enhance the capacity of an idealized "developmental" state (such as the dispersal of funds, the creation of bureaucratic capacity, etc). At the same time, the emphasis on "do no harm" corresponded to a scaling back of expectations for and commitment to the humanitarian mission and broader social engagement. OCHA's representative cautioned everyone at the meeting not to expect much in terms of enhanced standards of living for Angolans over the next couple of years. This was not a sentiment equally well accepted by all parties present. One UN official commented later: "It looks like the whole mission is just a sacrifice at the altar of Big Oil."

The meetings also revealed that actors and agencies competed over differing interpretations of fundamental ideals such as human rights, good governance and gender equity. This was expressed as a plethora of struggles between contending visions and aspirations—between and among both individuals and units and other partner and sub-contracted actors. For example, the UNHCR remained committed to the creation of a quasi-political body called the Human Rights Committee[7] in the northern province of Uige where it played the Lead Agency role. In OCHA- and UNDP- led provinces, both the project and the underlying principles had been set aside. The OCHA representative commented: [8]

> Initially OCHA was supportive of the parallel structure approach [to institution building], but now we are going in a different direction, towards engagement. We may be going in a horribly wrong direction. If so, we will move back to the first strategy. We are still relying on informal chats with key informants at various organizations, however.

The UNHCR, nevertheless, remained committed to the Human Rights Committee (HRC) and its grass roots methodology, and clearly viewed the HRC's principles and potential differently than some of the other members of the group.

Similar differences of opinion and perspective characterized other key issues. For example, the representative for the International Committee for the Red Cross (ICRC) expressed concern that attempts to insert gender equity requirements were, at times, insensitive to cultural norms and counter productive. The representative for YME, an international stream rehabilitation NGO, however, felt that international acquiescence to so-called cultural norms was often unstudied and unwarranted. He insisted that gender parity for village water committees had been unproblematic. He also argued that all-female water committees were more difficult to organize. But given women's sole responsibility for provisioning water to the household, it was unclear what underlay this dynamic, and if, indeed, it was deeply entrenched. Similarly, World Health Organization staff reported that the practice of yielding to male household demands for food dispersals had resulted in much of the food aid bypassing women and children, ultimately ending up at the informal markets of Luanda. At the least it was clear that the mental models upon the decision to disperse food to the household unit (and correspondingly models of household headship) were deeply flawed. Overall, interviews and meetings attended in both Luanda and Uige revealed a high degree of variance in the interpretation of gender equity norms and how they might best be applied, and to what end.

In short, the ubiquity of political negotiation over contending principles and projects, and the manifest lack of a coherent set of strategies or programmes that unified the Mission (or parts thereof), conflicted with both the conceptual clarity celebrated by Ruggie and others, and indeed, the clear plan or strategy I expected to see, based on a review of the general and Angola-specific UN documents. My interest was, however, piqued by several new observations:

1) The co-existence, in the discourse, of contending guiding principles and differing interpretations of key concepts such as human rights.

2) The extent to which the implementation context, among other things, comprised struggles and conflicts over the meaning of key UN concepts such as human rights and women's equality.

3) That there were likely important political implications attached to both what the discourses expressed coherently (i.e. the idea of the state) as well as the multiple, co-extant and competing minor discourses.[9] (This final observation would become the central theme of subsequent research.)

At this point, initial assumptions in favor of the UN—assumptions which took the organization and its strategies as more or less unproblematic—became untenable. Rather, it would be important to start from the observation that the UN is a complex social organization, partly defined by inexplicit discourses and political conflict among its staff and partner implementers.

A Project Re-conceptualized

Theory-bounded approaches typically decide up front what kind of data is relevant. The main criticism of such approaches is that methodology and epistemology can pre-determine findings.

> [A]*t a certain moment*, therefore, it is necessary to turn against method, or at least to treat it without any founding privilege as one of the voices of plurality—as a *view*, a spectacle mounted in the text, the text which all in all, is the only "true" result of any research [emphasis in original] (Barthes in Der Derian 1989: 7).

That is, in order to fully explore the implications of my Angolan observations, it would be necessary to take into account a richer more textured body of data, diverse enough to capture as many dimensions of complexity as possible; and only then would it be appropriate to assess how well the data maps onto existing theories and methodologies (see Chapter Nine), and/or to what extent theory-building is necessary for explaining how the pieces of the puzzle fit or fail to fit together. To this end, I sought to generate a body of data comprising multiple perspectives and angles, while simultaneously attempting to "fit" increasing layers of complexity into "something that works cognitively, that fits together and handles new cases" (Schwandt 1994: 127). An approach that takes all phenomena as potentially relevant requires a fundamentally different ontology. The project needed to be re-conceptualized. At this point, it became a theory-building project rooted in the principles of grounded theory (Strauss and Corbin 1994).

The Selection of Additional Country Cases

Mark Duffield (2001) recently described post-cold war peacekeeping as the merging of security and development. This is consistent with the Peace Support Operations continuum, which envisions overlapping processes of high-level diplomatic engagement (peacemaking), troop deployment (peacekeeping) and peace-building (reconstruction and development). Further, these defy linearity, just as conflicts defy easy and lasting resolutions. As a result, peacekeeping, overall, includes everything from election monitoring to children's sports programmes, troop deployment and local and national institution building. Duffield's work on the congruence between PSO thinking and development thinking more generally provides a convenient entry point for expanding a research project on PSOs to the development field more generally.

A decision to broaden the geographical base was taken in order to generate a sense of whether and how the dynamics observed in Angola (a highly chaotic context) were also evident across the region and in other (most different) contexts. Botswana, Namibia and Tanzania were selected on the basis of their very different histories, institutional, social and civil contexts, and contemporary levels of economic development, democratic experience, and human rights records. That is, in terms of Africa south of the Sahara these countries differ significantly in almost every contemporary and historical indicator across the social, political and economic fields.[10] They are "most different" cases (see Berg-Schlosser and Kerting 2003), albeit within a common regional context. As such, they could provide the opportunity to explore which features of the governance agenda tended to re-appear, independent of context.

However, these differences do not constitute the core subject matter here. Nor are they the subject of academic debate. At any rate, this is not a work of political historiography. Instead, the additional country cases serve as mirrors into which we look to see if the observations for the Angolan case are reflected meaningfully—with density. We look for patterns and for evidence of generalizability. The Angolan case study remains the central case study, rendering to the reader the most detail at multiple scales (see Chapter Eight; see also Wilson 2003; 2004; 2005 a/b), but the other cases supplement and deepen this analysis in important ways (see especially Chapter Seven).

Expanding Themes: From Human Rights to the Governance Agenda

As noted earlier, due to the breadth of peacekeeping activities, I initially decided to cut in thematically at human rights. In reformulating research parameters, the field of inquiry was broadened to good governance, human rights and democracy (GDH), focusing on the political and institutional rather than economic aspects, which are the purview of International Financial Institutions, such as the World Bank and IMF.[11] A key reason for adding democracy and governance to human rights is that the UN texts treat them as bundled and triangulated. Thus in some respects, an analysis of one without the other, in the context of UN thought, would be necessarily incomplete. The key reason for focusing on political and institutional dimensions is that human rights, democracy and good governance have widely divergent meanings and ontologies attached to them. In the World Bank lexicon, good governance, for example, tends to refer to standards of macro-economic efficiency. Outside the conceptual framework of market economics, governance tends to get linked to values associated with democracy, participation, etc. Thus, it is explicitly the latter with which we are concerned here.

Shifting from the UNHCR to UNDP

Despite having begun fieldwork at the UNHCR, subsequent fieldwork focused on the UNDP. The main reason for this is that both globally and in Africa, the UNDP has taken up the mantle of political reform. In May 2002, at the fifth African Governance Forum in Maputo, the UNDP emerged as the Lead Agency for governance in Africa, while the 2002 UNDP *Human Development Report*, entitled *Deepening Democracy in a Fragmented World*, unveiled a new set of objective and subjective governance indicators, distinguishing the UNDP as self-styled global arbiter. The focus on the UNDP also had the added appeal of looking beyond the World Bank and International Monetary Fund as familiar magnets of academic critique (Abrahamsen 2001; Bond 2005; 2006; Thérien 1999: Wilson 1999), while providing an opportunity to explore some of the dynamics of an agency whose centrality within the UN system appears to be once again on the rise (see Righter 1995).[12]

Additionally, the activities of the UNHCR in Uige were, in many respects, consistent with the thrust of UNDP activities in other provinces and more generally across Africa. For reasons related to the scope of the Internally Displaced Person (IDP) programme in Uige and its proximity to the Democratic Republic of the Congo, the UNHCR had been mandated Lead Agency there, while the UNDP had taken the Lead in the other provinces. As such, the HCR undertook a political institution-building role, working directly with the local and national government representatives, helping to guide, shape and extend government administration. The Human Rights Committee projects, for example, which will be discussed in-depth in Chapter Eight, were pursued by the UNHCR in the northern province of Uige, but by the UNDP in some of Angola's others provinces. In principle, the HRCs across Angola were meant to be substantively and structurally similar (Republic of Angola 2001).

Thus, since research was mainly concerned with the governance agenda and political institution building specifically, the shift to the UNDP made sense. It was not, however, necessary—under these peculiar circumstances—to treat the UNHCR research as fundamentally different from the later UNDP research, despite the clear differences between the roles, mandates and profiles of the two agencies.

From Local to Global

The experience in Angola highlighted the need to situate country-level activities within the global agendas, of which they form part. As such, I sought to situate the additional country case studies within both the regional and global governance agendas. In order to do this, I embarked on a series of deconstructions of the governance agenda at the global, regional and country levels, including both broad principled documents such as the *Human Development Reports,* and specific implementation *Road Maps.* It was then possible to make an assessment of how well the concepts and strategies flowed and fit together, and to what extent their journey from global to country, and ultimately country- and local-level expressions, were marked by fragmentation and contradiction. In other words, it was then possible to begin assessing whether the phenomena witnessed in Angola had some resonance in UN praxis more broadly.

Re-Focusing the Lens on the UN

In effect, the changes in the research project described above were indicative of a more important shift in focus. Whereas the initial project hoped to identify a set of prescriptions that would help PSOs achieve success more consistently, the new project sought to examine a slice (the governance slice) of the UN itself, in the hopes that re-focusing the lens on the UN as complex social environment would yield important insights for understanding the deeper structuring (or entangling) properties of the governance agenda. There was a fairly robust literature to turn to for support in making such a move (see also Chapter Nine).

International relations scholars have tended to focus on the geographical reasons for international organization (IO) dysfunction (non-rational behaviour), arguing that the UN does not, in fact, constitute an independent actor and therefore cannot be judged as though it were. The UN is often understood as a mere trade association of states (Mandelbaum 1994), "a response to problems of incomplete information, transaction costs, and other barriers to Pareto efficiency and welfare improvement for their members" (Barnett and Finnemore 2001: 403). In that various states clearly have different capacities to operationalize their ambitions and clearly hold positions of relative inequality in the UN, most notably in bodies such as the Security Council, the World Trade Organization, the World Bank and the International Monetary Fund, UN dysfunction is taken to be the manifest expression of international politics—power politics between states. From this vantage, the UN is bound to be frustrated in its pursuit of more lofty goals. International politics, however, was not the politics observed operating in the field. It may have direct implications for understanding the ambiguity of discourses designed to appease a large, diverse and highly unequal audience (Cox and Jacobsen 1973; van Ufford 1988), but in the field what I observed was the *operationalization* of multiple and conflicting perspectives on the discourses—various actors competing to operationalize their own *personal* understanding of human rights, gender equality, etc. This operationalization seemed, moreover, to have a dynamic effect all its own, independent of the other macro political processes of which they are part, and within which they are no doubt intertwined.

Theorists of IO proper (see Cox and Jacobsen 1973; Donini 1996; Ruggie and Kratchowil 2001; Weiss and Pitt (eds.) 1986) lament the conflation of international relations or international politics with the study of international organizations and bureaucracies. As Gallarotti (2001: 366) argues: "recent scholarship has increasingly strayed from the study of IO as distinct from World Politics" while ignoring "organizational failure" that contributes to" systematic failures" (367), and indeed the "trail of international events that leads to the graveyard of misguided social engineering" (377). There are, however, a plethora of studies supporting the importance of studying IO behaviour itself. For example, in 1989, Graham Hancock's

critically acclaimed *Lords of Poverty* exposed the UN's propensity to facilitate the "freewheeling lifestyles, power, prestige, and corruption of the multibillion dollar aid business." In 1986 John Galtung (17) predicted: "That
[the UN] will be used as instrument by the new international class of professionals in promulgating their class interests . . . seems likely." In 1995,
Rosemary Righter documented the UN's contemporary history of "intermi-
nable conferences, mountainous paperwork, and laundry lists of activities
that had only the most tenuous connection with the outside world" (15, see
also 155–184). Righter (177) also found the condition of the "international
civil service" to be deeply dysfunctional:

> So ingrained are slipshod UN management, political pressures on
> appointments, and the neglect of career development that the whole
> concept of international civil service now needs to be rethought . . .
> [T]here are hundreds of civil servants with the commitment and capac-
> ity to innovate trapped within the UN's prematurely fossilized bureau-
> cratic carapace. Any extended contact with the UN secretariats reveals
> widespread anxiety about the debilitating impact of managerial drift,
> ill-conceived programs, inter-agency rivalries, and inept or corrupt per-
> sonnel policies.

More recently, Kofi Annan joined the fray. In response to a critical report
launched in the shadow of the World Summit on Sustainable Development,
Annan admitted that "there are too many meetings and summits and that
reform is necessary at the world body meant to be the bedrock of multilateralism."[13]

There is, however, fairly persuasive evidence that the state of progress on this reform agenda is in a perpetual state of crisis—from peacekeeping (Jett 1999; Shawcross 2000) to macro-economic support (Abrahamsen
2001; Danaher 1994), to democracy (Gills *et al.* 1993; Snyder 2000), and a
fairly robust school of thought has settled on the evidence that many of the
reasons are endogenous. [14] Critics argue that the goals and accomplishments
of the vast number of meetings and conferences are only dimly intelligible,
while the practices and paper trails are, at best, labyrinthine and at worst
evidence that the UN bureaucracy exists mainly to serve the lifestyle interests of its extremely well paid staff. To be sure, it is difficult to disentangle
meaning from words, or substantive action from the production of reports.
For example, the *Human Development Reports* come with the caveat:
"The analysis and policy recommendations of this Report do not necessarily reflect the views of the United Nations Development Programme, its
Executive Board or its Member States." Whereas the introduction by Mark

Malloch Brown (UNDP 2002) asserts that: "Nevertheless, I believe that its central message is very relevant for the broader work of the UNDP and its partners." It remains, however, not to the credit of the UN as an organization that it simultaneously asserts and denies ownership of, perhaps, the most widely recognized UN publication in the world. It is in this light that a shift in emphasis was made towards an interrogation of the endogenous logic of the UN governance agenda.

RESEARCH STRATEGY, METHODS, INTERPRETATION AND DENSITY

The research methods chosen were not done so for the researcher to judge competing versions of the world as true or false, but to explore the political implications of the way the (constructed) world of the governance agenda "hangs together" (Ruggie 1999). If my observations in Angola were any indication, this "world" would have to be pieced together from multiple perspectives playing out at multiple levels. To this end, the goal was to solicit perspectives from multiple sources and levels, attempting then to "fit" accumulating nuances into "something that works cognitively, that fits together and handles new cases" (Schwandt 1994: 127). To this end, the deconstruction of UN texts was supplemented by perspectives of UN staff, members of civil society[15] and local academics, as well as contextualization within the broader literatures. The information gathered was then viewed through "interpretavist" lenses derived from a hybrid of grounded, constructivist, post-positivist and critical theories.

Discourse as Political Practice

As noted earlier, UN reports and documents were initially assumed to say something real about strategy and praxis. That is, it was expected that they would correlate to an independent/causal variable—the plan or strategy that, when operating well, *caused* development, democracy, human rights, etc., in some relatively straightforward way. This assumption began to unravel almost immediately in the field, with documents revealing multiple interpretations, and observation revealing social conflict over both the meaning and means of key objectives. That is, there was no easily delineated plan or strategy. What if, however, these features of discourse systematically produced, not development, but some other political effect (Foucault 1977)? In this spirit, I decided to take a second pass at UN stated objectives, undertaking an in-depth examination of key UN documents, from global to regional to the country level. Approaching some of these documents anew, I adopted a critical approach, structured around the methodological principles of content and discourse analysis. This reflected a conscious and epistemological shift towards understanding the UN texts as discourses and as practices in their own right with their own political effects and consequences in the real world. "[F]or example, the way people are positioned into roles through discursive practices, the way certain peoples, knowledge is disqualified or is not taken seriously in contrast to authorized knowledge, and so on" (Mills 1997: 149). In the terms of this project, key aspects of the GDH discourse tended to treat African *states* and their *governments* with great optimism, despite widespread evidence to the contrary; a propensity for corruption, predation and human rights abuses, engendering cycles of conflict, resistance, violent competition and disaffection.

Thus, it was assumed that these discourses were not simply epiphenomena of external political processes that constituted and constrained them, but rather political practices in their own right, with consequences in the real world. To compose African states as they are not, and then to set the wheels of a giant dysfunctional international bureaucracy turning to this tune, would certainly have consequences. As Thomas Weiss (2000: 795) noted recently, "ideas and concepts, both good and bad, have an impact on international public policy." That is, discourses do things; they have effects. Or, more strongly, "[p]eople use discourse to *do* things—to offer blame, to make excuses, to present themselves in a positive light, etc." (Gill 2001: 175).

> The notion of construction emphasizes the fact that we deal with the world in terms of constructions, not in a somehow "direct" or unmediated way; in a very real sense, texts of various kinds construct our world . . . The notion of construction, then, clearly marks a break with traditional "realist" models of language, in which it is taken to be a transparent medium, a relatively straightforward path to "real" beliefs or events, or a reflection of the way things really are (*ibid.*).

An important addition, however, is that texts (i.e. policy documents) do not simply embody one discourse, paradigm or take on the world. Rather, they often embody multiple discourses, which reflect "the complexity of the workings of power relations within society as a whole" (Fairclough in Mills 1997: 153). The corollary to this is that multiple possible meanings in any given discourse give rise to ever multiplying ways in which these core meanings can be read and understood; and by extension, effects are multiplied and dizzyingly complex. Yet, this complexity must also be read as having effects in the real world.

Thus, the "realist notion of language as simply a neutral means of reflecting or describing the world" was rejected and replaced with the assumption that discourses are central to understanding outcomes, that they effect outcomes, and perhaps most importantly, that these outcomes can be multifarious and complex, reflecting discourses that are multifarious and complex. From this perspective it is important not only to look at how accounts relate to the world, but also what functions they perform— whether original to intent or not. As a methodology, discourse analysis does not seek answers about the reality that is assumed to lie beyond the text, but about the functions of the text itself.

The Selection of Documents

The selection of documents was challenging for a number of reasons, which were illuminating for the way this challenge resonated with critiques of the UN organization more generally, specifically critiques that point to mountains of paper with labyrinthine links to each other. Specifically, democratic governance is asserted as a primary responsibility of the UNDP, but no statement was easily found clarifying how this relates to other key UN agencies that also claim to be centrally concerned with democratic governance. Nor is it clear what relationship democratic governance has to other concepts to which it is variously expressed as inextricably linked, such as human rights. As noted earlier, the UNDP even simultaneously asserts and denies ownership of the *Human Development Reports*. It does claim, however, to be guided by a commitment to the *Millennium Declaration* (and to some extent the New Economic Partnership for African Development—see related endnote), which is inextricably linked to key General Assembly statements and Reports of the Secretary General. These must stand in for the UNDP's regional approach in Africa,[16] as it has no specific regional agenda for Africa, but binds itself to cooperation with the UN system as a whole, and other stakeholders through the *Second Regional Cooperation Framework for Africa* (ECA 2001:2) under the intellectual auspices of the Regional and sub-regional summit conferences and their attendant prescriptions (now possibly superseded by NEPAD, although this is less than clear). The same is true for country documents. The UNDP does not have specific country documents prepared for every country in which it operates, but rather, variously, falls under the *Common Country Frameworks* (CCF) or *Development Assistant Frameworks* (UNDAF) or, as is the case with Botswana, appears to operate under both the CCF and the UNDP specific document the *Country Programme*.[17] The relationship between these or other documents, and the effect of several simultaneous programme documents at any level is not stated or apparent.

In this light, at the global level, I opted to review the 2002 UNDP *Human Development Report*, as well as selected chapters from the 2000 *Report* devoted to Human Rights. More generally, I also included the much-vaunted *Millennium Declaration* and its related *Road Map*, which includes a final section on *The Special Needs of Africa*. At the regional level, I included what appears to have been a near complete sample of the key Reports of the Secretary General, submitted to the Security Council, General Assembly and other components of the United Nations, with special emphasis on Africa: *The New Agenda for Development of Africa in the 1990s* (1993), and its related *Road Map* (1996), *The Causes of Conflict and the Promotion of Durable Peace and Sustainable Development in Africa* (1998), and its related implementation document (1999), as well as the African Governance *Concept Paper* drafted for the *Fifth African Governance Forum* (AGF-V) in Maputo (2002). Country documents varied in terms of availability. Typically, I opted for the most recent, at the time of my fieldwork, and/or the most comprehensive document. The result was a focus on the *Angolan Inter-Agency Appeal* (2001). In Botswana and Tanzania I relied upon the *Common Country Assessments* (1997: 2001) and for Namibia, the UN *Development Assistance Framework* (2001).

Deconstruction

As noted earlier, the plan was then to deconstruct and code the UN governance texts found at the global, regional and country levels. Martin Bauer (2002) suggests that after a number of passes have been made over the material, one can adopt a "coding frame." Because the de-constructed text is not meant to yield the hidden true meaning of a text, but rather to illuminate different meanings, functions and competing discourses within the text, the coding frame draws on principles of inquiry (see below on the "principles of rhetoric") designed to illuminate along a set of dimensions. With respect to the UN discourses, I wanted to ascertain and illuminate the extent to which my observations in the field were mirrored in and among the various levels of discourse—including the implementation *Road Maps*. Thus, I aimed to identify whether:

1) there were multiple and/or conflicting accounts of the meaning and means of the key concepts (good governance, democracy and human rights);

2) the extent to which specific definitions/discourses tended to dominate; and

3) whether the implicit ideas about the way the world works that flowed from the UN's "prescriptive descriptives" could be illuminated to better advantage.[18]

According to Bauer, the principles of rhetoric serve as a useful guide for generating a coding frame. "Deliberative rhetoric is found in the arena of policy, where debate centers on the best possible course of future action" (Leach 2002: 213). A rhetorical analysis signals the treatment of the text as a device for persuasion. In this light, the key words (GDH) were coded in terms of the "logos" "pathos" and "ethos" of the arguments/statements they appear within. "Logos refers to drawing conclusions from premises and observations; pathos stirs the emotions of the audience; and ethos refers to the display of the speaker's own authority to claim to frame" (Bauer 2002: 142). Within a text, various syntactical and semantic procedures also appear. Syntactical procedures include the frequency and ordering of words, their bundling with other words, and other stylistic features. In the texts studied, such syntactical features included the inter-changeability of "good governance" with "democratic governance" and the bundling of "human rights" with "rule of law." Semantic procedures include appeals to common sense and *universally* valid knowledge, the invocation of binaries, inexplicitness, evaluative descriptions, prescriptive descriptions, and admissions and concessions designed to inoculate the arguments against their most powerful shortcomings, etc. Finally, the identified features of the texts are used to reconstruct a knowledge through better illumination of the relationships between textual elements. According to Martin Bauer:

> People use language to represent the world as knowledge and self-knowledge. To reconstruct this knowledge, CA [content analysis] may have to go beyond the classification of text units and work towards networking the units of analysis to represent knowledge not only by elements, but also their relationships (*ibid*.: 135).

Throughout the book, I refer to this reconstructed knowledge map as the dominant discourse. It is the overall cosmology represented in the text. It illuminates "how the world hangs together" (Ruggie 1998), according to the text. Here, deconstruction helps us "to understand the placement and displacement of theories, how one theory comes to stand above and silence other theories" (Der Derian 1989: 6).

Future chapters illustrate that the dominant discourse within the texts examined is a story of the state as the foundational unit of the good life,

with its legitimacy always preceding the activities and processes (i.e. democratic means) that, ostensibly, legitimize it. The concept of "participation"
is disciplined in such a way that its primary function is to impute legitimacy to a pre-existing and/or externally devised order. Thus, participation
is often disciplined and divorced from the more radical notion of people
constituting political order.

The more interesting discovery, however, is that this discourse co-exists
and conflicts with multiple and competing minor discourses that make concessions to the dangers of elite capture, state repression, false universalisms,
etc. These contradictions are brought to a new level of intrigue by a subset
of discourse analysis insights that focus on the implications of multiple, co-
extant and competing discourses. For example, Fairclough (in Mills 1997:
153–154) argues that differently rationalized discourses about the same
thing do not simply coexist, they are in conflict. "In this way, Fairclough is
able to show that social relations are not simply the imposition of one discourse type on another (i.e. that of the doctor on the patient), but rather are
constituted by the clash of different discourse types for ascendancy within
interactions." Thus, in taking seriously that texts (even policy texts) have
more than one meaning we might add new dimensions and alternatives to
traditional international and IO theory. Importantly, "[t]his runs counter to
the modernist attempt to narrowly define the field of contestation and thus
more readily dominate it" (Der Derian 1989: 6).

Thus, the forthcoming discourse analysis reveals the co-existence of
dominant and minor discourses. To a large extent, this book illustrates this
in order to, ultimately, build a theoretical construct within which their co-
existence can be seen to have explanatory power with respect to dysfunctional development intervention.

Field Interviews

Interviews in the field were part of the effort to contextualize the governance agenda discourses and their effects. Three dimensions of perspective
were sought: First, interviews with UNDP Governance Unit staff members
were conducted in country. Each participant was asked the same set of
questions designed to elicit information about their understanding of: 1)
key concepts, 2) how coherent, effective and well-tailored the UN intervention was generally, and 3) core principles and processes of the mission (i.e.
"do no harm" or "constructive engagement"). The intent was to illuminate
the extent to which the goals and perspectives at the implementation level
were clear, coherent, and consistent, whether they mirrored complexities
and contradiction found in the discourse as a whole, and/or whether they
introduced something altogether new.

Second, I conducted a set of interviews with local experts (academics) and civil society organizations designed to illuminate the extent to which UN discourse and field staff defined problems and solutions in ways that were consistent with the perspectives of other interested actors. The intent was to explore the political implications of the UN's prescriptive descriptive, from the perspective of a wide array of stakeholders (i.e. lesbian and gay rights activists in Windhoek, the Center for Foreign Relations in Dar es Salaam, etc.). Thus, here I explore the "fitness" of UN discourses with competing discourses of GDH on the ground, evident from semi-structured interviews (Fontana and Frey 1994: Gaskell 2002) and locally published texts and grey literatures. This stage also entailed one in-depth case study: the Human Rights Committee project in the Northern Province of Angola, Uige, which because of its scale and boundedness, allowed me to interview nearly all UN and NGO staff, and government administrators.

Interpretivist Lenses

The shift from a theory-bounded to theory-building project required new interpretative tools and lenses. To create these, I borrowed from grounded (Strauss and Corbin 1994), post-positivist, critical (Kincheloe and MacLaren 1994), constructivist (Guba and Lincoln 1994), and discourse analyzes (Bauer 2002: Gill 2002: Mills 1997). From these emerged a hybrid lens through which to see and interpret with conceptual density[19] the multiple interpretations[20] and constructions, especially in terms of how they produced objects and social practices with real life consequences. At the risk of overstating the differences between paradigmatic approaches, I will nevertheless attempt to sketch the contributions each theoretical school makes to the project.

Grounded theory seeks to build theory and demands a commitment to the "forever provisional character of theory." (Strauss and Corbin 1994: 279). Thus, a grounded theory approach is recursive and unsettled; elaborated upon during the course of research and "grounded directly and indirectly on the perspectives of the diverse actors towards the phenomena studied" (280). In other words, many of the ultimate theoretical parameters of this project emerged during the research process itself, and in response to ever-accumulating bits of knowledge, and the process of trying to make them "fit." Grounded theory also requires exploring the expression of a phenomenon at multiple levels and from multiple perspectives (including those expressed at different times and in different places by the same actor)—keeping in mind that all of these are not obvious from the outset—to see how the various pieces of the puzzle "fit, how they might fit, and how they might not fit."

From post-positivism, I gained a concern for both regular and predict-able real life consequences, and for whether findings fit with pre-existing knowledge (see also Chapter Nine). In this spirit, the intent was, as James Der Derian (1989: 5) puts it, to:

> illuminate, rather than pretend to eliminate, the textual nature of the differences that produce and are sustained by international relations. This might better enable us to understand ourselves and others through the differences that make up everyday life in civil society and yet serve to justify homicide everyday in the international society.

Thus, post-positivism does not signify an interest in the purely theoreti-cal, as its critics argue. Rather, according to Guba and Lincoln (1994) the key difference between positivism and post-positivism is the concession that many of the shortcomings of the positivist epistemology can be com-pensated for by the abandonment of objectivity and its replacement with a search for *density*, a term that describes how well data floats in existing knowledge and fits as a theoretical framework. Correspondingly, I round out this book in Chapters Seven and Eight by attempting to illustrate how data from the four country studies fit together densely with existing knowl-edge, suggesting a propensity for the UN's GDH agenda to contribute to the construction and reconstruction of the space for authoritarian and elit-ist political orders to flourish.

From critical constructivism is borrowed a sense that the social world is constructed, and the:

> emphasis on the world of experience as it is lived, felt, undergone by social actors . . . [Constructivists] emphasize the pluralistic and plas-tic character of reality—pluralistic in the sense that reality is express-ible in a variety of symbol and language systems; plastic in the sense that reality is stretched and shaped to fit purposeful acts (Schwandt 1994: 125).

The constructivist lens reflects that much of the book is concerned with the *interplay between* complex and contradictory discourses of governance, democracy and human rights, and the production of some objects and relations as natural or given in the face of conflicting perspectives. At this nexus, the governance agenda constructs and produces, not only straight forwardly, but also by virtue of the complexities and contradictions that it *is* (see Mills 1997).

Conclusions as Density

The position here is that objective reality can never be fully captured and thus conclusions are forever provisional. Taking this epistemological stance allows for the fitting together of the multiple stories about reality expressed in the discourses with the multiple forms of social conflict at the country level to arrive, I hope the reader will eventually agree, at conceptual density—*but not proof*. That is, the core problematic described in the forthcoming chapters is the presence of multiple and conflicting discourses—in both the texts and practices of the governance agenda—and the potential for corresponding political effects (i.e. what is being produced). The combination of theoretical insights and research strategies described above are meant to provide the tools for investigating and interpreting this core problematic in a way that can yield explanatory *density* (as opposed to conclusive proof). In the end, theory is built that suggests avenues for further research.

That said, my ultimate concern is for the (potential) real life consequences of the way the governance agenda hangs together. It is ultimately from "thick" investigation into the interplay of multiple discourses that concerns flow about the propensity for UN discourses and practices to contribute to the construction and reconstruction of the space for authoritarian and elitist political orders to flourish (see especially Chapters Seven and Eight).

POSITIONING THE RESEARCHER

Rabinow and Sullivan (in Guba and Lincoln 1994: 119) argue: "The interpretative turn is not simply a new methodology, but rather a challenge to the very idea that inquiry into the social world and the value of the understanding that results is be determined by methodology." This is consistent with Levi-Strauss's interpretation of researcher as *bricoleur* (in Denzin and Lincoln 1994: 3):

> The bricoleur understands that research is an interactive process shaped by his or her personal history, biography, gender, class, race, and ethnicity, and those of the people in the setting. The bricoleur knows that science is power, for all research findings have political implications. There is no value free science. The bricoleur knows that researchers all tell stories about the worlds they have studied. Thus, the narratives or stories scientists tell are accounts couched and framed within specific storytelling traditions, often defined as paradigms (e.g. positivism, postpositivism, constructivism).

The admission of multiple (and potentially equally legitimate) discourses and interpretations coupled with reflectivist[21] sympathies (Smith 2001) requires the researcher to position herself within the research, confronting "the ethics and politics of research. The age of value-free inquiry for the human disciplines is over" (Denzin and Lincoln 1994: 1). To say this is to say something about paradigms, "a set of basic *beliefs* (or metaphysics) that deal with ultimates or first principles [emphasis in original]" (Guba and Lincoln 1994: 107). Paradigms rely on persuasiveness and utility rather than proof. They are comprised moreover of beliefs and values that have been the subject of philosophical discussion for millennia. They include such longstanding debates as human nature or the existence of God.

In this light, the forthcoming analysis is guided by the paradigmatic first principle that "knowledge is a significant instrument of power and control" (Reason 1994: 328), or as Foucault argued, *knowledge is power*, and thus power will be evenly distributed only to the extent that knowledge creation is shared and free from structural violence and physical coercion. This approach comes to me *via* my experience as a woman born into architectures of *legitimate* knowledge and *legitimate* ways of knowing handed down from a patriarchal past and with the effect of, *inter alia*, constituting woman as object within consequence-laden social practices. The hallmark of this past was the systematic exclusion of women from the production of *legitimate* forms of knowledge through a variety of physically and systemically violent means. These experiences are not, of course, unique to women, but cut across divisions and identities of race, class, religion, sexuality, etc. They contribute to a profound scepticism towards received wisdom, and in fact, towards the very notion of truth (see Crais 2001; Havel 1992; Parpart 1995; Vale 2003). Indeed, women's reasons for profound scepticism about truth are ubiquitous enough to almost be self-evident, as Maureen O'Hara reminds us:

> When every "system of truth" we've ever known, from oldest myth to modern medical science, has concluded that women are biologically, intellectually and morally inferior, that we are at once dangerous and naturally nurturing, that we are unsuitable for public office and should be protected and subjugated—then you bet feminists have a stake in conversations about "truth" and "reality"! (O'Hara 1995: 151)

Indeed as any serious intellectual must, I have learned to exercise profound scepticism when confronted by hierarchies and structures of authority and knowledge. I am disposed towards seeing those who hold positions of influence not as bearers of "any particular aptitude, but [as] privileged by their economic and social status . . . and [as inheritors of] the self-perpetuating character of the institutions created to provide leadership" (Rahman paraphrased in Reason 1994: 334). Likewise, as the reader will doubtless note, I am particularly uncharitable to claims to rational or *universal* knowledge, pronounced as such under the mantle of legitimately imposing such knowledge on others—often without even the pretence of their consent.

> From one perspective, the orthodox scientific worldview is the product of the Enlightenment and represents a liberating step for human society in releasing itself from the bonds of superstition and scholasticism. From another perspective, it is a movement to narrow our view of our world and to monopolize knowing in the hands of an elite few (Reason 1994: 328).

This position is consistent with my sympathy for the constructivist view that social reality is constructed; not existing out there, but between us. Thus, in the social sciences at least, the greater danger lies in exclusionary forms of knowledge creation than in not heeding the voice of the "expert," as Parpart argues (1995: 240), in sympathy with M. Hobart: "'Knowing is not an exclusive prerogative of some superior knowing subject' (Hobart 1993: 15–16). Thus he reminds us of the immense complexity involved in communication, in the power of knowledge to construct knowledge in ways that inhabit understanding."

This is why, perhaps, I see what I see when looking closely at the governance agenda: vague and contradictory iterations of governance, democracy and human rights programs, which on the one hand lay claim to *universal* knowledge about how to create the good polity, and on the other explicitly order some points of view out agenda setting. Here, I see the mobilization of bias (Bachrach and Baratz 1969). I see taken-for-granted categories and institutions integrated into UN models in ways that implicitly produce and organize hierarchies—and that not coincidentally place UN expertise at the pinnacle of that hierarchy. And ultimately, as the concluding chapter reprises, I am concerned about the ways in which both the coherent and incoherent, commonsensical and contested discourses seem to "produce self-fulfilling and self-sealing systems of action and justification, often with patterns of escalating error" (Argyris *et al.* in Reason 1994).

Thus, I may be conditioned to see these things because of my life experiences, because of who I am. I hope in the forthcoming chapters, however, to convince you, the reader, that they are in fact *there*, and pose real dangers to those who are the supposed beneficiaries.

CHAPTER OUTLINE

At no time does the forthcoming analysis attempt to arbitrate between contending technical approaches to solving the dilemma of poverty and powerlessness and big *T* truth. That is, it does not attempt to evaluate, for example, whether gendered political under-representation can, in fact, be redressed with quotas (UNDP 2002), or whether the normative behaviour of leaders really lies at the root of "bad" governance, and therefore is amenable to processes of socialization. No attempt is made to weigh the relative contributions of geopolitics versus African leaders and/or African forms of authority (Bratton and van de Walle 1997: Chabal and Doloz 1999: Clapham 1993: Reno 1998). There are no pretensions to settling the longstanding chicken and egg debate on whether there is a transcendental relationship between economic growth and democracy (Sen 2001; Diamond *et al.* 1996: Huntington 1994). Rather, the interest here is in exploring two key puzzles: 1) the political effect of co-extant dominant and minor discourses of good governance, democracy and human rights, which often contradict each other and lead nowhere, and 2) the potential real life consequences of these discourses and their contradictions.

Chapter Two reviews some of the academic literatures related to good governance, democracy and human rights. By emphasizing competing debates among scholars related to what constitutes *appropriate* working definitions, underlying principles, and *worthy* objectives, this chapter highlights the contested nature of these concepts. It levies challenges to the UN's remarkable claim that it has identified the "technology, know how and historical experience" to achieve the *Millennium Goals,* but fails to meet its targets due to "low levels of development aid from the industrialized North."[22] By comparing the definitions, principles and objectives found in the broader academic literature with those found in the UN's global discourse, the chapter introduces the rhetorical and disputed dimensions of such lofty claims.

Chapter Three provides a content analysis of the meanings of GDH found in selected UN global documents. The chapter uses the principles of rhetoric to code for semantic and syntactical procedures and patterns of persuasion. It also looks at how the GDH concepts are triangulated, and how related rhetorical devices network into a dominant discourse within which a very specific vision of the world is presented as "hanging together." Specifically, it suggests that while a wide range of devices, such as inexplicitness, mire the global documents, several key ideas nevertheless hold much of the rhetoric together. These are: 1) statements related to the *universal* legitimacy of UN knowledge/ the ordering of participation out of agenda setting; 2) the state as the basic and a priori unit of security and development; and 3) the implicit denial that people with power do bad things (the de-politicization of the development context; see Ferguson 1994).

Chapter Four documents the narrowing and re-focusing of the more radical transformational rhetoric used in the global aspirant documents (*Human Development Report, Millennium Declaration Millennium implementation Road Map*). For example, the *Human Development Report* threads human rights throughout a wide range of multifaceted claims, commitments and interdependent social and political processes, while the *Millennium implementation Road Map*—which ostensibly details what will actually be done—confines human rights promotion to "encouraging *governments*" to ratify human rights covenants.

Chapter Five compares the content of the global discourses with the regional documents and related *Road Maps* for implementation in Africa. In comparative perspective, the regional documents have fewer conflicting discourses, settling instead on a dominant discourse that constructs the UN as expert, the state as basic and *a priori* unit of security, and the almost complete denial of politics, at least its complex underbelly.

Chapter Six compares the global and regional layers of discourse with country documents and interviews with field staff. In many respects the country documents tend to advance altogether different principles, strategies and activities from the global and regional documents. For example, the media as a tool for "disseminating" information about the "roles and responsibilities of living in a democratic society" (CCF 2001: 4) is a popular idea at the country level, but which does not appear robustly at other levels of discourse. Nevertheless, the same dominant discourse identified above holds much of the country documents together.

Interestingly, interviews with field staff revealed various differences and divergences in the understanding of, and levels of satisfaction with, key concepts and implementation methodologies. Variances also characterized the form and rigidity of hierarchy, with some offices working fairly autonomously from models originating in New York and Geneva and/or having forums where top-down approaches could be contested (i.e. Angola), while other offices were more rigidly bound to the UN hierarchy—to the frustration of both local and international staff members (i.e. Botswana). Further, high staff turnover was evident in most offices; both Botswana and Namibia, for example, had recently undergone complete staff rotations, also seemingly truncating much of the institutional memory.

Chapter Seven contextualizes the UN governance agenda within recent and current practices of country governments. It relies on interviews conducted with local professionals (academics) and civil society organizations as well as locally produced studies, analyzes and the broader academic and grey literatures to interrogate UN idealism. Findings suggest that widespread political empowerment is, in fact, unlikely to emerge from the governance agenda as currently narrated. Overall, the chapter explores the social practices likely to be engendered by the UN's prescriptive descriptive, and their political implications (i.e. implications for the kind of social order being constructed). Five key themes relevant to the governance agenda are explored: 1) rule of law, 2) media 3) civil society, 4) elections, and 5) state-capacity-building.

Chapter Eight provides an in-depth case study of the Human Rights Committee project in the Northern Province of Angola, Uige, based on fieldwork conducted in 2001. This case study takes the analysis of Chapter Seven to a greater level of specificity. It illuminates the tensions and contradictions engendered by attempting to insert elements of the governance agenda into the existing, and manifestly not well understood, formal and informal political architectures of Uige. Chapter Eight is also a call to further research into how UN programs are received, interpreted, and innovated upon by those they intend to help.

Chapter Nine visits four well-established critical approaches to understanding UN effectiveness and dysfunction, and relates them to the thick description offered in the preceding chapters, as well as the conclusion that the governance agenda carries a propensity to construct and reconstruct authoritarian and elitist polities. Specifically, the chapter illustrates that findings fit together well with a variety of related literatures and studies that implicate the machinery of mainstream development thinking and organizational practice in the creation of substantive harm. This final chapter ultimately suggests that the complex and contradictory interaction between the dominant and minor discourses creates the illusion that UN development thinking is no longer top-down, elitist, and out of touch, and that therefore praxis will no longer instantiate the conditions of powerlessness that underlie poverty, vulnerability and marginalization. In mixing, even jumbling together, top-down and bottom up epistemologies, the governance agenda is many things to many people. Thereby, UN discourse bestows plausible deniability upon those parts of the bureaucracy that otherwise could not withstand the weight of the contradictions they engender. In this way, the ambiguous and ambivalent discourses (taken as a whole) allow the UN to hide from itself the parts of itself it cannot justify, but which it nevertheless seems unable to change. The discourse is the performance of irony.

Chapter Two

Policies and Institutions: "Unpopular among some—or even a majority—of the population"

This chapter compares and contrasts a wide range of academic literatures on good governance, democracy and human rights (GDH) in order to illustrate how complex and multi-dimensional these the concepts are. In each case, it asks: "If GDH, in general, are multi-dimensional and contested concepts, does the UN use them in ways that are nevertheless clear and consistent?" The short answer is no. In each case a brief review of global and African regional UN documents reveals that GDH are used in ways that are often vague and contradictory. It is this finding, and moreover its implications for UN praxis, which is probed in-depth in subsequent chapters.

GOVERNANCE DISCOURSE

A cursory review of the literatures on good governance reveals a marked lack of consensus on the meaning of the term. A surprising number of books and articles that make use of it neglect to define it at all (i.e. ODI 1992), while others use it in the title, then rarely use it in the text. For example in the index of Cohen *et al's Human Rights and Governance in Africa* (1993), "human rights" appears over 30 times, while governance appears not at all. Those books and articles that take pains to define all terms, such as Jon Pierre's edited collection *Debating Governance* (2000), reveal just what a vexing term it is. In Chapter Two, Paul Hirst begins by delineating the "five versions of governance" while in Chapter Four R.A.W. Rhodes begins with seven. Indeed, according to Jenkins (2002: 485) "[d]uring the 1990's, governance emerged as a catch-all term in both the study and practice of development."

Many analysts choose to explicitly define how governance will be used in a particular context. Shore and Wright (1997:6), for example:

> . . . use "governance" to refer to the more complex processes by which
> policies not only impose conditions, as if from "outside" or "above,"
> but influence people's indigenous norms of conduct so that they them-
> selves contribute, not necessarily consciously, to a government's model
> of social order.

Goran Hyden (1992: 7), similarly, defines governance as "the conscious
management of regime structures with a view to enhancing the legitimacy
of the public realm." Conversely, Serageldin and Landell (paraphrased in
Doing and Moore 1996: 114) define governance as "the use of political
authority and the exercise of control over society and the management of
its resources for social and economic development." More specifically, the
World Bank (2002: 99) argues:

> Good governance includes the creation and protection of property
> rights . . . It includes the provision of a regulatory regime that works
> with the market to promote competition. And it includes the provi-
> sion of sound macroeconomic policies that create a stable environment
> for market activity . . . *Good governance requires the power to carry
> out policies and to develop institutions that may be unpopular among
> some—or even a majority—of the population* [emphasis added].

In these definitions, governance is clearly linked to government, while its
normative content slides along a continuum from less to more support for
government-led development. Alternatively, some analysts use governance to
signify a desirable relationship between various more or less institutionalized
social, economic, state, non-state and trans-state forces (see Cox 1992: 162).
Jon Pierre (2000:4), for example, advances the proposition that:

> [G]overnance refers to a sustaining co-ordination and coherence among
> a wide variety of actors with different purposes and objectives, such as
> political actors and institutions, corporate interests, civil society, and
> transnational organization. The main point here is that political insti-
> tutions no longer exercise a monopoly of the orchestration of gover-
> nance. In these ways, governance could be said to be shorthand for the
> predominant view of government in the *Zeitgeist* of the late twentieth
> century. . . . It is also, presumably, more palatable than "government"
> which has become a slightly pejorative concept.

Jenkins (2002: 488), however, questions the integrity of the concept itself,
arguing that it may in fact be illustrative of "an instinctive reluctance to

face up to civil society's inherently precarious condition and sometimes ugly character, or to let democracy do its unpredictable work." Jenkins, like Shore and Wright, points to governance rhetoric as a mask for underlying political processes where powerful actors shape the quality and quantity of "civil society" by withholding funding and ignoring inconvenient studies and analyzes. The ascendancy of the governance idea, he argues, indicates that the international elite has a "palpable fear of democracy—or at least a strong desire to retain control over what should, by definition, be a local process of conferring legitimacy" (*ibid.*).

Aggregated, these definitions are similar insofar as they invoke processes of steering complex political and economic processes, while disaggregated they reveal how an undefined or short-hand use of governance can simply obscure loaded claims. As Goran Hyden (1992: 5) argues, the use of the term governance "enables us to suspend judgement about the exact relationship between political authority and formal institutions in society." Similarly, Schmitz (1995: 75–76) insists that "what the tethering of politics to governance does is to marginalize questions about authentic degrees of democratization within both government *and* society, in favor of questions of functional utility related to development performance" [emphasis in original]. Thus, in other words, on the one hand governance can signify an idealized social-democratic architecture—"a limited state controlled by representative government and bound by the rule of law, and largely self-organizing civil society independent of the state, but protected by the state's laws and administrative procedures" (Hirst 2000: 19). On the other, it can signify overlapping sites of governmental and non-governmental decision-making and influence, which at least theoretically are able to respond to the complex challenges of an "organizational society" (Presthus 1965 in *ibid.*)—"with large hierarchically controlled institutions on both sides of the public private divide that are either answerable to or only weakly accountable to citizens" (Hirst 2000: 20). Against the grain of these two polarities, Schmitz (1995) and Jenkins (2002) argue that the shift to "governance" obfuscates the dynamics of power, obscuring what ought to be the subject of local democratic decision-making.

GOVERNANCE IN UN DISCOURSE

Thus, while good governance has captured the imagination of the humanitarian machinery and largely supplanted the literature on good government, it is not immediately apparent what governance refers to in any given context. UN discourses are a case in point. To ascertain how the UN, writ large, approaches governance for Africa, the first key historical document to consult is the Secretary General's Report, *The Causes of Conflict and the Promotion of Durable Peace and Sustainable Development in Africa* (1998). However, while governance features prominently in the Report's rubrics, it appears a mere seven times in the text of its 107 paragraphs. The first instance refers to "colonial governance" (para. 71). This could provide important clues about how the UN is conceptualizing governance. Which actors participated in "colonial governance," through what processes and to what effect? But no elucidation is forthcoming. The following three appearances of governance link human rights, rule of law (para. 72), judicial institutions (para. 74) and the "effective management of resources" (para. 76) to "good" governance. In para. 78, it is asserted that "democratization can often build upon indigenous structures and traditional ways of inclusive governance." Again, we are left with a vague and inexplicit statement about the nature and processes of political authority. Later, in para. 105, "good governance" is asserted boldly as "what is needed from Africa." That is, "*Africa* must summon the will to take good governance seriously, ensuring respect for human rights and the rule of law, strengthening democratization, and promoting transparency and capability in administration. Unless good governance is prized, *Africa* will not break free of the threat and the reality of conflict that are so evident today" [emphasis added]. Yet, *Africa*, of course, does not act. People act. Governments act. Organizations act.

In the document, then, while governance tends to loosely correspond to key institutional pegs and processes, it is less than clear why "governance" and not "government" has been used. As Jon Pierre notes, it may simply be an attempt to evade the more pejorative "government." A clue to a more substantive reason, however, is found in its modifiers—"colonial," "inclusive," or "good." Specifically, the link between good governance and democracy and the link between democracy and inclusive traditional and indigenous structures links "good" governance (as opposed to colonial governance) to innovative "bottom-up" forms of decision-making—something distinct from government, as traditionally understood in representative-based theory. It is, then, very weakly presented as something functionally distinct from government. There is also an interesting contradiction. Good governance is at once what Africa lacks, in terms of human rights, rule of law, etc., but also what it already has in indigenous forms of "inclusive governance." Yet it is clear, ultimately, that the UN is not selling support for indigenous forms of governance. And the participatory credentials of traditional forms of governance, at any rate, might be challenging to substantiate—especially on gender equity terms (see Chapter Seven).

Usage in the *Millennium Declaration* (2000) also tends towards inexplicitness. The word governance appears only four times. First, the term is modified with illuminating results: "democratic and *participatory* governance *based on the will of the people* best assures these rights" to live and raise families in dignity, free from hunger, fear violence, oppression and injustice (para. 6: 2) [emphasis added]. The second (para. 13: 4) is a quite differently-centered bundled assertion that poverty eradication:

> depends *inter alia* on good governance. It also depends on good governance at the international level and on transparency in the financial, monetary and trading systems. We are also committed to an open, equitable rule-based, predictable, non-discriminatory multilateral trading and financial system.

The third usage is in the rubric for para. 24, "Human Rights, Democracy and Good Governance," but the term does not appear in any of the following points or resolutions. Thus, moving to the much vaunted *Millennium Declaration* for clarification achieves very little. The meaning of governance tends to be elusive, present in various bundles that, at once, suggest some hidden essence while also insinuating rather than revealing how that essence knits together various and divergent conceptions of participatory and effective institutions.

The basic pattern repeats in the 2002 *Human Development Report* (UNDP 2002: 1–9)—*Deepening Democracy in a Fragmented World*. For example, governance appears 17 times in the overview. Eleven times it is modified by "democratic" or references to participation. In the remaining six, meaning is linked to "rules for making markets work," "fair accountable institutions that protect human rights and basic freedoms" (2) and "accountability" (5). Moving to the global context, governance is linked to "pluralism" in terms of "expanding the space for groups outside formal state institutions to participate in global decision-making" and greater participation of and accountability to developing countries (7). Thus again, we find governance travelling through varied conceptual terrain, but notably, most strongly linked to democracy and key (pre-determined) institutions and processes, while simultaneously embodying both technical and more radical claims.

Overall a cursory review of the global and regional discourse is not very illuminating. Technocratized solutions often mask "prevailing orthodoxies which, when stripped of their putative universality, become seen as special pleading for historically transient but presently entrenched interests" (Cox in Schmitz 1995: 56). Vague, inexplicit and self-contradictory solutions can, for example, encourage the perception that governance as "rules for making markets work," and governance as people participating in the "debates and decisions that shape their lives," are sufficiently clear and symbiotic as to justify their conflation. In such cases "[t]he emperor's new wardrobe camouflages what ought to be contested" (*ibid.*), at least if the democratic and participatory dimensions are to be taken seriously. Thus, for all its dimensions, governance remains a secret cipher, a slippery signifier for what Africa lacks.

DEMOCRACY DISCOURSE

As illustrated above, democracy lends much by way of legitimacy to governance. Yet democracy is plagued with its own ambiguities, as Roland Stromberg (1996: 4) notes:

> Democracy is a fuzzy term. The word is all around us; it is constantly used in news media and everyday discourse to define our own culture and to shape our policies towards others who are said to be delinquent if they are "undemocratic" and may even need to have this nebulous entity thrust upon them by force.

As with governance, a cursory review of the democracy literature reveals a plethora of interpretations and a number of persistent cleavages. For example, Larry Diamond (1999: 6), one of contemporary politics' most renowned democracy experts, has concluded that "[e]ven if we think of democracy as simply . . . a system for choosing government through free and fair electoral competition at regular intervals, governments chosen in this manner are generally better than those that are not." In contrast, in their seminal volume *Low-Intensity Democracy*, Gills *et al.* (1993: 5) argue that "[i]n the absence of progressive social reform, the term 'democracy' is largely devoid of content. Indeed, it is in danger of becoming a term of political mystification or obfuscation, serving as euphemism for sophisticated modern forms of neo-authoritarianism." Similarly Graf (1996: 40) argues:

> Democratization, in its new discourse, holds out the prospect—or chimera—of developing without having to undertake urgently needed social reforms and dealing with the central issues of redistribution and social justice—reforms would jeopardize the structure of elite domination and the processes of transnational elite collaboration.

Linz and Stepan (1996:1) further define a completed democratic transition as one where the popular vote has indicated 'sufficient agreement has been reached about political procedures to produce an elected government . . . when this government *de facto* has the authority to generate new policies, and when the executive, legislative and judicial power . . . does not have to share power with other bodies *de jure*." According to critics such as ÓTuathail *et al.* (1998:5), however, even these minimal credentials, especially the last, are increasingly difficult to attain. They argue that domestic democracy is overwhelmingly compromised by globalization-from-above promoted by powerful corporate actors, orchestrated by politically-biased international institutions and "imagineered by transnational media and corporations which project consumer utopias." David Held has noted similarly that domestic democracies are threatened by the proliferation of issues that transcend existing democratic boundaries. That is, a basic lack of symmetry and congruence exists between "citizen-voters and decision makers" and "between the output (decisions, policies and so on) and their constituents." As examples, Held refers to changes in US or European domestic interest rate policies that profoundly affect other countries, transnational pollution, the effects of arms sales and procurement, etc. (1993: 25–26).

DEMOCRACY IN UN DISCOURSE

The meaning and implications of democracy are difficult to pin down. Nevertheless, "[d]emocratic principles have become the criteria for good governance domestically" (Khatami Statement in UNDP 2002: 64). What this means is that within UN discourse, legitimacy for the preoccupation with good governance derives primarily from the legitimacy of democracy. For example, the 2002 *Human Development Report* proposes that: "Advancing human development requires governance that is democratic in both form and substance–for the people by the people." Three reasons are offered: 1) democracy is an end in itself, 2) democracy allows people to put pressure on leaders to change harmful policies and thereby avert "economic and political catastrophes such as famines and descents into chaos," and 3) "democratic governance can trigger a virtuous cycle of development" by allowing people to "press for policies that expand social and economic activities" (*ibid.*: 3). In that democracy is good, governance must be as well.

Note that the meaning of democracy tends to traverse a number of conceptual territories. It is an end in itself and an illustration that the enlightened state has *granted* political freedoms *to* the people. Paradoxically, democracy is also political power that resides in the people, deriving its legitimacy from being popularly based, as well as the means whereby the people exercise checks and balances against those who, in fact, rule. David Held (1993:15) illuminates the fundamental tension in play: "Within the history of democratic theory lies a deeply rooted conflict about whether democracy should mean some kind of popular power (a form of politics in which citizens are engaged in self government and self regulation) or an aid to decision-making (a means of conferring authority on those periodically voted into office)." The conflation of these two long-standing facets of democracy tends to obscure the exact nature of the relationship between political authority and society being proposed.

Similarly, the *Causes of Conflict* (1998: 21) Report, mentions democracy nine (in-text) times, noting ambiguously that "democracy *gives* people a stake in society" [emphasis added] and that "the real test of a democratization process is not the organization of elections, *but whether those first elections are followed by others in accordance with an agreed electoral mandate*" [emphasis added]. That is, the image of democracy "giving" makes a relatively inexplicit statement about the relationship between democracy and the people. Similarly, evaluating the democratization process in terms of elections and adherence to electoral mandates is unambiguously minimalist, a stance elsewhere characterized as low-intensity and/or supportive of neo-authoritarianism (Abrahamsen 2001; Gill *et al.* 1993; Marks 2000).

Thus, democracy is filled with a particular (and minimalist) content while its contested definitions and inherent emancipatory potential are implicitly denied (Abrahamsen 2000: 67). The top-down/bottom-up question embedded in the heart of democratic debate is obscured as democracy from a "God's-eye view" simultaneously diffuses and co-opts the legitimacy associated with the *demos*. For example, Abrahamsen's (109–110) comparative evaluation of recent democracy movements in Africa concludes that accolades for Africa's recent wave of democratization obscure the inequities and entrenched power blocs it enables:

> [I]n many African countries democratization was a victory for the liberal conceptualization of democracy and those who had the most to gain from continued economic liberalization—the elite and the middle classes, as well as donors and creditors . . . Competing visions of democracy and alternative social policies were defeated and appear to have been marginalized within political debates.

Understanding what democracy means in real terms is further complicated by the tide of evidence documented by the 2002 HDR suggesting that "[e]ven where democratic institutions are firmly established, citizens often feel powerless to influence national policies." The 1999 *Gallup International Millennium Survey* noted that this had two dimensions. First, constraints emanating from international donors often neutralized or dramatically altered the trajectory of national policies, and second, that current democratic structures were *insufficiently democratic*. That is, in a survey of 50,000 people from 60 countries "only 1 in 10 said that their government responded to the people's will" (UNDP 2002: 1). Similarly, the World Bank (2005: 5) reported recently that according to *Afrobarometer* surveys and the *World Values Survey,* "[a]bout 75% of the respondents agree that African governments are doing too little for people trapped in poverty."

The democratic deficit[1] extends into the West, including recent influence-buying scandals such as those involving Enron in the United States and Elf in France, as well as longstanding trends such as exorbitant campaign spending, voter apathy, structural inequalities, and highly unequal distributions of wealth. However, the UNDP's chapter on "tackling democratic deficits" is overwhelmingly concerned with the "developing" world. In contrast to the 82 countries considered to be "fully democratic" (10), a litany of failed democratic transitions are listed, pointing to increasing poverty, corruption, crime, addiction, inequalities, etc. in such illiberal democracies as Zimbabwe and Kyrgyzstan, and new and transitional democracies in Eastern Europe, Africa, and Asia (63). Thus, paradoxically, despite noting that a large number of people in "fully democratic" countries do not consider their nations to be guided by the will of the people, the Report tends to define democracy in terms of the institutional and political architectures of these very same developed countries.

The HDR's overarching focus on the developing world is clearly an attempt to define democracy as something that developing nations, *in particular*, lack. They stand in opposition to the 82 *fully* democratic countries, who in being *fully* democratic, provide us with an accurate picture of what a democracy looks like—what it looks likely is largely what the West has achieved and upon which its comparative success is built. Democracy as the causal variable is implied, despite the fact that elsewhere causality is denied and democracy is justified mainly as and end in and of itself.[2] While the claim is made several times that countries can be "differently democratic" (4, 61), the Report sets out a very particular vision of democracy, which paradoxically, has been determined *for* people in the developing world, who at the same time and quite evidently have little to no access to decision-making structures in either their own countries or at the UN. It is therefore inevitable that the version of democracy on offer "operate[s] to endorse certain policy options and check others, encourage certain logics and inhibit others, support certain factions and weaken others" (Marks 2000: 57).

It bears repeating, however, that simultaneously, and paradoxically, democracy is characterized as something that is lacking across *all* nations, more generally. This lack manifests in the rise in unaccountable corporate power (68), voter apathy (69), and the lack of female representation in positions of political power (70), media monopolies (78), "unaccountable and unrepresentative militaries" (83), "corruption and elite capture," and "gaps in democratic practice" (65). Self evidently, these phenomena implicitly undermine the claim that "82 countries, with 57% of the world's people are *fully* democratic" [emphasis added]. Thus, a cursory review leaves many questions unanswered. Will the UN stop investing legitimacy in governments and state elites with patchy democratic mandates or credentials? Will their citizens have an opportunity to participate in modelling their own democracies? Why should developing countries adopt the clearly flawed model found in the West? Who will ultimately decide? If it is the UN or states whose governing apparatus has been captured by elites, in what ways is *democracy*, then, democratic?

HUMAN RIGHTS DISCOURSE

In terms of the UN's political mandate, good governance and democracy are almost always bundled with human rights. However, human rights are a notoriously vague and problematic concept, spanning everything from moral to legal, political to cultural, rational and post-rationalist quagmires. While human rights are generally understood to be those rights detailed by the UN's 1948 *Universal Declaration of Human Rights* and the related Covenants, "the idea of natural or human rights permanently entered into the mainstream of political theory and practice in the seventeenth century" in response to a number of intersecting and historically contingent pressures (Donnelly 1999: 82). Despite always making claims to universalism rooted in nature, most early treatises on rights excluded "women, along with savages, servants, wage labourers of either sex," etc. (*ibid.*). Like democracy, the association of rights with progress is due in no small measure to a sophisticated and resonant argument structure that has made it a useful, and often radical, tool for equality (Brown 1999: 105). That is:

> In effect, racist, bourgeois, Christian patriarchs found the same natural rights arguments they had used against aristocratic privilege turned against them in a struggle to incorporate new social groups into the realm of equal citizens entitled to participate in public and private life as autonomous subjects and agents (Donnelly 1999: 83).

Yet, this utility only partly allays concerns about ambiguities. Sceptics and supporters of the human rights regime alike admit that "different societies 'sign up' to the idea of universal human rights but disagree over the meaning and priority to be accorded to these rights" (Dunne and Wheeler 1999: 2–3). For example, "few countries in the world understand freedom of the press as broadly, and few countries in the world construe the right to social security as narrowly, as the United States" (Donnelly 1999: 99).[3] That is, "virtually everything encompassed by the notion of human rights is the subject of controversy" (Brown 1999: 103). This can be confirmed by even the most cursory review of the volumes of analysis devoted to the legal, practical, moral and normative questions that suffuse the discourse on rights (see Steiner and Alston 2000).

Two of the most enduring debates center on issues related to whether rights are, indeed, universal and who, if anybody, holds corresponding duties, "Observers from different regions and cultures can agree that the human rights movement with respect to its language of rights and the civil and political rights that it declares, stems principally from the liberal tradition of western thought" (*ibid.*: 361). For some analysts, this lineage is a clear constraint on claims to universality. Panniker (in *ibid.*: 384), for example, argues that "Human Rights are one window through which one particular culture envisions a just human order for its individuals. But those who live in that culture do not see the window." Similarly, Chris Brown (1999:104) has argued that "rights only make sense in the context of a particular kind of society . . . By adhering to the fiction of a universal grounding for rights independent of the particular kind of societies in which they are characteristically found, such advocates put themselves in a false position, and, perhaps paradoxically, weaken the credibility of their stand" (104).

For Brown and Panniker, rights clearly float in a liberal historical, institutional and normative *soup*. That is, rights are a legal device that evolved out of historically specific struggles, and within that context are appropriate—and effective—devices for challenging the status quo. Brown cautions, however, against conflating rights with the relative peacefulness and economic prosperity of liberal societies. Rights, he argues, piggyback on "features of the polity which have nothing to do with rights" (111). That is, where the institutional, legal, normative and economic architectures within which rights operate are absent, rights are less likely to offer meaningful protections. Similarly, Panniker cautions that where the *liberal soup* is absent, "Human Rights may turn out to be a Trojan horse, surreptitiously introduced into other civilizations which will then be obliged to accept those ways of living, thinking and feeling for which Human Rights is the proper solution in the cases of conflict" (387). That is, rights talk may undermine or dismantle existing and functional protections of human dignity with uneven and uncertain effect.

For others, such as Ronald Cohen (1993:4), rights are now and always universal: "At its most basic level, a human right is a safeguarded prerogative *granted* because a person is alive. This means that any human being *granted* personhood has rights by virtue of species membership" [emphasis added]. This position corresponds to the natural law tradition in which rights are understood to derive from the order of nature, and to be self-evident to all rational persons (see Sidorsky in Steiner and Alston 2001: 327). The benefit of the natural law position is that it extends rights to citizens of countries where rights are either not enshrined in positive law, or where such law is not enforced. There are several important drawbacks to the natural law perspective, however. Precise knowledge covering the specific content of rights granted by the order of nature and apprehended by reason has tended to be elusive, as has the answer to the puzzle of who or what has the corresponding duty to protect those rights. A key advantage is that natural law imputes rights with an open-ended and highly aspirant connection to greater and greater levels of human solidarity, equality, equity and flourishing (Brown 1999). Natural law is what makes rights a central tool for challenging all political, legal or moral regimes—and probably what accounts for their mimetic success and widespread and transhistorical appeal.

Thus, while technically human rights are not, in fact, *universal* (see Steiner and Alston 2001: 385), for many, this does not mean that they should not become so. According to Ken Booth (1999: 59), for example, it may be too early to tell if human rights are truly universal, but:

> It is a preposterous political position to argue that the idea of universal human rights is flawed because some groups cannot conceive the notion of rights. Are victims always to be left hostage to the selfish politics of the powerful? If we had to wait until everyone was persuaded before taking any step in life, we would still be in the Dark Ages.

Rhoda Howard (see Steiner and Alston 2001: 398–399) and Jack Donnelly (1999: 99) have both argued that while human rights may not be, by nature, universal, they have achieved a level of universality, and regardless of their western origin, provide an effective language for challenging contemporary forms of injustice and inequality. Howard, for example, argues that "[h]uman rights are a modern concept now universally applicable because of the *social evolution* of the entire world into state societies," particularly the "nature of justice" inherent to states and most fully active in "liberal and/or social democratic societies" [emphasis added]. That is, the just state is a "radical rupture from the many status-based, non-egalitarian, and hierarchical societies of the past and present" and offers the best contemporary social aspiration.

This brings the discussion to the recognition that part of what makes rights *rights* are the correlative duties implied. Presently, it is states who ratify the international covenants on rights, and the most straightforward right/duty relationship is between state and citizen, and secondarily between states, who agree to abide by international covenants in order to satisfy the common interest of international peace and security, and to pursue the common purpose of "encouraging respect for human rights and for fundamental freedoms" (UN Charter, article 1). Negative rights, such as those found in the *Covenant on Civil and Political Rights* require the state to not interfere in various aspects of people's lives, and to guarantee the rights of individuals against infringement by others. Positive rights, such as those found in the *Covenant on Economic Social and Cultural Rights*, require the state to be proactive in the creation of conditions where these rights can be satisfied, such as the right to education or social security.

To the extent that both types of duties inhere in states and not individuals, rights are state-centric, which is the site of significant flaws in the conceptual structure of rights, and moreover impedes their radical egalitarian promise. That is, the paradox of rights is that it is both states that abuse them and states which protect them. Why should we expect that states that show little regard for the freedom and dignity of their citizens one day will the next become the source from which all rights flow? In this, a wide range of observers, from analysts of transnational politics to feminists have found common ground. Critical scholars of transnational political economy, for example, argue that a rights regime that defines the relationship between state and society "is not only out of step with current power relations, it also tends to obscure them . . . International human rights law perpetuates the notions that private actors are, and by implication should be, only accountable to states, not individuals, and that other states are, and should be, only accountable to their own populations" (Jochnick 2001: 159). Jochnick (160) underscores his concern by reference to Texaco in the Amazon:

> For decades, the affected Amazon communities had suffered Texaco's abuses largely in silence, having been repeatedly told, both explicitly and implicitly, that they had no rights against the oil company and that the damage was a natural and inevitable price to pay for the country's development . . . Texaco has operated for years in the Amazon as

practically a state unto itself, with annual global earnings four times
the size of Ecuador's GNP, and with the active support of the US government. Even if the Ecuadorian government had been disposed to
control the company, few believed it could.

Similarly, some feminists have argued that the centrality of the state as "protector" of rights is misplaced, based on the faulty assumption that states are
neutral in the creation and perpetuation of power relations. Hillary Charles-
worth (in Steiner and Alston 2001: 216) has argued that the systemic pressures that render women more liable to being confined to a structurally
undervalued "private sphere" characterized by economic dependency and
multiple vulnerabilities are woven into the very fabric of stateness. If states
are not neutral, but "patriarchal, hierarchical, [and] militarized" entities
then a commitment to human rights requires that non-state actors have
more say in the formulation and enforcement of law (*ibid.*: 216). In other
words, while a strict human rights perspective maintains that states are best
placed and ultimately responsible for protecting human rights, others argue
that this belief masks the power relations created and maintained through
state action.

Interesting rebuttals to these arguments contend that these complexities can be accommodated by existing state-based processes. Karen Engle
(*ibid.*: 218–220), for example, in her *critique of the critique* of the role of
the state in policing the boundaries of the public/private divide, argues that
women are neither as excluded from the public sphere as some contend,
nor are they as anxious to see the private sphere, where many find important opportunities and protections, *penetrated* by international law. (Would
they be any more interested to see them *penetrated* by national law?) Further, she adds—somewhat contradictorily—"international law, particularly
human rights law, has been built by its own criticism. That is, every time
some group or cause feels outside the law, it pushes for inclusion, generally
through a new official document. The vast proliferation of human rights
documents, then, is as much a testament to exclusion as it is to inclusion."

Whether inclusionary rights-based strategies are generally effective
for vulnerable and marginalized groups is unclear. Martin Shaw (1999), in
a study of Kurdish refugees, argues that the "global society" purportedly
attempting to end egregious human rights violations only dimly and inadequately corresponds to the cosmopolitan democratic model Engle seems
to suggest. Rather, it tends to rely on indirect representation of "victims,"
co-opting their voices through media images and sound bites, repackag-
ing their concerns for western consumption. "Globalist ideas may represent inclusive global interests in an ideological sense, but how far do they

actually involve people across the globe" (221)? While some crises take on global significance "partly or mainly through mediation by television, scores of other crises remain . . . localized and fail . . . to secure similar mediation" (220). Similarly in his study of aid agencies in the Sudan, Mark Duffield (2001: 222) found that the elevation of rights in policies and statements over the last ten years did not translate into better protection for the world's vulnerable. Rather, NGOs tended to make a distinction between legal and normative aspects of human rights, going on to use their own subjective interpretations to justify pre-existing programmes. "[I]t is not the case of reforming the NGO to address human rights but the reverse: *it is the case of the aid agency reforming its concept of human rights to bring it into line with the work that it already does*" [emphasis in original].

Thus the meaning and promise of human rights is unsettled. Also, like debates on governance and democracy, popular human rights discourses are both delimited by, and transcendent of, the limits of the state-based conception of the political society. As a result, human rights can mean many things to many people and a reference in any given sound bite will likely evoke complex and contradictory associations.

HUMAN RIGHTS IN UN DISCOURSE

In the *Causes of Conflict* Report (1998), "human rights" appear twenty-eight times, mostly placing the onus upon African states and their elites to *extend* and *protect* rights. (Yet, many such states and elites are explicitly responsible for significant human rights abuses.) Rights tend to be linked to rule of law, governance and peace. For example, on page 11, respect for human rights and "the rehabilitation of civic institutions" are the foundation for lasting peace and development. On page 19, "[r]espect for human rights and the rule of law are necessary components of any effort to make peace durable. They are the cornerstones of good governance." A similar correlation is advanced on page 20: "Guaranteeing the fair and impartial enforcement of law is indispensable to the protection of human rights." Finally, the Report urges that "*Africa* must summon the will to take good governance seriously, ensuring respect for human rights and the rule of law, strengthening democratization and promoting transparency and capability in public administration" [emphasis added] (28). That is:

> A number of African States have continued to rely on centralized and highly personalized forms of government and some have also fallen into a pattern of corruption, ethnically-based decisions and human rights abuses. Notwithstanding the holding of multiparty elections in

a majority of African countries, much more must be done to provide
an environment where individuals *feel protected*, civil society is able
to flourish, and Government carries out its responsibilities effectively
and transparently, with adequate institutional mechanisms to ensure
accountability [emphasis added] (19).

In that human rights remain undefined, the emphasis implied by context
establishes a strong correlation with positive law and the creation of an
institutional framework, mainly in the western legal tradition. Specifically,
the link between human rights and the rule of law is made over and over
again, with law understood as a creative or ordering force. This accords
with what Mamdani (2001: 24) has identified as a central feature of western internationalism: "The architecture of the modern state was inscribed
in modern law, Western law. And rule of law was in turn central to the
construction of civilized society, in short, civil society." In other words, law
as manifested by the state creates the citizen, and the possibility of human
rights. However, as Chris Brown points out, "[r]ights associated with positive law are associated with particular jurisdictions and thus are not, as
such, *human* rights—but on the other hand, their ontological status is
secure" [emphasis in original]. Thus, the *Causes of Conflict* Report conflates human rights with rights-based legal systems bounded by states that
exhibit certain qualities and perform certain functions.

A still closer look at the use of human rights in the Report reveals
at least three interesting patterns. First, essentially, "human rights" do
not differ significantly from positive law "rights," or the "rule of law"
more generally. Second, it is evident that rights are state bound. Third,
human rights (as depicted) are implicitly understood as universal and self-
evident—such that no explanation of any kind is required to justify their
centrality in the text.

The UNDP's 2000 *Human Development Report* was devoted to
Human Rights and Development. It is therefore a good source to canvass
for more explicit information about what the UNDP understands by human
rights. Where the *Causes of Conflict* Report offered no explicit definition
or justification for its emphasis on human rights, the HDR asserts on the
first page of the Foreword yet another alternative way to understand rights
by conflating rights and freedoms: "Rights make human beings better economic actors." That is:

> Only with political freedoms—the right for all men and women to par-
> ticipate equally in society—can people genuinely take advantage of eco-
> nomic freedoms . . . And clearly it is not enough for countries simply

to grant economic and social rights in theory alone . . . People will work because they enjoy the fruits of their labour: fair pay, education and health care for their families and so forth. . . . But if the rewards of their labour are denied them again, they will lose their motivation. So economic and social rights are both the incentive for, and the reward of, a strong economy (iii).

Broadly, a key objective of the HDR is to draw out "the complex relationship between human development and human rights" (iii). At the heart of this relationship is "freedom." That is, "[h]uman freedom is the common purpose of both and common motivation of human rights and human development" (2). In this equation, development contributes by providing the tools needed to address "economic and institutional constraints," thereby "expanding people's capacity." Meanwhile, human rights contribute "moral legitimacy" and "legal tools and institutions—laws, the judiciary and the process of litigation—as means to secure freedoms and human development" (*ibid.*). There are seven freedoms in all: freedom from discrimination, want,[4] fear, and injustice, and freedom to realize potential, to participation, speech and association, and to decent work—without exploitation. They establish "the state's accountability for its human rights obligations and commitments under international law" (3). In other words, these freedoms are what states must seek to *extend* and *protect*.

The Report also establishes that the nature of duties implied by *human* rights are at times perfectly correlated to duties held by the state—and at others, imperfect in the sense that unjust practices can originate in complex social dynamics where the duty of reform falls to the community as a whole (24–26). As such, "laws alone cannot guarantee human rights." They require institutions, norms and an "enabling economic environment . . . Many groups in society, as well as governments, can strengthen all these relations" (7). That is:

> States have the first obligation to participate in the international human rights regime and establish national legal frameworks. But human rights activists and movements can also press for legal reforms—to give people access to legal processes, with institutional barriers removed (7).

Specifically, imperfect duties are invoked to argue that rights and duties are diffuse throughout society; civil society also has a duty to promote human rights awareness and to participate in related struggles. Further, state machinery is usefully supplemented by independent national commissions and ombudsmen (7). Yet, it is all troublingly technical. If we were to really see control over decisions about key aspects of "rights" democratized, the attendant freedoms privileged may be very different. For example, the strength of the global landless peoples' movements suggests that, in many parts of the world, freedom to decent work might be trumped by decent access to affordable land. In this light, the Report goes on to refute its own specificity. Echoing Jack Donnelly, it asserts that "human rights could be advanced beyond all recognition over the next quarter century" (13). Specifically, "Human rights—in an integrated world—require global justice. The state-centered model of accountability must be extended to the obligations of non-state actors and to the state's obligations beyond its borders" (9).

The *Millennium Declaration* stands in stark contrast to the *Human Development Report*. Within it, human rights are mentioned eight times, exclusively in the context of bounded state obligations situated within an international order based on sovereignty, non-interference, solidarity and tolerance. While comparatively, the HDR envisions a rather broad and inclusive model of global cooperation, the *Millennium Declaration* is self-consciously state centric:

> Responsibility for managing worldwide economic and social development, as well as threats to peace and security must be shared among nations of the world and should be exercised multilaterally. As the most representative organization in the world, the United Nations must play a central role (2).

UN discourse, then, reveals tensions between the concepts of *human* rights and *legal* rights. It also engenders contradictions by, at once, grafting human rights onto state power as well as aspirant models of global political pluralism, to which considerable progress in human rights advocacy can be attributed (i.e. global anti-apartheid struggle or women's rights movement). It engenders further tensions with claims to a universal commitment to human freedom and dignity while equally as often forming part of a technical programme linked quite openly to liberal philosophy. For example, on the one hand, "[h]uman rights and fundamental freedoms are the birth rights of all human beings" (UNDP 2000: 30); on the other, they are justified by their role in a technical programme: "legal tools and institutions—laws, the judiciary and the process of litigation—as means to secure freedoms and human development" (UNDP 2000: 2).

That is, human rights implicitly straddle a number of political, normative and economic configurations in ways that mask rather than disclose tensions and potential conflicts. More problematic still, is the almost total lack of differentiation between such heinous examples of state abuse as acts as torture, persecution and systemic acts of terror, and an economic system without *proper* incentive structures, thereby trading on the repugnance of the latter to justify narrow constructions of the former.

Thus, to look closely at UN discourses on human rights is to catch the institution simultaneously appealing to a wide range of philosophical outlooks and interpretations—while also attempting to establish itself as *the* pre-eminent political entity capable of defining and fostering human rights. Inconsistencies, however, suggest that the UN is far from a hegemonic actor that has already co-opted the emotive power of "human rights" to its own institutional goals. Rather, it participates in a broader discourse where a weakly articulated or inadequately represented "human rights" provides fertile ground for variegated outlooks and objectives. Various political forces compete to define the nature of rights deficits, to define what activities would fill in the gap, but this is an unsettled site of political struggle constituted, not by a common agreement on the importance of human rights—as it appears on the surface—but by the struggle to define what human rights in fact means, and which dimensions of rights will be prioritized. Here, clearly not all stakeholders participate equally in the conversation; not all stakeholders have the opportunity to participate at all.

CONCLUDING REMARKS

In part, governance, democracy and human rights have generated so much interest among theoreticians, academics and policy makers because they are versatile and contested, resonant and yielding. A cursory review of selected UN discourses suggests that as a whole, the institution mimics and makes use of this multidimensionality.

If the discussion in this chapter has left the reader more, not less confused about what these terms really mean, it is precisely because in both the broader literatures and in the UN discourse there really is no one definition, no clear core, no singularly defining moment. The meaning of governance tends to be elusive, present in various bundles that, at once, suggest some hidden essence while also insinuating rather than revealing how that essence knits together various and divergent conceptions of participatory and effective institutions. Similarly, democracy straddles a number of sometimes-contradictory political configurations, while projecting the ideal of *demos* (i.e. people as constituting government versus government as constituting the citizen), collecting on the attendant legitimacy, while potentially masking "a reality of oligarchy and technocracy, invisible power and bureaucratic-business domination, individual political alienation and differentiated social opportunity" (Marks 2000:73). Like debates on governance and democracy, human rights discourses are both delimited by and transcendent of the state-based conception of the political society, at once liberating while also rendering citizens beholden to the whims of state power, from whence human rights and their abuses flow.

Does all this mean, however, that UN approaches to GDH are simply confused and muddled, a messy discourse with equally messy praxis? Certainly some of the UN's strongest critics might agree. In the next chapter we take a much closer look at the global UN texts, and ultimately identify method in all the messiness.

Chapter Three
Human Development Reports: "Universally valued by people of the world over"

This chapter undertakes an in-depth content analysis[1] of the meanings of good governance, democracy and human rights (GDH) found in selected UN global documents, with a combined special emphasis on the 2000 and 2002 Human Development Reports (HDR), entitled Human Rights and Human Development and Deepening Democracy in a Fragmented World. The chapter applies the principles of rhetoric (see Chapter One) to interrogate the semantic and syntactical procedures and patterns of persuasion that add dimensions of meaning to the texts, beyond that which is explicit. Generally, using the principles of rhetoric to guide content analysis helps in the identification of implicit and explicit resort to claims of authority (ethos), appeals to emotion (pathos) and implicit assertions about the way the world is (logos). These combine to weave stories, within stories, within stories; an implicate[2] web within which meaning both resides and is obscured. Through content analysis, then, we gain a dense understanding of the stories presented in the texts, and how they are tangled, intertwined and often contradictory.

The conclusion of this chapter details how GDH are, in fact, triangulated and entangled, with the effect of implying both the way things are and what ought to be done about it. This "prescriptive descriptive" is from here on referred to as the "dominant discourse." Specifically, the analysis suggests that while a wide range of devices, such as inexplicitness, inoculation and contradiction mire these aspirant documents, several key beliefs about the way things are or ought to be, nevertheless, hold the documents together. These are: 1) claims that the UN is an (or the) authoritative and legitimate expert, 2) the model it proposes is both rational and universal, 3) claims that the state is the only and legitimate site for the insertion of UN technical assistance, and 4) claims that broad-based participation is "good," but not necessary or intrinsic to the overall governance agenda. That is, top-down externally-driven state-building activities are legitimized by their, ostensibly, rational and universal credentials.[3]

GOOD GOVERNANCE: UNIVERSAL ASPIRATIONS OF EVERYONE EVERYWHERE

The previous chapter noted that governance is an ambiguous concept. Relying on the analysis of Held (1993), Hirst (2000), Jenkins (2002) and others, several general approaches were identified. The first uses governance to signify a liberal political architecture, characterized by an impartial state operationalized by the rule of law, guaranteed by a separation of powers and monitored by an independent civil society and media. A second uses it to refer to an emergent condition where overlapping sites of government and non-governmental decision-making and influence structure the working out of complex and overlapping sites of power, which may also transcend state boundaries. A third questions whether the shift from a discourse of "government" to "governance" was, in fact, an attempt to obscure that *new* development approaches to government have failed to comprehend their terrain. Development practitioners generally ignored the wealth of knowledge generated during the 1990s that problematizes the nature, concentration and exercise of power within modern states (Badie 2000; Lipschutz 2000; Robbins 1999; Vale 2003; van Creveld 2000). That is, governance is used as a way of shifting ground to appease critics—while reasserting that identified areas of misallocation of political power are amenable to relatively minor technical solutions, and by association, are not structural (or epistemological).

    This section demonstrates that the use of governance in the UN's global discourse tends to refer to vague and inexplicit representative-democratic state/society model, devised by international actors to be executed by developing country *governments*. Citizens and members of civil society participate where and when the model deems appropriate, but their participation is disciplined by the model, and not part of a discussion on *what* model. Thus, governance is not so much represented as having a specific content, but rather as signifying the *proper* working relationship between the UN and developing country *governments*. It expresses that by working with the UN, governments can come to know what behaviour is consistent with good or democratic governance. In fact, as we see below, what comes through most clearly is that the process of working with the UN and taking its expert advice on board *is the very definition of* good governance. In other words, a government can satisfy the conditions of good governance by performing as the UN directs—independent of the nature of those commands or the relative effects on the life chances of citizens. Thus, while the HDRs shy away from explicitly, or at least unambiguously, defining good governance, they do set out the means: top down, externally-driven state-building. This state, by and large, is a blank slate, and its ontological privilege precedes democracy, good governance, human rights, even state legitimacy itself.

The 2000 Human Development Report

We begin with an important UN statement on the interface between human rights and political institutions: Chapter Three of the 2000 *Human Development Report* entitled *Inclusive Democracy Secures Rights*. This is the only chapter in the 2000 HDR dealing explicitly with political institutions. Governance appears only four times. First, "good" governance is counter-posed to the "evil" governance of Nigeria's Abacha regime. The other three times it is used as part of the compound "democratic governance," which is asserted to comprise democratically elected legislature, independent judiciary and independent executive, amounting to a separation of powers and therefore, accountability. Democratic governance is also asserted as the ideal framework for the realization of human rights because:

> it is based on the *extension* of civil and political rights notably the right to participate in political life. And by *allowing* a voice in political decisions, it can be instrumental in realizing other rights. Democracy builds the institutions needed for the fulfilment of human rights [emphasis added].

There are three striking features to this quote. The first is the implication that good governance corresponds to assumptions about how the representative-democratic state mediates competing interests and preferences. Strictly then, it is not in the first instance democratic since its structures are externally-driven and pre-determined, allegedly universally valid irrespective of context, local debates, etc. The second is the foundational or constitutive position of the state. Specifically, the state *extends* and *allows* the right to participate in political life. Third, the UN is making an authoritative claim that *it* is qualified to make this assertion; that it has the expertise to facilitate good governance. However, the markers of good governance the UN advances (separation of powers, elected legislature, etc.) are not so much beyond dispute or universally valid in any particular case as they are *presented as* universal, rational and objective—and juxtaposed to the "evil governance" found elsewhere. French political sociologist Betrand Badie (2000: 152–153), however, historicizes the taken-for-grantedness of the rationality underpinning the *inevitability* of the representative-democratic state architecture, reminding us that the "End of History" (Fukuyama 1992) has been foretold before:

> The current growing reference to multiparty systems and rediscovered pluralism [in developmentalist discourses] goes hand in hand with a formal justification of the one-party system practiced in the past. In both cases, there clearly appears to be the same effort of legitimation by association with, in the past, a Western, socialist, or Marxist institutional practice, and, currently, a neoliberal practice. In reality, this practice marks a turning point: it defines solutions destined to consolidate a weakened political order, and at the same time reassures the tutelary Western powers. Its effectiveness remains, however, uncertain since it attempts to save a political system that falls victim to its own cultural dissonance through principles forged by a legal system from without.

Badie, then, reminds us of the need to remain vigilant in the face of claims to universal truths and the excesses of *expert* knowledge (see also Parpart 1995).

The 2002 Human Development Report

As an illustration of the rising currency of governance in discussions about political reform, in chapters one through five of the 2002 HDR, governance appears about 105 times,[4] with the strongest link being to democracy (22+ times), and the most common definition, *inter alia*, widespread and substantive participation (16+ times). Otherwise, governance tends to be linked to, or defined as, various quasi-technical but ill-defined "development buzzwords" (see Moore and Schmitz 1995). For example, while governance is defined over 22 ways, such as fair and efficient processes, responsiveness, and the promotion of human rights, and defined as an absence of something (i.e. tyranny) a further 13 ways, including poverty, crime, or lagging development, few of these definitions boast much substantive elaboration, and fewer still give any hint about the means by which they are achieved or avoided. That is, to simply allege that "the practices and ideals of democracy have the capacity to . . . prevent the emergence of tyranny" (UNDP 2002: 83), leaves much to be desired, particularly with the growing salience of critiques charging that the promotion of democracy has often been a cover for legitimization of low-intensity democracy and neo-authoritarianism (see Gills *et al* 1993: Marks 2000; Snyder 2000). 'Tyranny," here, merely serves the function of the word *bad* and places governance in an oppositional relationship:

The denigrated term essentially functions to highlight the other term's significance; its formal function is to signify, or identify, the dominant term. The very differentiation and exclusion of this subordinate "opposite" defines the dominant term, which, as it were, draws a boundary around itself and declares: 'this I am, and not That" (Gregory 1989: xvi).

Further, many of the buzzword definitions of good governance turn up, unelaborated, as the means through which it is also created. Good governance not only alleviates poverty, it is the absence of poverty; it not only fosters participation, it is participatory; it is not only transparent government, it is created by transparency, and so on. Such inadequacies are nevertheless masked by claims to universality, obfuscating euphemism, and circular reasoning (see discussion on participation below).

In effect, then we do not find the recipe for good governance so much as we are encouraged to develop the sense of its general *flavour*. It would be difficult to glean from the Report *how* to deepen good governance; rather we are invited to "know it when we see it." It is a constellation of forms and events that assert relationships without proving them; imply processes without elaborating upon them. In other words, we are invited to recognize a narrow band of ostensibly rational-universal ends and means, such as rule of law, transparency, accountability, and women's equality, as both the activity and outcome of good governance, but not to notice how each point stands essentially unrelated to all other points or the goods they collectively promise. They are just lists. In our haste to concur that these are all good things, we can (are supposed to?) forget that it *matters* how these things are pursued. It matters that unwanted changes are foisted upon the unwilling in the name of good things, and that in the process, much of the social fabric is often frayed beyond repair. It is as though there were no history, no politics.

Further, if for every change we were to ask—"Who performs it?" or "Who extends the *right* to it?" or "Who creates the conditions for it?"—we overwhelmingly find *the state*. Or we find an ill-defined partnership between international donors and the state. This partnership is only *de facto* rendered inclusive through *participation*, which is, at least for now, deferred in the name of universality (see next section). The problem is, of course, that states and technical developmental conditionalities have logics of their own, sometimes detached from, and unresponsive to, the needs of the individuals they profess to represent (see Buzan 1983). Problems arise when the state is not an emanation of the collective will, but a form of power that imposes and colonizes (Chabal and Daloz 1999; Vale 2003). For the state is not just a corporate person or collective entity, but a medium by which elites capture and justify power (see Ferguson 1990; 1994). The state is an apparatus of power. Much the same has been said, of course, of the UN (Cox and Jacobsen 1973; Galtung 1987; Hancock 1989; Righter 1995).

The location of participation within the logic of the text makes for an important illustration of the shortcomings of the UN's commitment to popular participation and consultation. While the 2002 HDR consistently and frequently defines good or democratic governance, *inter alia,* as widespread participation in political decision-making processes, paradoxically participation is variously integrated into different and sometimes contradictory parts of the text with the effect of obfuscating *the lack of* democratic or participatory processes. Specifically, the use of participation tends to obfuscate whether participation is, in fact, a regulative or constitutive aspect of (democratic) governance (see Wittgenstein 1953 in Hollis 1994).

Constitutive rules define or constitute the essence of an activity (i.e. democracy *is* participation), while regulative rules refer to those that merely *ought* to be followed (i.e. democracy *ought to be* participatory). Obfuscation is obtained through an interesting fudging of the borders between constitutive and regulative rules, a border that Hollis (1994: 153) helps to illuminate:

> The distinction is not always clear, but the difference is roughly that, if one breaks regulative rules, one is not playing the game well or appropriately, whereas, if one breaks the constitutive rules, one is not playing it at all. *Ambiguity about borderlines is often useful to theorists and players alike and certainly does not imply that there is no vital difference* [emphasis added].

The difference between regulative and constitutive rules is useful for understanding the claim made in the 2002 HDR that one can still contribute to good governance where participatory elements are weak to non-existent— just not very well, or with "mixed implications for democratic governance" (UNDP 2002: 108). That is, the Report implies that lack of participation transgresses a regulative rule of etiquette; one *ought* to demonstrate a participatory element, but its lack does not necessarily constitute a breach of good governance. In fact, its lack is justified by the need to address more fundamental goals, as the Report (108–109) argues using as example World Bank processes to negotiate Poverty Reduction Strategies:

> While "[i]n rare cases does interaction involve the kind of collaborative planning and decision-making envisaged in the description [of participation] of shared control over decisions and resource . . . problems are perhaps not accidental, because the desire of international institutions

to build a participatory capacity-building and policy-making process has clashed with the need to disburse debt relief as rapidly as possible.

By implication, we are invited to see that it is appropriate (according to *objective* standards such as urgency and need), but not optimal, for participation to come into play after the constitutive structures—of, in this case, the Poverty Reduction Strategies initiated by the IMF and World Bank—are in place. More specifically, the text repeatedly asserts that "democratic governance means that . . . [p]eople have a say in the decisions that affect their lives," yet nowhere is it stipulated that *the people* determine, or even necessarily participate in the making of the so-called "[i]nclusive and fair rules, institutions and practices that govern social interactions" (51). For example, in the previous quote, while "the IMF and World Bank describe the [Poverty Reduction Strategy Paper] process as one in which the borrowing country and its people take the lead" (108), key emphasis is put on "debt relief," allowing the Report to explain away participatory deficits as secondary to the *primary* objective. Not surprisingly, a recent report by a Sussex University academic found a "broad consensus among our civil society sources in Ghana, Malawi, Mozambique, Tanzania and Zambia that their coalitions have been unable to influence macro-economic policy or even engage governments in dialog about it" (McGee 2002). [5]

Primary and *universal* objectives go a long way towards explaining why participation is rarely a first ordering principle. This, despite the fact that the World Bank itself notes that in the absence of a participatory processes which can help to determine how gains from debt relief should be spent, by whom and according to what kind of accountability structures, there are few guarantees that "the money thus freed would actually advance social development and reduce poverty" (World Bank 2001: 2). As such, the emphasis that the HDR puts on debt relief as a signifier for an unambiguous good, coupled with the admittedly poor participation obtained in defining its parameters, doubles as an effort to side-step relations and processes of power that dominate the determination of "fair and equitable" rules. For example, while it is clear from the Report that the World Bank and IMF have taken the lead on defining the content of Poverty Reduction Strategies (108), elsewhere the Report also illuminates severe structural problems at the Bank and Fund. While, "female representation at the highest levels remains low"—0% and 8% at the IMF and World Bank respectively, (115), the Report nevertheless asserts that "[w]here participation has been limited to ad hoc consultations, workshops and meetings, there is little evidence that it has affected decision-making or accountability" (109), and the implications for "democratic governance" are merely *mixed*. Further, not only is this participatory deficit a result of an overly ambitious desire to rapidly disburse debt relief, but "[i]ndeed, these institutions have often been under intense pressure to disburse debt relief from the same civil society groups that are pressing for deeper participation" (109). Thus the lack of consultative processes is, in the final analysis, the fault of civil society itself.

Thus, when the HDRs conflate good or democratic governance with participation, there is something rather misleading going on. Evoking participation no doubt helps to shore up the legitimacy of the governance agenda by implying that the agenda is *democratically legitimate*, and therefore not the product of the imaginations of rarefied international bureaucrats. If this is a slight of hand, it relies on blurring the lines between participation as *constituting* or merely *embellishing* good governance. How can it be other than constituted by participation? This answer, expanded upon in the next few paragraphs, lies in the Reports' propensity to substitute claims to universality for a popularly endorsed mandate.

In the section entitled *"Broadening the Scope of Human Development: Why Participation and Why Now?"* (UNDP 2002: 53–54), the UNDP advances the argument that while "societies and people value capabilities differently depending on their situation," the HDR only advances "capabilities" that are "universally valued by people of the world over" and "fundamental in the sense that the lack of it would close off many options in life." The implication is that whatever the UN has identified as the key elements of the good state are, by definition, core universal aspirations of all people everywhere. At the same time, to be a citizen in such a state is also a core universal aspiration of all people everywhere. The universal and inevitable state as the foundation upon which the very notion of the political depends, then, is a central myth of the HDR and the crucial assumption that renders top-down processes as participatory expressions of the common will. That is, we are asked to suspend belief and historical knowledge and to see all states, essentially, as the central embodiment of the collective will. It allows us to impute legitimacy[6] to a state that is not necessarily legitimate in the eyes of its citizens, and to see UN consultations with the government of such a state as consultations with the people who will live with the consequences.

For sceptics, however, the lack of real participatory credentials will still leave open the core epistemological problem of knowledge: "by what criterion do we know that a belief is true or at least that we are justified in holding it" (Hollis 1994: 146)? For example, claims to universal knowledge or expertise made by historically contingent bureaucrats of a certain class have long been problematic among certain streams of critics. James Ferguson (1994:18), drawing on Foucault, described the problematic thus:

The thoughts and actions of "development" bureaucrats are powerfully shaped by the world of acceptable statements and utterances within which they live; and what they do and do not do is a product not only of the interests of various nations, classes, or international agencies, but also, at the same time of a working out of this complex structure of knowledge.

In Sum

According to the HDRs, then, as long as governments embrace the expert advice of the UN, they are practicing "good governance"—no matter how far off the public will (see Abrahamsen 2001).[7] Thus, despite conflating and defining good governance as participation and participatory processes over and over again, participation is not really what governance is about. The impression that it is, however, is achieved by presenting the content of good governance up front, then defining this content as universal aspiration of everybody everywhere. Thereby, following UN expert advice is good governance by virtue of being the expression of the will of the people, apprehended not by democratic mandate, but some *higher* knowledge of *universal* aspirations.

Yet, it must be noted that this last section looks at governance in isolation from key linked concepts, such as democracy and human rights—which could mitigate or balance the shortcomings of the good governance discourse. Thus, in the following sections, we shall explore the position of democracy and human rights in the discourse.

DEMOCRACY: VALUES COMMON TO PEOPLE EVERYWHERE

The concept of democracy is central to understanding governance, because "[d]emocratic principles have become the criteria for good governance domestically" (Khatami statement in UNDP 2002: 64). Democracy is also the central good or principle in the two texts being examined here. As noted in the previous chapter, however, democracy is a highly contested concept. As aspiration, democracy holds the promise of transcending systemic power clots and poverties, and resonates in the popular imaginary as an ideal value upon which to premise demands for popular, substantive, and even radical change to extant political systems. Yet, as technical model (for the purposes of international development), democracy tends to mirror western models, and in that act of mirroring, empties itself of much of the democratic project it seeks to ascribe to itself. By relying on the implicit claim that the basic structure of democracy has already been determined, (see Fukuyama

1994; Huntington 1994: Linz and Stepan 1996), it is claimed that political systems no longer need to be democratically determined *per se*; local struggles are in some sense irrelevant. Paradoxically, the *other world* can have democracy imported, even forced upon it (see Stromberg 1996: 4). Van Canenburgh (1999) attributes this fuzzy logic to unchecked idealism, and cautions:

> Some pressing questions need to be asked which may disturb those idealists. Specifically, what kind of intended and unintended effects can we expect from policies to promote democracy in developing countries? What are the assumptions about democracy, implicit and explicit, that constitute the basis for these policies? Do donor governments take sufficiently into account the context into which they are attempting to promote democracy? And to what extent can democracy be influenced from outside?

Here, questions linger as to whether the historically contingent structures fought for and won by the ancestors of western Europeans stand in for those of Tanzanian villagers (for the affirmative, see Habermas 2001: 113–129, for the negative see Badie 2000). That is, there is some question as to whether democracy is an open-ended participatory process or a predetermined set of institutional structures to which political struggle will eventually conform.

A related issue is the blurry distinction between "the people" and "those who, in fact, rule," which critics argue (Abrahamsen 2000; Cox 1987; Marks 2000) obscures relations of domination embedded within contemporary forms of democracy. At one level, the state or country is represented as an unproblematic emmanation of the popular will. At another, chapters 1–5 of the 2002 HDR, for example, engage substantively with contemporary signs of democratic deficit, such as voter apathy, transnational power, persistent inequalities, etc., and unambiguously recognize that states are not free of pernicious biases stemming from unequal power relations and democratic deficits. For example, on page 65, the Report asserts that "[e]ven where arrangements for accountability exist, they do not function well in many democracies." It later goes on to provide two main reasons:

- Democratic institutions are subverted by corruption and elite capture.

- Democratic institutions have inadequate reach, and there are gaps in democratic practice.

The tension is not simply one typifying Southern forms of democracy, however, but also one within the North, as well as embedded within domestic and global political structures, generally. The Report concedes, for example, that: "Large parts of the public no longer believe their interests are represented in institutions such as the IMF, World Bank, UN Security Council and WTO" (112). In fact, the spectres of elite capture, democratic deficit, public cynicism and disillusionment loom large throughout the Report.

Paradoxically, the Report often implicitly or explicitly juxtaposes the 82 *fully* democratic countries (10) to those with institutions that are 'subverted by corruption and elite capture" (65, 68, 78), while also treating the state as, alternatively, nowhere and everywhere the expression of the perfect sovereign will of the people—all the while denying that such distinctions are even being made at all. Thus, while the governance stream tends to depict the state as a blank slate or empty vessel, the empty space into which an insertion of technical components (elections, political parties, legislatures, etc.) can be made, the democracy stream tends to obscure the relationship between state and society being proposed, while simultaneously admitting and denying that the standard model of democracy is significantly flawed.

The 2000 Human Development Report

Democracy appears 110+ times in Chapter Three of the 2000 *Human Development Report* entitled *Inclusive Democracy Secures Rights,* with (human) rights being, by far the strongest correlate. Leaving rights aside, as we explore their meaning in the next section, chapter three also provides a clear sense of the "forms and events" comprising an ideal democratic institutional configuration. Embedded within discussion of these forms and events are a tangle of assertions, simultaneously asserting and denying that historical and contextual specificity matters, while states and societies are variously conflated and delineated. For example, democracy is defined, *inter alia,* as "free and fair elections," which depend on the active involvement of internally democratic political parties; while the caveat is entered that outside of advanced liberal polities "political parties" are often little more than individual or family fiefdoms (65), this does not affect the centrality of parties in the overall picture. Rather, it is suggested as solution that "ideally, parties would agree voluntarily to [codes of conduct] and negotiate towards consensus on the text, which might later be incorporated into law" (66). Thus, paradoxically, on the one hand, the Report seems aware that: "[i]t needs to be acknowledged that African political parties are not like their western counterparts. They are primarily based on primordial ties such as ethnicity or locality and they tend to lack a clear policy platform or ideological orientation" (van Canenburgh 1999: 98).On the other hand, the Report maintains the centrality of political parties, even to the extent that they are considered desirable and necessary even where their contingent expression embodies a subversion of democratic principles. Paradoxically, it is also appropriate for these "family fiefdoms" to negotiate amongst themselves, and even incorporate their elite consensus into law (see Chapter Seven on rule of law).

One explanation for this curious attachment to political parties in contexts where their desirability and effectiveness is clearly problematic is what Halpern (1997: 57–58) terms "prototypical thinking." "People tend to think in terms of prototypes or "best examples" of a category . . . Thinking in terms of prototypes biases how we think." Van Canenburgh (1999: 98), in her study of policies designed to promote democracy in Africa, draws a comparable conclusion: "Western governments and NGOs tend to see what they want to see in Africa, and to imagine that politics everywhere operates in the same way. They therefore assume that certain characteristics such as the introduction of multi-party competition actually reflect a process of democratization." Thus, we find that the essential structure of democracy requires political parties, free elections, an independent media, separation of powers, rule of law, civil society, etc., even to the extent that rendering these as mere caricatures of how they actually exist in the West seems sufficient. For example, despite the plethora of studies and analyzes that suggest that *pro forma* elections do little to curb the possibility of violence or re-distribute power, the only reason given for holding free elections is so that "individuals are acknowledged as an important part of *the system"* [emphasis added] (57).

According to Barnet (2002: 61), drawing on work by Charles Tilly and Robert Jackson: "Third World state formation will be different from Western state formation precisely because Third World state formation is occurring in a different historical context." While the 2000 HDR asserts that "countries" can be differently democratic, the *ideal* configuration is identified as the "inclusive" model of democracy. This is contrasted to both majoritarian and liberal democratic models. According to the Report, the former regime type is one that fails to protect rights, the latter is one that abuses rights. In contrast an inclusive democracy is:

> *built on the principle* that *political power is dispersed* and shared in a variety of ways—to protect minorities and to ensure participation and free speech for all citizens. Inclusive democracy emphasizes the quality of representation by striving for consensus and inclusion, not the brute electoral force of the majority. An inclusive democracy also *appreciates*

the need to promote civil society organizations, open media, rights-oriented economic policy and separation of powers. It thus creates mechanisms for the accountability of the majority to the minorities [emphasis added] (57).

If these are some of the forms and events of the right kind of democracy, however, we are still left with the riddle of power, such as who decides on the basic principle? Who builds? Who disperses political power? And who, in an inclusive democracy, does the appreciating? That is, as an abstract concept, inclusive democracy itself cannot be the one that *appreciates* the need to *promote* civil society, etc. At one point, the Report asserts that a shift is required from state-centered approaches [to democracy] to pluralist multi-actor approaches—"with accountability not only for the state but media, corporations, schools, families, communities and individuals" (13). The wisdom of the point is not often revisited, however, and more importantly isn't threaded throughout the analysis, nor is widespread accountability explicitly linked to a corresponding diffusion of power.

How the UN answers the riddle of power embedded within notions of "inclusive democracy" may lie in the assertion that many *states* have much to *learn* and *recognize* (see 64)—but this emphasis on *realization* only works if *states* are, in fact, an expression of popular will and problems like elite capture, patronage and misappropriation of state resources (often flagrant and widespread) are fundamentally the result of ignorance and oversight not complexes of power operating at the level of the state.

The 2002 Human Development Report

The word democracy appears in the 2002 *Human Development Report* close to 600 times. In our most relevant Chapters, Two and Three, *Democratic Governance for Human Development* and *Deepening Democracy by Tackling Democratic Deficits*, it appears approximately 320 times. The reference to "inclusive democracy" from the 2000 Report has disappeared, and has been replaced by the compound "democratic governance." Nevertheless, both chapters share substantive similarities with the 2000 Report, especially in relation to the emphasis on rights and rule of law (as discussed below in the section on human rights), separation of powers, and other electoral markers. There are notable differences, however, which tend to suggest a better overall engagement with the critical democratic literature. The most substantive changes are: 1) a retreat from the position that rights and democracy are instrumental to growth and development (Which is replaced with an appeal to democracy as a *universally* sought after end in and of itself.) and 2) a new emphasis on diverse forms of democratic deficit, as opposed to an emphasis on only those states that do not protect human rights (liberal-majoritarian), and those which abuse human rights (illiberal).

The 2000 Report relied on a rather drawn-out chain to imply that the promotion of democracy and development were symbiotic, and thus democracy was justified on technical merit. That is, democracy "is the only form of political regime compatible with respecting all five categories of rights" (56), and "[r]ights make human beings better economic actors . . . So economic and social rights are both the incentive for, and the reward of, a strong economy" (iii). The 2002 Report, in contrast, cites evidence to merely bolster the assertion that democracy and growth are not incompatible (56). Democracy itself is justified because "[d]emocracy is a universally recognized ideal, based on values common to people everywhere regardless of cultural, political social or economic differences" (55). Yet, this must certainly depend on what one means by democracy. While the Report argues that societies are free to be differently democratic, democracy is, among other things, "inseparable from human rights," "founded on the primacy of law, for which judicial institutions and independent and impartial, effective oversight mechanisms are the guarantors" while "a parliament representing all parts of society" is essential. But are these the only ways that sovereignty can be dispersed and divided (see Keating 2001: 27–28)? Keating argues at the conclusion of his comprehensive comparative multiple case study that "[i]f democracy is to be strengthened, it must be located where the *demos* is, not where theorists [or the UN] would like it to be . . . There are, as we have seen, new political spaces beyond the state, whether above, below, or alongside, and these are the loci of new democratizing pressures" (166).

Elsewhere the Report appears to acknowledge this possibility: "People everywhere want to determine their destiny. The kind of democracy they choose need not follow a particular model—the North American or the Western European, for example. The *model must be adapted to* [why not developed in?] local circumstances and history [emphasis added]" (61). Yet, even here there is ambiguity: "people need not follow a particular model," yet, "*the* model must be *adapted.*" Thus, the Report both asserts and conflates a *universal* desire for democracy with the more or less basic *universal* components of democracy it prescribes, despite the widespread use of qualifications and immunizations against the kinds of criticisms that appeals to false universalisms have provoked in the past—and of which the UN appears to be acutely aware.

This brings us to the second important deviation from the 2000 HDR—the 2002 Report's focus on diverse and widespread deficits. Indeed, the lengthy list of democratic deficits that plague all democracies to varying degrees demands some sustained focus on the configurations of power being proposed—and the processes and relations through which sovereignty is, or is not, dispersed and divided. From the perspective of a critique of power, for example, the long list of democratic deficits does not amount to a list of technical problems, but signposts to where power in the system does, or will coagulate. In other words, as Foucault suggests, perhaps the problem is not how to find technical solutions to the *persistent* shortcomings of democratic support programs, but rather to determine what is served by models of democracy that *persistently* reproduce certain kinds of democratic deficits (see Abrahamsen 2001). In effect, among the various forms of African states (see Shaw 2001), the reinforcement of sovereignty performed by UN support has often "conferred formal privileges which leaders found useful as they attempted to consolidate their power, legitimize their regimes, and enhance the economic opportunities for their jurisdiction—or, in some cases, themselves" (MacLean 2001: 149). Do not these elites, in turn, prove useful[8] to the flow of international commodities in oil, diamonds, minerals, timber, coltan, gold, etc? Are they not part of the fiction that weak and quasi states are somehow sovereign and equal nations in and to themselves—a foundational myth of the UN?

As Habermas describing his widely vaunted "deliberative democracy" model (2001: 116–117) notes, however, "a law may claim legitimacy only if those possibly affected could consent to it after participating in rational discourses . . . [Further], the fairness of bargained agreements depends in turn on discursively justified procedures of compromise formation." Nevertheless, the democratic model given, ultimately, does not prove that its institutional forms rest upon the "communicative conditions for a reasonable political will formation" (Habermas 2001: 117). Rather, in privileging both states and governments as the engines of change—especially in African contexts where the state already tends to organizationally outflank all other power configurations within its boundaries—the model carries the distinct tendency to harden and intensify the democratic deficits it decries.

In implicit self-defense, the 2002 Report attempts to inoculate arguments and diffuse tensions by arguing that, ultimately, we should accept that "[t]he role of the people is not to 'decide issues' but to 'produce a government'" (see Schumpeter 1987 in Marks 2000: 50):

> [Democratic deficits] are to be expected of representative democracy, which above all is a system of political competition, not one intended exclusively to empower citizens, generate high or direct participation

in government affairs or produce economic or social justice . . . [Nor does it] guarantee social justice any more than it guarantees economic growth, social peace, administrative efficiency, political harmony, free markets or the end to ideology (UNDP 2002: 83).

By way of justification, the Report goes on to add that the real value of democracy is that "the institutions, practices and ideals of democracy have the capacity to challenge the concentration of political power and prevent the emergence of tyranny" (83). Here again we see the re-affirmation of the norms, forms and events the UN conflates with democracy, and the implicit denial of the politics of this claim, advocating a weak role for the *demos*, and by extension, participation, by asserting that it is the "institutions, practices and ideals" that have "power," not the people. Susan Marks (2000: 52) argues however, that "[t]he effect of such a model is to concentrate attention on forms and events, and correspondingly to shift the emphasis away from relationships and processes":

> [S]ignificance lies in providing some of the institutions and procedures associated with modern democracy, while leaving established centers of power substantially intact "Low intensity democracy" is one of a number of phrases that have been coined to highlight the relative formality of this conception of democracy. Others include "cosmetic democracy" and "façade democracy."

In Sum

The Report implicitly invokes crucial ambiguities about the relationship between state and society and the relative roles of substantive participation and, ostensibly, universal institutions, practices, and ideals. As witness to this drama, we are enjoined to become complicit in forgetting that democracy, perhaps more so than governance or human rights, is found where *the shape* of collective power is perpetually *in the process* of being determined by its members. As often as not, the HDR describes a destination, not a journey, "a point in space, rather than a process over time . . . a realization of an event" (Marks 2000. 66). However, "[a]gainst the promise of self-rule and political equality stands a reality of oligarchy and technocracy, invisible power and bureaucratic-business domination, individual alienation and differentiated social opportunity (*ibid.*: 73)."

Yet, the concept of human rights, with which governance and democracy is triangulated, may still mitigate or redress the shortcomings and ambiguities noted above.

HUMAN RIGHTS: ON LIVING HAPPILY EVER AFTER

The previous chapter argued that, like debates on governance and democracy, popular human rights discourses are rooted within, and transcendent of, representative-democratic political communities bounded by states. Further, it concluded that the meaning of human rights was versatile and malleable. As a result, human rights can mean many things to many people and a reference at any given moment will likely evoke complex and contradictory associations. In the West, at least, these associations are likely to lend legitimacy to whatever claim is being made. That is, if one were to say that "[d]emocracy is the only form of political regime compatible with respecting all five categories of rights" (UNDP 2000: 56), then one is clearly saying that democracy is the most desirable of all political regimes. At the same time, human rights are often understood as synonymous with citizen's rights and transcendent of them, correlating to, ostensibly, higher transcendental values such as the sanctity of life, self-determination, freedom, etc., which place duties on humanity generally.

As a matter of historical contingency, however, rights are legal and moral limits to the power of the state, and part of the legitimacy bargain, which rests on the state's duty and capacity to protect—and not violate—rights. Without rights, the obligations citizens have to a state apparatus grow thin and murky, as does state legitimacy. Where rights are *protected* or *extended*, however, the state/society contract is typically taken to be solid and valid. Rights, then, are an important statement about, and determinant of, the obligations and duties between state and society. When present they constitute the state as legitimate and the state/citizen relationship as legitimate. Thus, while the governance stream tends to represent the state as a blank slate (onto which it can write its intervention), and the democracy stream tends to deny the requisite of substantive participation by way of uncritical universalisms (in order that it can insert a pre-determined institutional configuration), the rights stream unites the destinies of state and citizen, re-affirming the sanctity and inevitability of the union. In this way rights marry the citizen to the state, entrenching the belief, ultimately, that no other political configuration is as fundamental to the good life.

In this light, in what follows we take a systematic look at the UNDP's global discourse on human rights. Overall, many of the same patterns as those discerned in the case of democracy and governance re-appear. Neither Report shies away from granting that states with unaccountable elites and captured state institutions complicate the achievement of human rights; nevertheless, both prescribe an internationally devised set of institutional forms and events to be inserted at the level of the state and infer that these will set in motion processes whereby elite capture will wither, accountability will flourish and multifaceted "freedom" will ensue.

The 2000 Human Development Report

The 2000 Report explicitly correlates rights to universal/ timeless rational-legal rights, which correlate to duties held by the state: "the state is omnipresent in any discussion of human rights, as culprit and protector, as judge, jury and defendant (58)." The Report then goes on to provide for states the institutional template that corresponds to a good or legitimate state. It also provides citizens with guidelines on what sort of engagement with the state is appropriate and UN sanctioned. Further, it argues implicitly that when citizens participate in this way, they *de facto* accept the ruling bargain. For example:

> When individuals are acknowledged as part of the system, they tend to take responsibility for it and make efforts to maintain and improve it. Voting is the opportunity to choose government, and faith in the process of electing representatives confers legitimacy on the institutions of government (57).

That is, voting corresponds to the "basic right of participation." Ironically, the mere act of trying to transform the system is grounds for its legitimacy. In other words, the mere act of voting is seen to legitimize the post-election (and often pre-election) architecture of power, whether this it is the intention of the voter or not. Paradoxically, in most cases low voter turn out—or not voting—does not have the converse effect.

Further, under this model, the institutions of government are not necessarily created by public processes. Rather, they must simply correlate to key features of the *universal* democratic system, *adapted where appropriate to local conditions*. For example, consider this handy laundry-list for states proposed on page 56 [emphases added]:

- *Holding* free and fair elections contributes to fulfilment of the right to participation.

- *Allowing* free and independent media contributes to fulfilment of the right to freedom of expression, thought and conscience.

- *Separating* powers among branches of government helps protect citizens from abuses of their civil and political rights.

- *Encouraging* an open civil society contributes to fulfilment of the right to peaceful assembly and association.

Cooper and Packard (1996: 23) argue, however, that these *universal* institutions and structures are too easily collapsed into hollow formalism, while potentially contributing very little to the guiding principles professed:

> The insistence on "good government" reproduces much that was previously said about the "good economy": a bland assertion that the West has defined objective standards for others to meet, a generalized set of categories (elections, multiple parties) that define those standards, irrespective of the actual debates that might be going on in specific context over how more people might acquire meaningful voice in their own lives.

Further, with no irony intended, the Report goes on to note that "many democracies fail to protect or promote human rights" because, *inter alia*:

> Elected governments frequently lose legitimacy and popular support when they behave in an authoritarian manner. When elite groups act as if they are above the law or when elected representatives arbitrarily remove judges, civil servants and others, faith in democratic institutions *weakens* [emphasis added] (59).

That a system in which "elected officials" are free to behave as they choose should be considered a democracy is strange; that democratic institutions fail to elicit faith under these conditions is not surprising; that such widespread deficits do not force the UN to reconsider its facile models is bizarre. Nevertheless, the 2000 Report appears resistant to the idea of substantive participation in agenda setting. While inoculating its position by lamenting a wide range of rights-related democratic deficits, the Report remains unable to provide any evidence of a shift towards participatory and open-ended processes. Instead, it is wedded to a commitment to *de facto* legitimacy by participation by way of periodic and episodic referenda on pre-determined institutions and agendas, and of course, bland universalisms.

For example, the first paragraph under the rubric of "Widening Participation and Expression" begins with: "A precondition for building inclusive democracy is ensuring the *right to elect representatives*" [emphasis added]. The first sentence in the second paragraph is: "A key element in deepening inclusive democracy is a *legal framework* that protects the right to participation and free expression [emphasis added]" (66). As noted earlier, such frameworks not only protect, but structure the conditions under which participation can take place. Further, in the absence of any substantive elaboration, we are left to assume that the "right to participation" *is* the right to elect representatives under conditions of the UN's choosing— nothing less perhaps, but also nothing more.

Thus, while the Report inoculates its propositions over and over by identifying human rights deficits and also admitting the dangers inherent in facile interpretations of representative democracy's tenets, it nevertheless de-politicizes the state in order to justify it as the only viable engine for rights, while simultaneously disciplining the idea of substantive participatory conversation about the content of the means to the satisfaction of human rights. That is, again, no evidence is provided to suggest that the *universal* model or attendant processes are open for debate.

The 2002 Human Development Report

Human rights appear in the 2002 Report approximately 95 times, less than democracy or governance. Coding revealed a marked emphasis on civil and political rights, the behaviour of government, and secondarily, on participation through ombuds*men* [sic] and commissions. Rights more generally, the Report argues, can be achieved through the ratification of international treaties and covenants. Primarily, rights are promoted through institutions and legal practices that regulate the behaviour of states and citizens. Rule and administration of law, international law and constitutional law are central, as are social movements *based on transnational goals and values*. There is little non-state and no non-international activity that correlates to rights.

However, as Pierson notes (1996: 137), "having a formal framework of rights is no guarantee that these rights will be upheld. The Soviet Constitution of 1936, for example, embodied an impressive array of civil and political liberties, virtually none of which were respected." The same could be said of many contemporary constitutions. South Africa, for example, has enshrined gender and racial equality in its constitution, while remaining one of the most racially unequal societies in the world with shocking statistics on gender-based violence.

Additionally, the legal and coercive apparatus of the state is often viewed by *citizens* with suspicion and fear. The 2002 Report (66), for example, documents that "[s]urveys of poor people find that at best, the police and judiciary are considered unresponsive—at worst aggressive abusers of judicial rights." In response, the 2002 Report (72) places much emphasis on *a few good state officials* who promote the integrity of corrupt and partisan law and order machineries. For example, in India, judicial activism, itself, is what prevented the Prime Minister's attempt to eliminate judicial review of parliamentary powers. It was also judicial activism that opened the courts to "public interest litigation involving the human rights of the poor and powerless." Similarly, in Apartheid South Africa, it was "human rights lawyers and a few sympathetic judges that kept the judicial process from losing all credibility." All other things being equal, judges who are *sympathetic* with the plight of the vulnerable and marginalized are preferable, but investing an otherwise predatory legal system with legitimacy by virtue of the *sympathy* of a few good elites is cold comfort in the face of more substantive reforms that prevent the systematic colonization of these offices by a few *bad apples*.

Simultaneously, we find the focus on elite leadership tempered by reference to participation as the *motor of progress*:

> Participation promotes collective agency as well as individual agency—important because collective action through social and political movements has often been a motor of progress for issues central to human development: protecting the environment, promoting gender equality, fostering human rights (UNDP 2002: 53).

Yet, the Report goes on to assert that "[p]utting participation at the heart of human development strategies raises a question about the scope of human development: which capabilities are part of human development . . . ? [T]he human development approach requires deciding which capabilities are most important for public policy." In other words, participation raises the questions: how can one be sure that people will identify the capabilities that are most important for public policy? And what if participatory identification of capabilities diverges from those identified by the HDR? In response, the Report asserts that the HDR (by definition?) only advances "capabilities" that are "universally valued by people the world over" and "fundamental in the sense that the lack of it would close off many options in life" (53–54).

Ensconced in the knowledge that the experts have accurately identified the architecture, the key actors and, most importantly, the *universal* priorities, participation is, again, rendered redundant, simultaneously evoked and denied. Thus, while the right to participation receives pride of place, it is an *ad hoc* participation in a political life whose boundaries have already been drawn, thereby "forcing politics into formalized institutional structures"

(Marks 2000: 71). But even if a few good elites could provide the backbone for UN models, the power of the state, particularly in developing countries, is often penetrated by asymmetrical global relations and rivalled by other actors, such as multinational corporations, whose global reach, profits and lack of accountability may engender them with more sway than the (weak or quasi) states within which they operate (see Jochnick 2001: 159). In this case, rendering states as the vehicle to protect and satisfy human rights may be, at least, wishful thinking.

There is, however, nothing inherent within the concept of human or legal rights that precludes them from dispersing duties more symmetrically across power landscapes. Some versions of global governance, for example, promise a dynamic and responsive architecture where duty rests not only with states, but with international bodies and transnational networks and partnerships, including corporate codes of conduct, coalitions of the willing, international criminal tribunals, (Brahimi 2000: Risse-Kappen 1996; UNDP 2002) etc., and guaranteed by more robust forms of local/global accountability (Held 2000; Hirst 1997). Here, we catch a glimpse of the vast potential that the human rights concept embodies in the modern age (Donnelly 1999; Habermas 2001). We glimpse at the non-state actors and movements who have been able to seize what is in effect a powerful constitutive of the modern state-society legitimacy problematic, and turn it to their own agenda, as Keck and Sikkink (1999: 79) note:

> We can trace the idea that states should protect the human rights of their citizens back to the French Revolution and the US Bill of Rights, but the idea that human rights should be an integral part of foreign policy and international relations is new. As recently as 1970, the idea that the human rights of citizens of any country are legitimately the concern of people and governments everywhere was considered radical. Transnational advocacy networks played a key role in placing human rights on foreign policy agendas.

As a consequence of transnational human rights activity, then, (some) states have experienced a reconstitution of their prerogative to act as the final arbiter of their own performance and sovereign legitimacy (see ICISS 2001). The shifting loci of duty[9] threatens to de-center states in the rights equation, and raises spectral questions such as "How might persons exit an imposed citizenship that entails significant—or even minor—breaches of human rights" (see Scott 2003)? "What obligations can a woman living under a gendered state have to that state?" "What obligations does an international authority-order premised on the protection of human rights have to her?" "What responsibilities do those who contribute to and benefit from a gendered state bear?" In other words, in a chain of values that includes sovereignty, citizenship and various legal, normative and aspirant forms of human rights, the latter vies convincingly for the role of first ordering principle precisely because it establishes the conditions and limits of legitimacy *per se*[10] and defines the point at which, if a contract does, in fact, exist between state and society or state and individual, that contract can be considered broken.[11]

In Sum

We find that much of what passes for human rights talk focuses on the state and its ability to *protect* and *extend* human rights. Paradoxically, this state is simultaneously the perpetrator of human rights abuses and source of general insecurity as well as the only fundamental unit of the good life and source from which all human rights, and the conditions for their satisfaction, must necessarily flow. Despite shifting landscapes of transnational power, the model relies upon a deep and implicit assumption that states are the only form of political community through which human rights, and indeed human dignity, can be achieved. Little to no consideration is given to the dangers inherent in encouraging, or even requiring, the people who live within the borders of rights-abusing or merely weak and/or neglectful states to re-orient their vision of the political and political community toward a tacit consent to the legitimacy of the state *in order to gain access to human dignity*, nor is much given to a more fundamental constitutive role for local people or networks in this very specific political future (see Chapter Eight on human rights promotion in Angola).

It would again, however, be false to overstate the level of clarity and cohesiveness obtained in either of the Reports—or to claim that their role is to lay out a detailed builders' plan (see Chapters Four and Five for a critique of the *Road Maps* for implementation). The processes and relationships whereby rights are satisfied, and various desirables such as freedom and development are obtained, remain sufficiently whimsical as to leave a good number of holes, crevices, questions and red herrings. At this juncture, we will move on to the last section of this chapter, an exploration of the richer dominant discourse evident in the triangulation of GDH woven into the HDRs.

CONCLUDING REMARKS: THE REST OF THE STORY

Van Canenburgh (1999: 94) argued recently that "[t]he current generation of international policies to promote democratization must be examined in particular in the context of an earlier concern for human rights, from which in some sense they flow." Indeed, the 2000 HDR argues that "[d]emocracy is the only form of political regime compatible with respecting all five categories of rights—economic, social, political, civil and cultural" (UNDP 2000: 56). At the same time, democracy and human rights have also been intricately linked to governance, as the UNDP (2002: 64) argues: "Democratic principles have become the criteria for good governance domestically." As a means to conclude this chapter, we will briefly explore the interplay of relationships between good governance, democracy and human rights, and the living implications of the web of meaning embedded within the UN's dominant discourse.

As noted in previous sections, human rights have a radical side, but this not systematically invoked by the HDRs. Rather, rights tend to refer to *citizen* rights more so than *human* rights—the latter of which can (in theory) place a general and diffuse duty on anyone who is in a position to satisfy them, rather than being explicitly state-bound. Correspondingly, the UN's misnamed *human* rights play their key role as that which constitutes *a fated and inevitable* relationship between state and subject—"but not always in ways that more uncritical admirers have supposed." That is, "while citizen's rights imply an entitlement to some form of provision or restraint by the state, they are generally subject to interpretation or even revocation by state authorities" (Pierson 1996: 28). Yet, note that the UN renders such extensive state powers unproblematically in its 2000 HDR Report (69): "Economic policies have large effects on the rights of people. Those people hurt by decisions have the *right to know*—and to participate in debate and discussion. That does not mean that they have veto power, since many economic policies can hurt a few people *justifiably*" [emphasis added].

In effect then, it is important to note that the UN's version of *human* rights is one where rights flow from states, as the 2000 (58) Report admits: 'the state is omnipresent in any discussion of human rights, as culprit and protector, as judge, jury and defendant." And, paradoxically, the emphasis is on the legitimacy of the state as *extender* and *protector* of human rights, rather than on human rights, *per se*. It is also a version that constitutes the inevitability of the relationship between state and citizen, in that rights can *only* be extended and protected by states; according to the UN, without states, there is no possibility of human rights.

But, citizenship is not only a matter of rights (granted in exchange for legitimacy), it is also one of duties, not the least of which is to refrain from undermining the *legitimacy* of the state (sedition, treason, rebellion, subversion, etc). Thus, by constituting the relationship between state and subject and naming it as the (only) source of human rights, rights become a device

that works to seal off avenues for the withdrawal of legitimacy from patriarchal, repressive, captured or kleptocratic states, etc. If you want rights,
you must claim them from your government, even if it is your government
which is abusing them.

Notice now how the concepts of democratic or good governance
triangulate with human rights. Governance is key to the state-system restoration equation because it provides for *how* non-democratic or illiberal
states become *legitimate* states without actually, well, being *demo*cratically
legitimate. Governance, as we've noted, signifies a relationship of tutelage
between UN experts and developing country governments. The concept is
used, then, to assert the power of UN expertise to guarantee future (and
thus present) state legitimacy. That is, the good governance paradigm is
used as a way to invite governments aboard the program that certifies that
they are enroute to becoming legitimate. It is a tricky move to accomplish
because there is really very little that is participatory, consultative or democratic going on. In effect, a top-down and externally-driven project must be
passed off as democratic. This is achieved by resorting to the claim that the
forms and events promoted are, in fact, *universally valid*. Once more, they
are universally valid *and therefore* democratic. Good governance is the *universally* valid process experts have devised to set democracy in motion; this
process is based on universal forms and events that people *would* choose
themselves—if they could. They are, we are invited to believe, substantively
identical to what democratic processes would yield, and thereby, the democratic governance agenda ultimately backdates the legitimacy of the entire
process, when in the imagined future—in fact the imagined now—the imagined end justifies the lived experience of the means today. We know this,
because the UN says so, as the self-styled arbiter of what is universally valued the world over, by everyone, everywhere.

Democracy works in much the same way by positing a universal model
of democracy which governments are enjoined to *adapt* for their purposes/
context. By setting out the model, the UN ring fences and disciplines what
counts as democratic behaviour—thereby making sure that democratic processes don't yield anything that is not *universally* valued. That is, as aspiration, democracy holds the promise of transcending systemic power clots
and poverties, and resonates in the popular imaginary as an ideal value
upon which to premise demands for popular, substantive, and even radical
change to extant political systems. As technical model, however, democracy
tends to mirror western models, and in that act of mirroring, empties itself
of much of the democratic project it seeks to ascribe to itself. The democracy agenda, then, catches the UN in the act of pre-determining where and
when citizens shall participate in the decisions that affect their lives, and,

more importantly, what constitutes appropriate participation. The result is a fundamental tension between aspirant ideals that envision people choosing their own form of democracy and a technical models that privilege the UN acting through the state apparatus to determine the *greater or common good*. Ultimately, then, in absence of appeals to universality, the UN's democratic governance model is one that posits—but does not prove—that it can satisfy the "communicative conditions for a reasonable political will formation" (Habermas 2001: 117).

Rights, then, in conjunction with democracy and governance, provide and legitimize the boundaries within which *citizens* must act in order to try to effect change in government behaviour. Citizens interested in obtaining rights from rights-abusing governments must adhere to procedures x, y and z, which paradoxically, and simultaneously, increase the legitimacy of the state (i.e. voting).

The irony for people in developing countries is, of course, the tangled clots of power that claim sovereign prerogatives over territories (see Ferguson 1990; Okafor 2000)—and the people who reside there—are not always interested in, or capable of, either refraining from perpetrating citizen or human rights abuses or creating the conditions where rights can be satisfied. The irony for the UN is that this simple fact remains among the *raison d'être* of both the Reports, and thus cannot easily be swept aside. The Reports wrestle earnestly with the inadequacies of their own accounts—which as a multilateral agency, the UN has only limited freedom to articulate. That is, the Reports admit crucial problems such as elite capture and the statistics that reveal that *majorities* in *fully democratic* countries are tending to feel disenfranchised and cynical. Yet, these admissions make very little difference to the overall model proposed, which is largely state-centric and only weakly democratic. Repeatedly, the Reports attempt to inoculate themselves against the admitted fact that the model proposed has great potential for abuse and dysfunction, while championing a dense and tangled implicate order, which, ironically, paves the way for elite abuse and democratic dysfunction (see especially Chapter Seven).

It is the multiple and complex ways in which the GDH concepts are defined and triangulated to seal off challenges to the state and/or the state system that is the underlying logic of the texts—from here on in known as the "dominant discourse." Thus, there is a pattern or method to the simultaneous politicizing and de-politicizing of both the governance agenda and the state into which it is to be inserted, the simultaneous evocation and disciplining of participation and the simultaneous appeal to both particularism and universalism. As the following chapters discuss further, viewing these features through the prism of dominant and minor discourses renders the tangled, complicated and often contradictory assertions of the HDRs more intelligible, possibly even more insidious (see Chapter Nine). Taking both the dominant and the minor discourses into account suggests that the Reports are, *inter alia* (and not necessarily intentionally), an elaborate obfuscation designed to de-stabilize the fact that the dominant discourse is inherently top-down and non-participatory, and legitimized by specious claims to universal (and therefore self-justified) values. The repeated use of inoculations, the relentless inexplicitness and the implicative tendencies of the text render the message in such a way that it begs to be understood in multiple, even contradictory ways. What does this serve?

Chapter Four

The Millennium Road Map: "Urging states," "Encouraging governments" and "Working within the United Nations"

The previous chapter documented both the top-down and bottom-up epistemologies inhabiting the governance agenda in the global level discourse. It assigned the label of "dominant discourse" to the top-down and state-centric approaches, in that they were most coherently expressed and widely seen throughout the Human Development Reports. It assigned the label of minor discourses to the bottom up and more participatory approaches, in that they tended to be more weakly, vaguely expressed and easily dismissed. This chapter reprises our analysis of the global-level discourse. It examines how GDH are expressed in the Road Map towards the implementation of the United Nations Millennium Declaration, henceforth referred to as the Millennium Road Map. This Map is meant to outline the practical strategies for implementing the Millennium Goals, and is the central document describing how global aspirations will be realized. What is explored below is the extent to which the strategies the Map advances tend to express the top-down, state-centric dominant discourse or the more participatory minor discourses. The chapter also details how coherently strategies are expressed.

INTRODUCING THE MILLENNIUM ROAD MAP

The *Millennium Declaration* was meant to embody the central or core aspirations of the UN and related commitments made by its member states. It does not stand alone, however, but reflects and complements other global strategy documents such as the *International Development Goals* (IDG) and *Human Development Reports*. Nevertheless, the *Millennium Declaration* is the most recent system-wide guiding statement to which all agencies pledge commitment.[1] As noted above, these global documents are not intended to serve as a blueprints or strategies, themselves, but rather as guiding lights for a wide range of actors, policies and support programmes.

The aspirations detailed at the global level are supplemented by *Road Maps*—most recently by the: *Road Map towards the implementation of the United Nations Millennium Declaration* (2001). The *Millennium Road Map* is divided into seven key areas of concern. Section V (36–40) is devoted to "human rights, democracy and good governance." It:

> reaffirms that fundamental human rights are the foundation of human dignity and must be protected. It outlines the power of democracy to effect change and empower citizens and reaffirms the need to work collectively for more inclusive political processes, with genuine political participation (4).

In the previous chapter, a number of questions were posed about the content of these objectives. For example, are human rights necessary and sufficient for human dignity? If human rights must be protected, who will protect them? If, in the end, it is the state, how are human rights different from citizen rights? Do rights really have the transformative power the UN claims; or rather do they simply float well in affluent liberal polities? And more critically, what hope is there for human dignity where states are pernicious and predatory?

Further questions were provoked by the fuzziness of the relationship between state and society in the UN account. Does it rely upon a certain willful blindness about *darker* potentials of state power? In particular, concerns were raised about the relatively narrow interpretation and uneven integration of popular participation. For example, to what extent is a strategy that seeks to pre-determine the forms and events, and to some extent the outcomes of, democracy, truly democratic? What if those forms and events limit participation to spheres that are relatively unimportant to the real anatomy of power? Concerns were also raised about the relationships between the local and global. How well do the various architectures of power at various scales map onto how the UN's version of GDH conceptualizes power?

The *Millennium Road Map* claims to speak informatively to the questions raised by the HDRs, by detailing the link between aspiration and what it terms "strategies for moving forward." For example, the *Map* (37) asserts that:

> Human rights are an intrinsic part of human dignity and human development can be a means towards realizing these rights. A rights-based

approach to development is the basis of equality and equity, both in the distribution of development gains and in the level of participation in the development process.

Interestingly, two out of five strategies for respecting and upholding human rights are: 1) "integrating human rights into all development activities," and 2) "integrating human rights norms into United Nations system policies, programmes and country strategies" (37). Technical questions associated with the *how* aside for the moment, however, it is nevertheless surprising that at the end of 2001, the UN was still advocating to *itself* that it ought to apply human rights friendly processes towards the goals of achieving "full protection and promotion in all countries of civil, political, economic, social and cultural rights for all" (36). It is in this context, then, we look to the *Road Map* for a better understanding of the praxis that accompanies the aspirations detailed at the global level.

GOVERNANCE AS WORKING WITH GOVERNMENT

Previous chapters identified, governance, in the global discourse, as tending to refer to a relationship of tutelage between international donors and developing countries. It is not, itself, a broadly participatory process, but rather attempts to create conditions where specific forms of participation in state decision-making become possible. It was also noted that the way the governance discourse is structured tends to leave open questions related to top-down social and political transformation inserted at the level of the pre- or non-liberal state running a risk of empowering an unaccountable political elite and disrupting existing socio-political and economic forms. Further, it was noted that the governance agenda is not commensurate with contemporary standards of legitimacy (i.e. freely and democratically chosen and consistent with human rights norms). Rather, it is taken as inherently good, resting on the UN as the repository of rational *universal* truths and the state a the basic and fundamental unit of the good life (see for example UNDP 2002: 53–54). Thus, the agenda promises that outcomes will be good because they are based on rational and *universal* truths and aspirations. It is implied that the people affected, therefore, do not *have to* participate in the formulation of policy for these to be legitimate. UN policies are legitimate by virtue of being rational *universal* truths. The problem for recipients, of course, is that development wisdom has achieved mixed results at best to date (Cooper and Packard 1996; Parpart *et al.* 2002).

Governance appears in the *Millennium Road Map* 22 times. By rubric:

- Peace security and disarmament: 4
- Development and poverty eradication: 10
- Protecting our common environment: 0
- Human rights democracy and good governance: 4
- Protecting the vulnerable: 0
- Meeting the special needs of Africa: 4
- Strengthening the United Nations: 0

The textual structure of the *Map* is such that a goal is given, paragraphs of elaboration follow, and finally strategies for moving forward are detailed. For example, the *Road Map* advances the following goal:

> Make the United Nations more effective in maintaining peace and security by giving it the resources and tools it needs for conflict prevention, the peaceful resolution of disputes, peacekeeping, and post-conflict peace-building and reconstruction (11).

Part of the elaboration of this goal is:

> Mechanisms of social stability and societal justice usually develop hand in hand with improvements in living standards. This process is a dynamic one, with basic development goals reinforcing the need for *good governance,* and in turn *good governance* practices providing a framework for peace and development [emphasis added] (11).

Here we witness the now familiar formulation wherein the most basic development goals are conceptualized as the instantiation of the UN institutional model (defined as good governance), and dependent on good practices (also defined as good governance). While it is by no means clear what the relationships and processes are or upon what claims to authority and legitimacy that are based, the *dynamic process of good governance* is nevertheless asserted as that which makes peace and development possible.

The *Road Map*, in contrast to the global discourse, links its goals and paragraphs of elaboration to substantive "strategies for moving forward." In this case, the strategies that correlate directly to the elaboration paragraph above are:

- "Urging states to act on the recommendations made in the report of the Secretary-General on the prevention of armed conflict."

- "Strengthening national capacities for addressing structural risk factors by providing United Nations advisory services and technical assistance."

In response to a pre-identified problem, a pre-determined (read: universal) model is advanced. Both the model and the state into which it is inserted are represented as apolitical. The question becomes one of simple UN/government partnerships and knowledge transfers. Nothing by way of explanation, justification or statement of participatory or consultative process is offered. At the same time, however, "strategies for moving forward" tend be rendered in such broad strokes as to beg purpose for the *Road Map* itself. That is, it is not clear how they differ from the *Human Development Reports* and other like documents. For example, in an effort to "have achieved a significant improvement in the lives of at least 100 million slum dwellers," the *Road Map* includes as a strategy for moving forward: "Ensuring good urban governance and planning by forging public-private partnerships" (24). Is this a *Road Map*?

In the section on "human rights, democracy and good governance," governance appears four times. First, it is noted that "the promotion of gender equality is a strong focus of United Nations activities,[2] which are designed to ensure the equality of women in all aspects of human endeavour and as beneficiaries of sustainable development, peace and security, good governance and human rights" (38). Strategies include: "[e]ncouraging governments . . . ," "[s]upporting national efforts . . . ," "continuing efforts to encourage parties to conflicts . . . ," and "[w]orking within the United Nations . . ." Notably, all strategies take the state—or (violent) contenders for the state—unlikely to have strong female representation— as the point of insertion.

The following appearances of governance (39–40), correspond to a strong commitment to participation:

> Ensuring democracy requires good governance, which in turn depends on inclusive participation, transparency, accountability and the promotion of the rule of law . . . The United Nation assists governments in strengthening their legal frameworks, policies, mechanisms and institutions for democratic governance.

Nevertheless, here, again, strategies are limited to: "[e]ncouraging states . . . ," "[c]ontinuing United Nations work . . ." [p]roviding assistance to government . . ." and "[s]upporting government."

Overall, the *Road Map* is more systematic and clearly delineated than the *Human Development Report*, but in essence and detail, their contents are substantively similar. "Governance" is used to signify forms and events through which the misdistribution of power across the political system, ostensibly, becomes amenable to technical adjustments. These are devised by international experts and executed primarily by developing country governments, rendered as little more than agents of a benign developmental state and conduits for UN expertise. The one key difference from the HDR is that the *Map* places a far greater and more explicit emphasis on working directly with states, and little to no emphasis on the darker side of state power or caveats associated with development work. Similarly, commitment to more participatory forms of decision-making (and agenda setting?) is expressed, but even here top-down processes continue to dominate. For example, the *Map* includes one goal dealing specifically with participation: "To work collectively for more inclusive political processes, allowing genuine participation by all citizens" (39). Yet, all the related strategies call for dialogue primarily with the state.

In conclusion, then, the *Map* does not mitigate the questions and contradictions invoked by the other global discourses considered in the previous chapter. Rather, it tends to intensify them by giving greater emphasis to states as the only insertion point, while de-emphasizing—to an even greater extent—the role of participation in the transformation of state/society relations. Further, the top-down processes of governance are more clearly visible and less obscurely rendered. Are the shortcoming in the strategies associated with governance sufficiently balanced by goals and strategies associated with democracy and human rights to be offset?

DEMOCRACY DEFINED AND IMPOSED

The previous chapter notes that descriptions of democracy in global discourses tend to be vague. Specifically, descriptions obscure the relationship between state and society being proposed, leaving open the possibility that the institutionalization of selective components of democracy in weak and quasi states could today, as in the past, truncate rather than enhance people's contributions to conversations about where their communities are going and how they want to get there (De Rivera 2001; Gills *et al.* 1993; Jackson 2000; Marks 2000). In many respects, they carry the propensity to simply cast a veil of legitimacy over minority and elite rule (Marks 2000; Gills *et al.* 1993). Further, in that the story of democracy is one that implicitly disciplines participation, *explicitly ordering participation out of the agenda setting process*, it is paradoxically undemocratic, handed down, imposed.

Democracy appears 31 times in the *Road Map*, mainly in the sections on "human rights, democracy and good governance," and "meeting the special needs of Africa."[3] In terms of the former, democracy is defined as "fair and periodic elections, an independent judiciary, a transparent government and a vibrant civil society." In response to how to promote and consolidate democracy, however, the *Map* responds simply: "an election alone is not a solution; small minorities are often at risk in democracies and a well-functioning democracy is one that operates within the context of a comprehensive human rights regime" (37).

The *Map* claims that the United Nations has assisted in democracy promotion by holding international conferences focused on "identifying essential democratic ideals, mechanisms, and institutions, and implementation strategies." The demographic constitution of these conferences is not given; however, it is noted that key target areas identified include (38):

> *building* conflict resolution capacities, *combating* corruption, *building* and *supporting* civil society, *enhancing* the role of media, security sector reform, *supporting* public administration structures and decentralization, and *improving* electoral and parliamentary systems and processes. *Protecting* the rights of women, minorities, migrants and indigenous peoples is also essential" [emphasis added].

Who is going to perform all these transitive verbs? At minimum, the links and constellations proposed beg elaboration. Who is building, supporting, improving and protecting? Why these and not other targets? How do they fit together? Which are most/least important? And so on. Similarly, take for example the following ambiguous assertion on page 8: "The rule of law is ultimately enforced through the application of democratic principles and international human rights and humanitarian norms." What does this mean?

Further, the 2002 HDR argued that "people everywhere want to determine their destiny. The kind of democracy they choose need not follow a particular model" (61). Yet, here we see emphasis on a very particular model, or at least a constellation of familiars, coupled with a marked lack of emphasis on processes though which people come to determine the nature and trajectory of their own political community. That is, there is a critical lack of specificity included on *how* and *why* the forms and events proposed will transform authoritarian states into states whose legitimacy can plausibly be considered to be derived from *democracy—demos*: Greek for people. This is the same criticism that has been levied against the US plan to create democracy in the Middle East. It is a fault line that tends to run through democracy promotion more generally: "what's missing from it is the how; the actual process," said Thomas Carothers of the Carnegie Endowment for International Peace, a dovish think tank."[4]

In the 'strategies for moving forward," we find a special emphasis on "encouraging states," "providing assistance to government" and 'supporting government efforts," particularly in areas related to developing human rights standards, electoral and parliamentary structures, legislation reform, media support and "efforts to involve civil society" (40). As always, we are left with the uneasy question: "What if governments and/or state elites have other plans?" What is clear is that strategies tend to accord legitimacy to the state apparatus and by extension it elites, not to the extent that democratic credentials have been established, but rather—and minimally—on a fuzzy combination of territorial control and external recognition. Masking this essential fact is an emptiness residing at the heart of the *Map's* rendering of democracy, characterized by an uneven, vague and non-specific commitment to participation mixed with an uncritical faith in state-centred and top-down approaches to building democracy.

While some emphasis is placed on creating minimal conditions that *could* contribute to expanding the role of society (and its various members) in decision-making and agenda-setting, these are couched in relentlessly vague terms, many of which depend on the assumption that the real problem is that developing country governments do not *understand* democracy, or its components such as gender equality and freedom of speech. Here again critiques of the Bush administration's strategic ideology for the Middle East resonate: "The problem with most Arab [sic] leaders isn't that they don't understand democracy, it's that they have no intention of giving up power."[5]

The *Map*, then, mirrors the ambiguity found in the global discourse in failing to provide any clear sense of what is actually *demo*cratic about the forms and events it proposes. The *Map* differs, however, to the extent that it is relatively more idealistically state-centric. Further, global and transnational democratic deficits that are given some critical treatment in the global discourse are, in the *Map*, conspicuous only in their absence.

HUMAN DIGNITY AS STATE-BUILDING

In the previous chapter, it was argued that human rights tend to be conflated with citizen rights, with the effect of ordering the state into the center of the architecture of human dignity. A failure of state building, in this case, extinguishes the possibility of realizing human dignity. This *story* is not without its caveats, as Florence Bernault (2000: 127) argues, in relation to the history of human rights on the African continent:

From the end of the nineteenth century to the 1960s the representatives of colonial domination used human rights as political tools to exert control over local societies and to reserve political privileges to the whites. During this crucial period, therefore, human rights developed less as philosophical ideas of human dignity than as specific, historical relationships between emerging modern states (colonial governments) and reluctant civilians (the "natives").

More recently, tensions between state and society include widespread human rights abuses perpetrated by or at the behest of state elites and other actors (i.e. major oil and diamond interests[6]) who use quasi-governments as a shield behind which the responsibility of international actors for gross human suffering can be evaded (i.e. displacement, exploitation, ecological devastation). These tensions can be particularly acute in Africa where state elites often have little to gain from divesting and diversifying power and freeing the political arena for open contest. In response to these tensions Bernault (137) argues for a substantive reckoning with the fundamental ambivalence at the heart of the rights project:

> [T]he rise of human rights . . . emerged historically as a particular configuration of politics as a specific relationship between the state and citizens. In the West, they helped articulate the rights of individual citizens as powerful protection against potential state abuses. Today, African states largely function as dictatorships. Concentrating wealth and retaining monopoly on legitimate violence, they present considerable threats to the freedom of individuals, while claiming to bear the sole initiative in handling human rights.

Thus, tensions are engendered by a narrow focus on empowering states to define and protect human rights. In terms of implementation, for example, this has tended to privilege wishful thinking about state behaviour while de-emphasizing the importance of integrating human rights standards into more broadly empowering processes (Parpart *et al.* 2002). History attests that the danger that state elites will use whatever additional capacity donors put at their disposal (i.e. budget support, police resources, etc.) to consolidate and entrench their own power base, is clear and present.

Nevertheless, the *Road Map* declares that strategies for moving forward include "[s]upporting the practical application of a rights-based approach to development" (4, 37). This corresponds to one main type of activity: supporting government efforts to bring national laws and institutions into line with international human rights standards. Concomitantly, there are a number of special emphases, including the "right of education for girls" (20, 21), calling on governments to implement and enforce gender-sensitive legislation and policies" (25), and the drafting of the Universal Declaration on the Genome, which stipulates that "no research concerning the human genome should prevail over respect for human rights" (36). Interestingly, human rights does not appear once in the goals, paragraphs or strategies of section VII, "Meeting the special needs of Africa." This is discussed in more depth in Chapter Five.

In sum, the *Map* provides a hierarchical, state-centric and legalistic framework for human rights advocacy. It depicts the UN as the core source of expertise and source of ultimate (and expanding) technical and moral authority, and states as international *subjects* that receive benevolent and protective UN expertise. Simultaneously, a dangerous illusion is cast: states both *are* and *will be* the fundamental unit of the good life. Yet, this is otherwise not self-evidently true, certainly not in Africa and other peripheral societies experiencing periodic state failure. Placing the state at the core of the human rights concept, however, implicitly rebuts alternative perspectives that question whether the state, as such, is all that likely to enhance the quality of living of its *citizens* in the absence of other historically contingent and grassroots countervailing pressures (Brown 1999; Oppenheimer 1975; Tilly 1987). Paradoxically, as noted in the introduction of this chapter, the UN itself is still in the process of integrating a rights-based approach into its own activities (36–37).

Related strategies are based on the assumption that when states do not protect human rights it is because they do not know how, or do not have the capacity (para 207: 38). Thus, a "practical rights based approach" refers mainly to "encouraging governments to fulfil their human rights obligations" (37), "[s]upporting States in integrating human rights mechanisms" (38), "[a]ssisting States in developing documenting programmes for their citizens, adults and children alike, which can provide key access to fundamental rights" (39), "reviewing national criminal laws and their enforcement in order to protect the rights to freedom of opinion, expression and information" (40), etc. That people might have to gain leverage over the state apparatus to realize basic human dignities is not even considered at the level of implementation (*Road Map*)—only at the level of rhetoric (HDR).

Thus, the *Map* confines itself to the UN-state nexus. For example, while it acknowledges that "[t]here has been a clear shift in attitudes . . . Once considered the sole territory of sovereign states, the protection of human rights is now viewed as a universal concern," it points only to "recent conviction for genocide, rape, war crimes and crimes against humanity handed down in the International Criminal Tribunals for Rwanda and former Yugoslavia," as evidence (37),[7] signalling its own centrality in the definition of what counts as *universal*. There is no mention of human rights as lived experience in the context of the environment (section IV), or trade (25, 27), pharmaceuticals (23), debt relief (28), access to land or clean water, etc. Nor, in marked contrast to the HDR, is there any mention of the emerging transnational dimensions of rights and duties, such as those linked to the power of transnational actors or global-local relationships that could allow communities and individuals to directly broker the content and mechanism of rights and duties in a broader range of relationships.

Further, other than encouraging and supporting states,[8] the marriage of human rights to participatory and/or rights-based processes is ephemeral. There are a small number of isolated assertions where strategies for moving forward include: "[i]ntegrating human rights in all development activities focused on the economic, social and cultural well-being of each member of society," and that "a rights-based approach to development is the basis of equality, both in the distribution of development gains and in the level of participation in the development process" (37). Yet, at best, it appears that the "rights-based" approach is premised on faith in the consolidation of the state and constitution of the people as citizens and subjects as a necessary condition for human dignity. This may be true, but, only to the extent that human rights finds essential meaning in the constitution of the state/society relationship. If human rights describe not the relationship between state and society but aspirations for human dignity and flourishing including such goods as human security, access to clean drinking water, self-determination, etc, it is no longer clear that constituting, consolidating and legitimating a specific (and largely paternalistic) relationship between existing states and societies is sufficient or even, in many cases, appropriate. Especially in the real world context where states are, in fact, apparatuses penetrated by a host of instrumental power relations. States are often in the service individuals, cliques, factions and class, ethnic and gendered interests, even where rights regimes function *comparatively* well.

CONCLUDING REMARKS

The dominant discourse found in the *Human Development Reports* is well evidenced in the *Millennium Road Map*. Discussions that feature governance catch the UN in the process of building up a house of cards justifying relations of tutelage between UN experts and national elites in ways that side-step almost completely questions of voice and accountability, and the distribution of power more generally. Additionally, there is nothing clearly democratic about the processes that, ostensibly, promote democracy. Human rights are most often conceptualized as a device to render the state central to the realization of human dignity—even where the state constitutes the gravest and most immediate threat to human security. While some emphasis is placed on creating minimal conditions that *could* contribute to expanding the role of society (and its various members) in decision-making and agenda-setting, these are couched in relentlessly vague strategies, many of which depend on the assumption that the real problem is that governments do not *understand* how to promote and respect democracy and human rights. Overall, if the "strategies for moving forward" can be seen to have any credibility at all, this would depend on an artful forgetfulness about the relations of power and exploitation that underpin contemporary democratic and human rights deficits.

Chapter Five

From Global Ideas to Regional Road Maps: "The moderating role of central authorities"

In this chapter we take our first turn into the UN implementation labyrinth by looking at the African regional level discourse and its relationship to the global. The key objectives are: 1) to trace similarities and differences between different layers of discourse, 2) to determine how the dominant global-scale governance/democracy/rights discourse translates to the regional level, and 3) to assess ambiguity and inexplicitness in the regional discourse.

In order to accomplish this, Chapter Five examines the way Good Governance, Democracy and Human Rights (GDH) are used in the regional Reports to the Secretary General—the New Agenda for the Development of Africa (1993) and the Causes of Conflict and the Promotion of Durable Peace in Africa (1998)—and their related Road Maps (1996: 1999). It also examines the section on the "Special Needs of Africa" in the more recent Millennium Road Map (2001), ostensibly the most recent regional Map. The chapter illustrates how significant differences and similarities exist between the treatment of GDH at global and African regional levels. Specifically, when seen in comparative perspective, the regional documents make significantly fewer overtures to participatory, inclusive or broadly consultative processes, while offering a more straightforwardly top-down vision of UN/government interaction than the global documents. Equally significant, some regional documents completely erase traces of the UN commitment to human rights by not mentioning them at all. This is despite the centrality of human rights in several of the country-level strategy documents, as we will see in the next chapter.[1] Thus, the chapter provides a thick description of the regional discourse in order to illuminate how it becomes, in many respects, a more steamlined expression of the dominant discourse found at the global level; that is, top-down, state centric and non-participatory.

INTRODUCTION TO REGIONAL DISCOURSE

The global discourses theorize GDH in ways that raise a number of flags. For example, the previous chapters argued that the term *human* rights is something of a misnomer when used to signify the more narrow and conservative *citizen* rights, which correspond to rights extended by, and duties corresponding to, the state. Support for these kinds of rights ought to carry the caveat that states do not always have the capacity, legitimacy or interest in protecting human rights, or even refraining from gross abuses. That is, even if functional capacity and expertise could be inserted into any given state apparatus, there is no guarantee that the human rights situation would improve. More problematic still, state elites may simply use enhanced state capacity to strengthen and entrench their own position.

More optimistically, however, the global Reports and *Road Maps* have, over time, engaged with a progressively wider set of criticisms and policy questions. Thus, for example, the 2002 HDR is far more centrally concerned with the specific manifestations of global inequality associated with globalization than the 2000 HDR was. To date, however, many of these concerns remain not well integrated at other levels of UN discourse. There is, for example, scant evidence in the regional discourse of an open engagement with outside criticism. For the most part, regional discourses demonstrate few attempts to acknowledge well-established criticisms of UN praxis. That is, despite a dense web of studies and analyzes that document the effect (or lack thereof) of each subsequent UN development decade on intensifying survival pressures in Africa (see chapter nine), the regional documents make few allowances for or concessions to these literatures. Rather they tend to depict African states, societies and people as blank slates upon which UN solutions can be drawn more or less without complication— despite the fact that this has rarely been the case.

For example, the concept paper for the *Fifth African Governance Forum (AGF-V)*[2] (2002: 14) places special emphasis on the lack of good knowledge available at the local level in order to justify "the moderating role of central authorities." The following passage is worth quoting at length:

> While it is indisputable that community participation in the planning and implementation of their own development is a welcome phenomenon as it improves the quality of investment choices, this "democratic"

and "participatory" ideal does not always obtain in the localities that still suffer from insufficient access to the requisite knowledge and information that is strategic to arriving at informed choices. Because of its being linked to the principles of democracy and majority rule, the concept of decentralization often tends to place a higher premium on the *process* used to reach a decision than on the quality of outcome from that process. And then, in a rather illogical manner, an assumption is made that because the choice has been reached in a participatory and democratic manner, then that choice must be good (meaning it will better serve the interests of those that made it). And yet, it is not unrealistic to visualize a situation whereby a whole community with insufficient information on alternative choices and the likely impact of various options could unanimously and democratically settle for a *wrong* choice of priorities. The moderating role of central authorities is, thus, still important even under de-centralized systems [emphasis in original].

Thus, we find a special emphasis on the likelihood that local participants will be incapable of making good decisions and that communities as a whole are as likely to make bad as good democratic decisions. This may be true, but experts, conversely, do not seem to suffer from the same probability of folly—yet their knowledge of the situation is often as likely to be incomplete.

In this light, the stage is set for a thick description of the details and tone of UN regional discourse. The chapter concludes with a brief summation of the similarities and differences between the global and regional discourses.

Governance: Agenda for Development

Good governance appears in the 1993 *Agenda for Development of Africa* six times. Essentially, it features as part of a triangle of goods—alongside the consolidation of democracy and "the catalytic role of the state" (18). Together they form the "political environment in which the New Agenda can be successfully implemented." In conjunction with a number of other donor priorities such as "structural adjustment," "environmental protection" and "human resources development" (5), good governance is also an aid conditionality. Simultaneously, it is juxtaposed to "systems of governance that often led to abuses, violations of human rights and gross injustices" (16), specifically the oppression of opposition and clamp-downs on freedom of speech.

Thus governance is embedded in the now familiar tensions between the state, society and the international system. For example, on page 15, the Report refers to the importance of consolidating "democratic systems of governance" (15). Here an attempt is made to strike the uneasy balance between conditionalities and the top-down/externally-driven processes they invoke and bottom-up political transformation. The Report advocates that African countries and donors work towards "strengthening the still weak political and administrative structures that prevent most *African governments from establishing a national consensus* [emphasis added]." This is complemented by the assertion that "[t]he consolidation of the political transition process will also require broad popular participation in the decision-making process." Thus, paradoxically, good governance as a partnership between government and donors is supposed to both *establish* the national consensus, as well as consult with it. More detail would be helpful here, but none is provided. The moment of transition from bad to good governance is presided over by a symbiosis between democratic, government-led and donor mandated transformation; yet the apportionments of authority, as well as citizen participation, are critically obscure. Thus, while political participation is lauded, we can only guess at what political expression this might take on the ground.

A final interesting feature is that the report recognizes that governance can be good or bad. Yet, bad governance does not appear to have any external dimensions—only good governance does. That is, international actors can help to foster *good* governance, but *bad* or *evil* governance is wholly endogenous (i.e. not dependent on international donor flows or commodity chains or inappropriate conditionalities, etc.).

Governance: Causes of Conflict

In the *Causes of Conflict* Report, governance features prominently in the Report's section headings, appearing seven times in its 107 paragraphs. The first instance refers to *colonial* governance (para. 71), but little if any weight is given to the external linkages that sustained the dynamics of the colonial states (see also Cammack 1997; Davidson 1974; Grovogui 1996). Contemporary state pathologies are, by comparison, treated as similarly endemic and bounded, as illustrated by the following quote:

> The difficult relations between state and society in Africa owe much to the authoritarian legacy of colonial governance. Because there was little need to seek political legitimacy, the colonial State did not encourage representation or participation. The result was often social and political

fragmentation, and sometimes weak and dependent civil society. A number of African States have continued to rely on centralized and highly personalized forms of government and some have also fallen into a pattern of corruption, ethnically based decisions and human rights abuses. Notwithstanding the holding of multiparty elections in a majority of African countries, much more must be done to provide an environment in which individuals feel protected, civil society is able to flourish, and Government carries out its responsibilities effectively and transparently, with adequate institutional mechanisms to ensure accountability.

Yet, paradoxically, the use of colonial governance works to deny the external dimensions of contemporary bad governance while simultaneously positioning the authoritarian state as both the source of malaise *and the appropriate driver of change*. The remaining references to governance link it to human rights, rule of law (para. 72), judicial institutions (para 74) and the "effective management of resources" (para. 76). Finally, paragraph 105 asserts simply that good governance is "what is needed from Africa."

Thus, overall, we find that governance accords with how it is used in the dominant discourse. Specifically, it is a partnership between the United Nation's system and individual African governments. For example: "Strengthening judicial institutions is a very important way in which the international community can help African countries to promote good governance" (Para. 74). Similarly, while "respect for human rights and the rule of law are . . . cornerstones of good governance," these are "signals" that "governments" send to donors to "demonstrate its commitment to building a society in which people can live freely" (Para. 72). Likewise, paragraph 76 notes that "[g]ood governance also requires the effective management of resources. Improved public sector management in Africa must therefore continue to be a high priority for *the United Nations system and for African Governments* [emphasis added]." Only governments, alone, however, can enact bad governance.

Governance: AGF-V

The fifth *Africa Governance Framework (AGF-V)* places its emphasis on political transformation and decision-making squarely in the context of broad-based participation—or rather the caveats to be associated with it. For example, the introduction notes that:

One important assumption is that the reduction of poverty is more likely to be assured when people for whom pro-poor interventions are meant are allowed, through empowerment, to effectively participate in these interventions. Nevertheless, the paper cautions that while this assumption may be generally valid, its applicability under conditions currently prevailing in an average African state must be re-examined more critically, for experience on the continent provides limited proof in support of this.

This justification for emphasizing leadership and expertise, however, con-flicts with the admission that "experience in developing countries reveals that few decentralization initiatives have managed to engage local commu-nities in effective "bottom-up," planning mechanisms" (6). That is, limited proof is used as a justification to *de-emphasize* participation rather than as a signal that programmes are insufficiently participatory.

Thus we find that participation in the AGF-V is similar to participation in the HDR. At once, it admits the legitimacy of demands for "participatory and inclusive mechanisms in the planning sphere," while simultaneously hedg-ing on the commitment to the open-endedness a real participatory approach would necessitate. In this, the AGF document shares with the 2002 HDR a deep concern that participatory processes will result in popular demands for policy priorities that are *wrong*. Thus, where we see participation invoked, we simultaneously see it disciplined and marginalized.

In Sum

The regional discourses, then, tend to confirm the meaning of governance identified in previous chapters and characterized here as the dominant dis-course from the HDRs, and even more coherently expressed in the *Millen-nium Road Map* (see Chapter Four). That is, it is a concept that invokes participation, while simultaneously betraying deep scepticism about it. What role or voice citizens might have is critically obscure. More central is the relationship between the United Nations system and African govern-ments, and more specifically, government capacity to enact UN recommen-dations and conditionalities, which do not admit the possibility of being wrong or the very real risk of their contributing to *bad* governance.

Democracy: Agenda for Development

Democracy appears six times in the 1993 *New Agenda for Development*. It is unambiguously presented as the responsibility of "African countries" to "intensify the democratization process." This responsibility is juxtaposed to the responsibilities of the "international community at large," which include "the search for a solution to the debt problem, the provision of additional resources and the support for African efforts towards economic diversification" (3). This separation of responsibility accords with a general delineation and segregation of democracy from other developmental goals. That is, governments are responsible for democracy; the international community for the content of development goals. For example, in one of the few allusions to democracy the Report highlights that:

> While the mounting democratization wave is associated with widespread freedom and respect for human rights, there is an overwhelming need to improve further the systems of governance vital to maintaining peace and stability, *as well as governance that promotes development* [emphasis added] (16).

Thus, here and elsewhere the Report implies that democracy, all other things being equal, is desirable, but not necessarily a process through which development becomes activated. In fact, it is separated from peace, stability, governance and development. It is hived off.

Not only is it hived off, but then the question is raised whether people acting democratically are even capable of making the decisions and sacrifices required by development. This emphasis manifests as the concern that popular participation carries the risk that people will choose *wrongly*:

> The rising tide of democratic movement in Africa is a sign that a new era for political change is emerging within the region as the demand for a pluralistic system, accountability and freedom of speech is spreading over many countries. *It is hoped that this movement will lead to social organization that is compatible with the efforts and sacrifices required for sustained development* [emphasis added] (18).

Thus, the Report asserts that "the transition towards democratic systems of governance . . . requires efforts by both African countries and their development partners" (15), as well as strengthening of the state apparatus and popular participation in decision-making (16). However, how popular participation links to the other manifestly non-participatory features of democracy described, remains unclear.

Democracy: Causes of Conflict Report

The *Causes of Conflict* Report, in comparison, mentions democracy nine times in-text. The emphasis is markedly different from the *Agenda for Development* in that it accords democracy the power to mitigate the likelihood of conflict while helping to "guarantee political rights, protect economic freedoms and foster an environment where peace and development can flourish" (21). The rather different conception, role and status accorded to democracy may be related to the conflict lens adopted by the Report, with emphasis placed on "[d]emocratic channels for pursuing legitimate interests and expressing dissent" (28). That is, democracy is presented as a process that, when present, significantly mitigates the likelihood of conflict.

Nevertheless, the *Causes of Conflict* Report ultimately settles instead for a narrow conceptualization of democracy, asserting that "[t]he real test of a democratization process is not the organization of first elections, but whether those elections are followed by others in accordance with an agreed electoral timetable" (21). Thereby democracy's participatory dimension is simultaneously unleashed and tamed—confined to the ballot in four-year intervals. Chapter Seven provides a fuller discussion of the dangers associated with the conflation of democracy with elections.

Democracy: AGF-V

The *AGF-V*, like the *Agenda for Development*, walks a fine line between conservative concerns about the ability of the demos to know and understand the complexity of the issues involved and make appropriate decisions (14), and slightly more open-ended conceptions of the political project (10–11):

> [D]emocracy, in general, and decentralization in particular, must accommodate the interests of the majority and minority, the poor and the rich, the privileged and the disadvantaged. In the above context, a government that ignores the needs of large sections of the population in setting and implementing policy is not perceived to be capable government.

Thus we see democracy and de-centralization paired with conceptions of government as relatively autonomous—and hopefully benign—free from the fetters of existing structures of accountability. It is a very strange way to formulate the problematic of democracy, indeed.

In Sum

At the regional level, the distinction between government (and the development-elite) and *the people*, generally, is pronounced, normalized and legitimized. That is, the expectation of a government *of the people* is deferred while the architecture of a government or governing/development elite partnership, that is separate from and responsible *for* the people, is reinforced. This version of democracy is *complemented* by a marked ambivalence towards the extent to which popular and participatory decision-making would be consistent with fostering development in complex conditions. While the HDRs also betray this ambivalence, they do not attempt to justify a limited commitment to participation in the same way as the regional documents do.[3]

Human Rights: Agenda for Development

Human rights appear four times in the *Agenda for Development*. Overall, they are represented as part of the package of preconditions for aid dispersal. But, they are not justified; no attempt is made to claim a timeless or universal quality or to establish their role in a more technical agenda. It is, therefore, not possible to find a consistent meaning or priority afforded to human rights in the *Agenda for Development*. At best rights are considered some kind of by-product of democracy—and notably not governance—distinct from security, development and governance:

> While the mounting democratization wave is associated with widespread freedom and respect for human rights, there is an overwhelming need to improve further systems of governance vital to maintaining peace and stability, as well as governance that promotes development (16).

Human Rights: Causes of Conflict Report

In the *Causes of Conflict* Report, human rights appear 28 times (see Chapter Two for a more thorough discussion), and overwhelmingly as part of an ill-defined technical model, or perhaps (and less coherently) a point in a vague representative-democratic institutional constellation, which makes equally vague promises about its ability to mitigate the likelihood of violent conflict.

Human rights, themselves, however, again are not defined. Rather, they are seen as correlated to rule of law and as, *somehow*, related to the overall institutional framework being proposed. Specifically, the link between human rights and the rule of law is made over and over again, with law understood as a creative or ordering force.[4] Thus, essentially, human rights do not differ significantly from positive law rights, citizen rights or the rule of law more generally. In this, human rights become synonymous with rule of law—a shadow or by-product of it, with no ordering or emancipatory force of its own (see Chapter Seven for further discussion on this point).

Human Rights: AGF-V

Sandwiched between global and country documents, the latter of which often place human rights at the center of UN praxis, the *AGF-V* does not mention rights at all. Interviews with UNDP field staff tended to suggest that this might be reflective of extra-discursive political bargains with African political elites whose values or interests often conflict with those enshrined in human rights principles.[5] For example, interviews with the UNDP in Botswana revealed that the government was not amenable to having human rights become a part of the local governance strategy. Nevertheless, three of the four sets of country documents reviewed placed human rights at the center of country programs, and no other regional documents examined omitted rights completely. Thus, there is no obvious paper trail explaining why and which documents exclude or minimize key aspects of the governance bundle (GDH).

In Sum

The global discourses tend to variously describe rights as the responsibility of governments to *extend* and to *protect*, and variously as more radical expressions of transcendental aspirations. The *Causes of Conflict* Report, by contrast, describes rights as the outcome of a state's legal architecture. Within the Report, rights play a central role, but that role constructs the state as the primary means through which rights can be achieved. That is, if rights are the goal, the legal architecture of the state is the means. Oddly, the *AGF-V* concept paper fails to mention rights at all. Thus, taken as a whole, the regional documents simultaneously invoke and deny the radical promise embodied by the human rights concept. This is essentially consistent with the dominant discourse identified in earlier chapters.

REGIONAL ROAD MAPS

At the time that research began, there were three implementation *Road Maps* that corresponded to the three regional documents discussed above (only tangentially in the case of the AGF-V): the 1996 *Implementation of the United Nations New Agenda for Development on Africa in the 1990s;* the 1999 *Development of Africa: Implementation of the recommendations in the report of the Secretary-General to the Security Council and the General Assembly, specifically the implementation and coordinated follow-up by the United Nations system of initiatives on Africa;* and the 2001 *Road Map towards the implementation of the United Nations Millennium: Meeting the special needs of Africa.*

The *Road Maps* tend to suggest that the dominant discourse first identified in the HDRs is more explicit and central to the activities and processes the UN undertakes at the regional level. At the same time, however, new dimensions appear, such as the socialization of elites, while others fade or become increasingly unevenly expressed, such as the centrality of human rights.

Governance: New Agenda Road Map

The implementation *Road Map* "reviews some critical development issues affecting the implementation of the *New Agenda* and recommends measures to accelerate this implementation, and generally foster sustained and sustainable growth and development in Africa." It mentions governance directly 10 times, and remarks that good governance is a "priority" issue facing Africa, and "a prerequisite to sustained and sustainable growth and development, including poverty reduction" (2, 11).

> To improve governance, it is important that African countries pursue and strengthen further the democratization process and enhance an institutional framework that ensures the rule of law, promotes a strong and participatory civil society, allows free and independent press, ensures the functioning of an independent, efficient and reliable judicial system and civil service and a strong partnership between government and the private sector, as well as non-governmental organizations and grass-roots organizations (2).

However, in order to actually accomplish these goals, the *Road Map* gives a rather thin regurgitation of the very same assertions. That is, "[t]o consolidate the democratization process and improve governance, further *concrete steps* need to be taken at the *national* level [emphasis added]." These are worth quoting at length in order to illustrate the similarity to the passage quoted above from the introduction and overall level of generality (8).

> (a) To create an institutional framework that: (i) assures wider participation in decision-making and implementing processes and facilitates the emergence of a strong viable and assertive civil

society; (ii) promotes open dialogue with all groups, be they ethnic, religious or regional; (iii) intensifies the democratization process; and (iv) guarantees the rule of law, accountability and transparency of government;

(b) To allow free and independent media and encourage scrutiny by the free press of Government and/or public agencies and bodies;

(c) To ensure the establishment and functioning of an objective, independent, efficient and reliable judicial system,

(d) To institute mechanisms for promoting peace, political stability and security

(e) To create a developmental State by establishing an efficient, motivated and dedicated civil service and by maintaining a strong partnership between government and private sector.

Generally, these points have merit, but they don't provide any more detail than the statement of aspiration that gives rise to them. They are not, in effect, *concrete steps*. Further, to the extent that they implicitly deny very real strategic and conceptual problems embedded within themselves, they are worrisome. Serious criticism has been levied against the *objectivity* of law and the two-tiered system of justice that has emerged in the West and which has been replicated in the South. For example, a key shortcoming of the legal system in Botswana is the absence of legal aid,[6] which effectively excludes a large portion of the population from participating fully or equitably. Similarly, in Namibia, Canadian legal frameworks have been adapted to uneven success and legal experts argue that the widely divergent institutional and cultural contexts make for an awkward mismatch.[7]

Thus, similar to the *Millennium Road Map* reviewed in the previous chapter, we find very little of substance in the implementation guidelines to signpost the specific emphases and processes that will ultimately give concrete expression to abstract ideas. There is an emphasis on participation, but only within the context of a pre-determined institutional framework. There is an emphasis on the state as agent of transformation, but this is not balanced with the knowledge that state elites and apparatuses have *darker* sides. Further, while the international presence looms large, it is simultaneously sublimated and denied. That is, it is the source of knowledge and expertise and the driving force of change, yet this is not acknowledged, and as such neither can the host of critical issues associated with external governance and accountability that accompany this dynamic be incorporated honestly into the central problematic.

Only three specific initiatives are mentioned. These detail internationally funded programmes to train government representatives on questions of peace and governance (23), World Bank and IMF policy advice "to increase the ability of governments to manage socio-economic policies as well as to support the promotion of good governance" (36). These are entirely consistent with governance as the insertion of UN/international expertise at the level of the state, as seen in all the other texts reviewed so far.

Governance: Causes of Conflict Road Map

This *Map* stands apart from others with respect to the level of detail and its willingness to be specific. That is, the *Map* gives a good accounting of what types of activities have been pursued, who is responsible, and how these actors and activities link together. For example, the first paragraph relating to "strengthening good governance" discusses the African Governance Forum Initiative and reveals the partnership between the World Bank, UNDP and ECA (Economic Commission for Africa). As will be discussed in Chapter Seven, in some countries, this initiative is the central component of UN governance support.[8] It is also one of the few initiatives that can be traced from its roots in the global and regional discourses down to actual country programming, *as well as correlated to actual country-level activity*. The *Map* also disaggregates African countries and discloses, in many cases, which countries are receiving what type of assistance, with relatively good detail (see para. 13, 14, 17, etc.), including the key UN partners with which African governments are working, and in some cases, key bi-lateral donors as well (para 18, 65, 66).

The *Map* also implicitly recognizes that reliable data, is, in fact, a significant problem:

> As an integrated part of the Africa Governance Forum process, the joint UNDP/Department of Economic and Social Affairs comprehensive databases and analyses of governance are expected to enhance the in-country capacity for coordination and lead to sustainability (16).

There should be no doubt that a lack of reliable data has been a persistent and significant obstacle to the technical agenda asserted across the rhetoric, yet this is rarely admitted.[9] The *Causes of Conflict Road Map*, then, provides substantive information for understanding the meaning of governance in terms of concrete actions and processes. It describes workshops and forums for national governments—and to some extent local and municipal governments (para.14)—to receive technical advice and to show evidence of learning. The key areas of emphasis are assistance in accountability, transparency (para. 12), "human rights, justice and the participation of civil society" (para. 13), professionalism and ethical standards in the civil service (para. 13), capacity building for decentralization and local governance, "technical advice on human rights and labour law revision" and training for labour judges, drafting of media legislation, (para. 14) reform of public institutions, training of judges, "small grants for the development of civil organizations" (funded by the government of Australia), and election support (para. 18).

Such workshops and forums are likely designed for the transfer of knowledge from international experts to national governments, and as such are entirely consistent with what we have come to recognize as the dominant features of governance. While the participation of civil society is included as key governance initiatives for the Departments of Economic and Social Affairs in Burundi, Liberia, Mozambique and South Africa, no examples of implementation are given, invoking again the sense that participatory processes are of second order importance.

Governance: Millennium Road Map—Special Needs of Africa

The *Millennium Road Map* (2001) also includes a section on "meeting the special needs of Africa." Here, governance equates mainly with the objective to "give full support to the political and institutional structures of emerging democracies" (43). The related strategy for moving forward is:

> Supporting the democracy and governance programmes of the New African Initiative, which includes targeted capacity-building focused on public sector management, administrative and civil service reform and strengthening parliamentary oversight (44).

Thus, we find a clear correlation between governance and government. The only other use of governance is the reference that the HIV/AIDS pandemic will contribute to a "profound unravelling of . . . governance . . . devastating to every sector and every development target . . . [including] good governance" (45). The reference is characteristically vague, and one can only speculate as to the meaning.

In Sum

In sum, then, the regional *Road Maps* confirm that, where governance is relatively clearly expressed (which is not often), it refers to a relationship of tutelage between the international and developing country *governments*, and that overall few participatory credentials obtain, despite the invocation of participatory rhetoric.

Democracy: Agenda for Development Road Map

It was noted above that the *Agenda for Development, inter alia,* expressed the belief that *the people* are not always capable of discerning the *right* paths to development and prosperity. Correspondingly, the commitment to democracy expressed was predictably conflicted. The implementation *Map*, however, has a somewhat different emphasis, tending to draw stronger links between democratization and complex forms of multi-actor governance by, at once, conflating and equating them with:

> an institutional framework that ensures the rule of law, promotes a strong and participatory civil society, allows free and independent press, ensures the functioning of an independent, efficient and reliable judicial system, and civil service and a strong partnership between government and the private sector, as well as non-governmental organizations and grass-roots organizations" (2).

Very hopeful, but unfortunately, this passage exhausts the level of detail provided (see also 8). We do not glimpse the corresponding programmes or action plans. The level of detail provided, then, would be more appropriate in the *Agenda for Development*, itself, rather than it's *Road Map*. In fact, one might be ask what functions these *Maps* serve, since they are often, more or less, indistinguishable from their concept documents, and, on a whole, fail to provide a *Road Map* to anywhere.

A second discussion on democracy (22) is in keeping with the *Agenda's* focus on democracy as beginning and ending with African governments. The *Map* notes that the end of the Cold War resulted in progress towards democratization in many countries, but without making any reference to the geopolitical pressures at play. Rather, it simply asserts that "[h]uman rights and popular participation are today [as opposed to during the Cold War] widely accepted *ruling* principles [emphasis added]." We are left to speculate where—and in which countries and echelons of power—these changes of attitude have taken place; and equally, what are the drivers. The final mention of democracy notes only that *"a panel of high-level personalities* . . . reached conclusions and made concrete recommendations on a number of important issues [including] democracy" [emphasis added] (33).

Democracy: Causes of Conflict Road Map

The *Map* for the *Causes of Conflict* Report, as noted above, provides much higher quality information, and thereby serves as a better guide to understanding how the rhetoric on democracy translates in the field. For example, in Mozambique, rhetoric translated into a UNESCO project "on strengthening democracy and good governance through development of the media" (para. 17). The *Map* also documents bilateral support from the Norwegian government for expert advice and knowledge transfers. These are the only two initiatives mentioned, however. A second emphasis is placed on democracy as a priority identified by African countries in the General Assembly Resolution 46/151, the Cairo Agenda, and the successor agreement to the Lome Convention.

Thus, as in the case of governance, the *Causes of Conflict* Map illustrates clearly that the UN's commitment to democracy goes little beyond encouraging existing elites to "intensify the democratization process." That is, intervention is limited to efforts to change the intellectual climate in ruling regimes, coupled with media support in Mozambique. Unfortunately, then, whereas the *Causes of Conflict* Report linked democracy with lower levels of conflict in transitional societies, the conclusion to draw from the *Map* is that this insight has, at best, uneven expression in praxis.

Democracy: Millennium Road Map—Special Needs of Africa

Similar to the *Agenda*, the *Millennium Road Map* links democracy and governance, and makes some vague allusions to institution building, and "encouraging Governments" (44). It also draws the reader's attention to an increase in the number of democratically elected governments since the end of the Cold War (43), without providing any hint as to the geopolitical pressures that have fuelled conflict, and prolonged the life of despotic regimes, and generally played a significant role both in complicating and facilitating political transformation in Africa since independence (see also Abrahamsen 2001: Nyang'oro and Shaw 1998: Wilson and Mwaka 2004). In this way, Africa's democratic deficit is seen as completely endogenous and the UN and *international community* can implicitly absolve itself from the responsibility it shares.

In Sum

The UN must, as much as possible, blur the mistakes of the past. Admitting that previous claims to universal knowledge may, in fact, have been misguided or spurious would necessarily call into question contemporary claims to *universal* knowledge. This would fundamentally challenge the claim that human dignity and prosperity *do not* require greater popular access to the agenda setting process. This in turn would necessitate a greater commitment to substantive popular control over where developing societies are heading and how its various members want to get there. In the light of a UN that cannot deal honestly with past failures we find in the regional documents the same thin version of democracy seen in earlier sections and chapters—a pre-determined set of *universal* institutional forms and events, which deny the importance of fully disclosing the dynamics at play, admitting contextual and historical specificities and, ultimately, of participation in agenda setting. We also find the emphasis on high-level meetings and the opinions of high-level personalities masquerading as a new emphasis on the socialization of elites. Or is this supposed to pass as democratic participation?

Human Rights: Agenda for Development Road Map

It was noted above that the regional reports tend to see human rights as both a guiding principle and an outcome of a state's legal architecture. The implementation *Road Map* for the *Agenda* makes mention of rights five times, but the only substantive remarks are in reference to progress on the accession of African states to the Convention on the Rights of the Child, and its similarity to the (former) Organization of African Unity's Charter on the Rights and Welfare of the Child.

Human Rights: Causes of Conflict Road Map

By contrast, rights are well threaded throughout the *Causes of Conflict Map*. A number of initiatives are named, as are their corresponding UN agencies or bi-lateral donors. Significant emphasis is put on the ratification of treaties and knowledge transfers, particularly in conjunction with technical legal advice, awareness and sensitization campaigns, some with very promising components such as the UNHCR initiative to "protect and care for children and adolescents in refugee situations" (para. 30).[10] Yet even here there is no mention of the structural conditions underlying the global refugee crisis.

Respect for rights is also depicted as a conditionality for aid and debt relief, with the implication that what rights do is "create a positive environment for investment . . . enhance competitiveness . . . openness to trade, rationalized tax structures, adequate infrastructure, transparency and accountability as well as the protection of property rights" (para. 49; see also para. 63, 65, 66).

Human Rights: Millennium Road Map—Special Needs of Africa

The Millennium Road Map's section on the special needs of Africa makes *no* reference to human rights. This is something that scholars of Africa will no doubt want to watch over the next few years. Will there be a diminishing emphasis on rights in subsequent country documents? Will there be a phasing out of rights-based programming? Will rights programming become ever more ambiguous and rhetorical? Will the UN nevertheless continue to invoke rights as its guiding light while phasing it out of key strategic documents?

In Sum

In sum then, we see the universal and transcendental qualities that define human rights and set *human* rights apart from other kinds of rights regimes receding further and further into the background. Nowhere do we see an emphasis on rights actually translating into the direct empowerment of citizens. Rather the emphasis is on the responsibility of governments to get on board with the UN's human rights norms by signing international treaties and covenants, and ultimately, on situating rights within a legal architecture designed to expedite the UN model of a good state and good state/society relations. This is a state that *extends and protects* rights in ways defined by the UN, not local conditions. It is also a rights regime in which citizens participate in highly circumscribed, and ultimately externally defined, ways. It rests on UN claims to *universal* knowledge (UNDP 2002: 53–54) rather than being amenable to local knowingness and lived experience.

GLOBAL TO REGIONAL SUMMARY

Governance

In the global discourse, governance refers to an ill-defined constellation of political institutions, identified and bundled together by international experts and executed by developing country governments (see Chapters Three and Four). Paradoxically, this same ill-defined bundle is also linked to global democratic deficits and inequalities, such as elite capture, influence peddling and gender inequities, which afflict both developed representative democracies and under-developed and undemocratic regimes alike, albeit to different extents. However, despite signs of systemic distress and rhetorical moves to the contrary, the governance agenda seems poised to simply impose itself upon those whose poverty has become the *raison d'être* of the humanitarian machinery. It countenances few opportunities for broad-based participation in agenda setting, leaving much dependent on the *universal* wisdom of international experts, while clinging to the largely discredited fantasy that third world states can be assumed to be synonymous with the apolitical and benign, if largely mythical, developmental state.

The corresponding *Millennium Road Map* does little to mitigate the contradictions invoked by the uneven and qualified commitment to participation and democratic governance. Rather, it tends to intensify them. That is, the *Road Map* makes little pretence to participatory or consultative processes while also placing an even greater emphasis on governments as the only partners for UN sponsorship. Unlike the HDR, the corresponding *Road Map* never recognizes that these states may not be democratic, and may even be predatory and highly corrupt, living off the excesses afforded by international legitimacy and donor resource flows.

At the regional level, what role citizens might play becomes even more obscure. The discourse emphasizes a commitment to a pre-determined model or structure for good or democratic governance, in which the state and international donors are central. In some instances, however, it goes even further than the global discourses by actually *de-emphasizing* the role of popular participation in agenda setting, while emphasizing the potential for people to *choose wrongly*.

Overall, however, the regional *Road Maps* are vague and superficial. They express a commitment to a wide range of participatory institutions for dialogue, but provide no specific information about what this might mean. The exception is the *Road Map* for the *Causes of Conflict* Report. Within it, the processes of implementing good governance are limited to the provision of workshops and forums for governments—and to some extent local and municipal governments (para.14)—to receive technical advice and to show evidence of learning. Thus, where information is less ambiguous, it tends to accord with the dominant rather than minor discourses. This means that one of the only things we can say for sure about the governance agenda, so far, is *that it creates conditions for the transfer of knowledge from international experts to local governments*. We can also say that there is little to suggest that this is a two way process, or that much room exists for more substantive participation. We can also say that there is a plethora of other complex and contradictory dimensions to the governance agenda, but there is little to suggest that these claims correlate to substantive or systematic programming (see especially the Namibian case in Chapter Seven).

Democracy

The global discourse on democracy gives weight to the democratic deficits that plague all states. Oddly, however, in response to evidence of widespread democratic deficit, a concerted campaign to bring the popular voice into the political process is *not* what is prescribed. Rather, the same old institutions and practices are simply dished out and served up cold to developing countries. Here, we might take special note of the "objective and subjective indicators of governance" found in the 2002 *Human Development Report* (see Chapter Seven), which tend to be minimalist.

The relevant *Map*, correspondingly, fails to provide any clear sense of what is actually *demo*cratic about its democratic support programmes. They are pre-packaged, then delivered to governments, after which time people are apprised of when and under what conditions they can actually participate in the conversation about where their communities are going and how their various members want to get there. By then, of course, much of the agenda has been set.

The regional discourses tend to follow the tone of the *Millennium Map*. Specifically, the distinctions between government (and the development-elite) and the people are pronounced, normalized and legitimized. *That is, it is taken for granted that the governing elite must rule the people, protect them, and police them*, and not vice versa. The UN state is moreover a leviathan state rather than a democratic state.[11] This version of democracy is *complemented* by a marked ambivalence about the extent to which popular and participatory decision-making would be consistent with building development in complex conditions.

Interestingly, the regional *Road Maps*, overall, tend to disassociate the UN from the processes of building-democracy, emphasizing instead the responsibility of governments themselves. They also reveal the UN as more concerned with other developmental *goals* such as investor climate and media freedom. These are linked to democracy, but the nature of that relationship is left obscure. Overall, the role of international actors is underplayed. Finally, in a particularly duplicitous move, the downward geopolitical pressures the Cold War exerted on democracy over the last 50 years are implicitly denied by rendering Africa's problems as completely endogenous.

From global idea to regional *Road Map*, then, democracy changes. It goes from being everyone's problem to being the sole responsibility of African governments. Ultimately, democracy is advanced as somehow separate from the development project, writ large, and then delegated to governments. What happens below the government level seems to be of little interest to the UN. There is, then, nothing that suggests that rhetoric about the promotion of democracy is actually going to translate into UN support for power sharing across the political and social spectrums. *Rather, it seems set to empower elites to structure their own democratic legitimacy for international consumption.*

Human Rights

The global discourse on human rights recognizes rights as citizen rights. These define the legitimacy bargain between relatively powerless citizens and powerful states, which promise to *protect* and *extend* rights of citizens in exchange for submission to the authority of the state. At the same time, the global discourse recognizes that grassroots pressures are "the struggles of poor and marginalized to claim their rights and to overcome institutionalized obstacles" (UNDP 2002: 79), and this includes struggles not only against the interests of their own state elites, but systemic global interests more generally. There is a clear but unresolved tension, then, between rights as citizen rights, with the minimal function of regulating the relationship between "the people" and "those who in fact rule," and rights as a mechanism for re-ordering power landscapes and structures of opportunity, more generally. This tension is a crucial one in the context of tangled complexes of global power that can eclipse states, particularly weak states; more crucial still, in the context of criticisms that even *fully* democratic states have significant democratic and rights deficits (UNDP 2002).

The corresponding *Road Map* declares that strategies for moving forward include "[s]upporting the practical application of a rights-based approach to development" (4, 37). This corresponds to one main type of activity, however; supporting government efforts to bring national laws and institutions into line with international human rights standards—even while the UN itself admits that it has not fully integrated human rights norms and practices into its own programming and operations (as women are undoubtedly already aware). Thus, we find that other than encouraging and supporting states,[12] the marriage of human rights to struggles for liberation, freedom and equality is an ephemeral one. More over, the rights-based approach appears to work towards consolidating states and constituting people as citizens and subjects, *and only thereby* does it hope to set the conditions for human dignity.

While the global discourses tend to variously describe rights as the responsibility of governments to *extend* and to *protect*, and variously as more radical expressions of transcendental aspirations, the *Agenda for Development* explicitly treats rights as something African governments are expected to "prioritize" in exchange for donor support. That is, rights do not inhere in people, but rather in the good graces and interests of governments,[13] which the UN rewards with cash incentives. The *Causes of Conflict* report, more explicitly, describes rights as the outcome of a legal architecture that defines the state as protector. Within it, rights play a central role, but that role is the construction of the state as the primary means through which rights can be achieved. Oddly, the *AGF-V* concept paper fails to mention rights at all. Similarly, the *Millennium* and *Agenda Road Maps* also very nearly exclude human rights, which receive *no* mention in the *Millennium's* section: "meeting the special needs of Africa." The *Causes of Conflict Map*, in contrast, places a clear emphasis on the promotion of rights—but again, centrally as encouragement to states to ratify Treaties and Covenants. It is important to note, however, that the *Causes of Conflict Map* also contains clear references to bi-lateral initiatives that accord, relatively, with more aspirant interpretations of human rights. That is, here the state does not feature front and center as duty holder and *protector* of rights; rather rights are integrated into more broadly conceived economic "programmes and projects," which identify a larger and potentially more broad-based number of insertion points for aid and technical transfers. The potential here is for direct-action and process-oriented human rights promotion.

CONCLUDING REMARKS

Comparing global and regional discourses reveals a number of interesting differences and similarities in the way key terms and concepts are represented. The most pronounced differences correspond to the almost complete erasure of even the pretence of participatory or broadly-based consultative processes. That is not to say that concessions to such core democratic values are not expressed, but rather that when they are, they are characterized by such inexplicitness, and contradicted so frequently by the dominant discourse, that they really cannot be invested with much seriousness.

The most pronounced similarity is, of course, the same pattern of dominant and minor discourses. The dominant discourse accords with top-down insertion of UN expertise at the level of the apolitical developmental state. It also tends to accord with the kind of activity given concrete expression in the *Road Maps*—working in and through governments. The minor discourses accord with such progressive ideas as broad-based participation, rights-based programming, gender mainstreaming, etc. These tend not to be expressed very coherently in the *Road Maps*, nor are they very well elaborated upon more generally.

Chapter Six
Country Level: "Systemic dissemination of information so as to promote universal understanding"

Chapter Six continues our journey through the UN labyrinth to the country level. It provides a thick description of the versions of GDH found in country documents of Angola, Botswana, Namibia and Tanzania. It also explores impressions and interpretations of field staff collected through semi-structured interviews. There are two main observations documented below.[1] One is related to the country discourse in global/regional comparative perspective. The second relates to the impressions of field staff. Specifically: 1) The country documents, at times, advance new and different understandings of GDH, as well as different approaches to achieving them. For example, human rights, while almost totally absent from the regional discourses, are advanced as the raison d'être of two of the UN missions studied, Angola and Namibia, while also playing a significant role in a third, Tanzania. Further, new at the country level is the central role afforded to the media as the means through which to "disseminate" information about the "roles and responsibilities" of living in a democracy. 2) Interviews with field staff provided interesting glimpses of subjectivities and complexities upon which a field Unit is built, revealing significantly different interpretations and levels of satisfaction with key concepts. There were also significant differences in organizational constraints experienced by different field offices, particularly with respect to office independence from directives emanating from New York and Geneva. Some Units interviewed worked fairly autonomously from strategies originating in head office and/or had forums where top-down approaches could be contested (i.e. Angola), while other offices were more rigidly bound to the UN hierarchy—sometimes to the frustration of both local and international staff members (i.e. Botswana). Dynamics at the implementation level were further complicated by high mobility in most offices. A majority of staff interviewed had been based in country for less than six months, with the exception of Tanzania. Both Botswana and Namibia, for example, had recently undergone a complete staff rotation, also seemingly truncating much of the institutional memory. In effect, for example, the Namibian field office, while having produced a plethora of text, had extremely limited field operations.

A WORD ON THE SELECTION OF CASES AND DOCUMENTS

As noted in Chapter One, countries were selected for their high degree of variance across a wide range of indicators—social, economic, political and historical. This would make it possible to observe whether country-level differences and similarities in UN programmes varied significantly in accordance with substantive contextual differences. It would also make it possible to observe whether country level strategies shared substantive similarities despite these contextual differences.

The *art*[2] of choosing which documents to examine was also discussed in Chapter One. To re-cap briefly, at the country-level, there were often several documents from which to choose, and no clear guidance on which was considered by any level or Unit of the UN to be more relevant or comprehensive. Typically, I opted for the most recent at the time of fieldwork and/or most comprehensive document. Ultimately, I chose to focus on the *Angolan Inter-Agency Consolidated Appeal* (2001). In Botswana and Tanzania I relied upon the *Common Country Frameworks* (1997; 2001) and for Namibia, the UN *Development Assistance Framework* (2001). (see Chapter One for further discussion on document selection).

GOVERNANCE: MORE VARIATIONS AND NUANCES

Governance appears in *Angola's Appeal* (2001) only four times in 210 pages; Botswana's CCF (1997[3]) once in 10 pages, Namibia's UNDAF (2001) 60 times in 208 pages; and Tanzania's CCF (2002) 15 times in 12 pages.

Within the *Angolan Appeal*, meaning was split between what has, so far, been the conventional usage of governance—that is, a relationship of tutelage aimed at skills and capacity building within government—and the concept of NGO governance, which describes efforts to build skills, capacity and accountability within the NGO sector (read: civil society). In terms of the former, governance support referred to "capacity building of local authorities at municipal and community levels" (149). In terms of the latter, it was to "convene 12 management workshops . . . covering the topics of NGO governance, participatory needs assessment, strategic planning, programme planning, monitoring and evaluation, human resource management, financial resource management and funding" (159).

It appears, then, that the *Inter-Agency Consolidated Appeal* promotes a state building exercise that seeks to strengthen civil society while simultaneously building capacity within the state apparatus. This stands in contrast to the majority of the references in the global and regional texts, which tend to place a far greater emphasis on working with and through states, while becoming critically vague on issues related to the promotion of civil society and the inclusion of participatory or consultative practices. In this sense, then, the *Appeal* is *more radical* than other UN documents we've seen to date.

In the case of Botswana, governance is mentioned only in the following statement: "Botswana has a long history of democratic practices and good governance." A similar sentiment is expressed in the recent joint UN/Government document pertaining to Botswana: *Local Governance for Poverty Reduction: the case of Botswana* (2002). For example: "Although Botswana has a good track record of democratic governance, and the government has formally committed itself to promoting democratic decentralization, the strength of decentralized institutions remains limited" (11). In the case of Botswana, then, it is not exactly clear what governance means, and why the term government is not used. What is described, rather, is good government, which is seen as largely achieved.

The Namibian UNDAF (2001) places priority on the twin goals of poverty and HIV/AIDS. In this context, it also seeks to coordinate activities on a wide range of cross-cutting issues, specifically, "gender equality, human rights, democracy, *good governance*, transparency and accountability, *compliance with international standards*, equity, environmental sustainability, community empowerment and partnerships between government and civil society" [emphasis added] (12). The iteration of governance and government/civil society partnerships as two different things appears a number of times in the *Framework* (see 51). So does the theme that governance accords, generally, with questions of government, and more specifically law and order. Thus, there is a clear indication that governance and *government* are being used interchangeably. In fact, the following is one of the few documented, explicitly governance-related programmes underway:

> As part of its support to the Good Governance Programme, UNDP, together with UNESCO is involved in a Support to Technical Services

(STS) project, which will provide for in-country training of prosecu-
tors, police and social workers to establish sexual offence courts in
Namibia (24).

There is, then, a tendency to conceptualize governance in terms of working with and through government exclusively. That is, the document makes
clear that the UNDP concentrates its efforts "upstream"[4] and:

> [a]t the request of governments and in support of its areas of focus,
> assists in building capacity for good governance, popular participation,
> civil empowerment, private and public sector development and growth
> with equity, stressing that *national plans and priorities constitute the
> only viable frame of reference for the national programming of opera-
> tional activities for development within the United Nations System*
> [emphasis added] (163–164).

Yet, paradoxically, one of the main themes of the *Framework* is the lack of
a clear definition for good governance. One of the main goals of the Inter-
Agency team is "in close co-operation with all stakeholders, to define and
reach agreement on, concepts such as poverty, poverty reduction, a human
rights approach to programming and *good governance* [emphasis added]"
(48, 58, 175).

In all the documents examined, this is one of the few instances where
the subjective and normative dimensions of the terms are addressed; there
is recognition that definitions are contested and, perhaps, contextual. This
stands in stark contrast to the global and regional documents, which tend
to rely on claims to universality rather than open the door to a more reflex-
ive engagement with what counts as of UN *knowledge*.

In contrast to Botswana, the Tanzanian CCF is densely threaded with
the governance concept. Specifically, "[t]he government recognizes that a key
basis for sustained economic growth and human development is good governance. Thus, it has given governance issues the highest priority within the
context of a good governance framework . . ." (3). This context includes
"rationalization of the public sector," de-centralization, sectoral development
("agriculture, education, and health"), "*inculcating* a culture of accountability
and transparency" and "*introducing* and *sustaining* the concept of a participatory, pluralistic and democratic society" [emphasis added] (3). Concomitantly,
there is a relatively well-detailed accounting of projects and progress (para.
12), including local/de-centralized governance support. As elsewhere, we can
only speculate as to who "inculcates" and "introduces," and who receives.

The CCF also puts significant emphasis on "increasing community-level participation in decision-making" (6). In direct contradiction with the regional *AGF-V* (2002) document examined in the previous chapter, which is relatively sceptical about the virtues of participation, the CCF (8) argues that: "Experience has shown that development efforts are much more successful when there is a high level of ownership of the development process, generated by participation in decision-making whether at the village, district, or national levels." More conventionally, governance is also linked to "reinforcing multiparty democracy," and putting a "[l]egal and institutional framework in place so as to enhance democratic and accountable village governance" (3).

Similar to the Namibian UNDAF, the Tanzanian CCF also notes that "[t]he experience and lessons in the work of the UNDP in governance indicates a need for reconfiguring the programmes as to merge normative issues with the activities in the areas of development management" (4). In related footnotes, normative issues are defined as "prevention of corruption, civic and human rights and democratic accountability," while development management issues are "poverty monitoring and aid coordination." Interestingly, here we find some indication (if ultimately fairly indistinct) that the nexus of technical and normative issues both exists and invites scrutiny.

In Sum

We find that the Angolan and Tanzanian documents accommodate broad conceptualizations of governance that envision a key role for NGOs, with the Tanzanian CCF even including a commitment to broad-based participation more generally. Conversely, the Botswana and Namibian documents define governance narrowly as the purview of government (often synonymous with governance), and in the latter case specifically related to law, order and government administration. At the same time, the Botswana and Angolan documents do not admit the normative and unsettled dimensions of governance, while the Tanzanian and Namibian ones do.[5] Across the cases, then, governance is an unsettled concept, in some ways reflecting, writ large, the complexities of the *Human Development Reports*. Yet, when taken on a case by case basis, we see, at times, very different definitions being invoked. In the next chapter, we explore just how case appropriate these country-specific interpretations are. In the final chapter, we explore the utility for the UN bureaucracy of this—taken in global to local perspective—overall quite messy discourse space. That is, what purpose does it serve?

DEMOCRACY: EVEN MORE VARIATION AND NUANCES

It is perhaps unsurprising that Angola's 2001 *Consolidated Inter-Agency Appeal* makes no mention of democracy, considering the disastrous effects of the last UN-orchestrated elections in 1992. In a country as large as France, Spain and Germany combined—at war since 1974, or 1961, depending on definitions—and in which two rival armies estimated to total two hundred thousand men were to be demobilized, the UN election mission UNAVEM[6] II comprised 350 unarmed military observers, 126 armed police observers and 400 observers to cover all 18 provinces and 600 polling stations. "[T]he total budget for seventeen months of operation was only $118, 000" (Anstee 1999: 592). Six months prior to the elections, "Washington provided UNITA[7] with 30 million in covert aid" (Adekeye and Landsberg 2000: 169). During the disarmament, demobilization and pre-election phase, UNITA re-mobilized for total military onslaught, and soon after preliminary election results revealed an MPLA[8] Dos Santos presidential victory, UNITA launched a conventional war that destroyed much of Angola's remaining colonial infrastructure. The MPLA was caught essentially demobilized and unprepared. The resulting civilian casualties were catastrophic; it is widely estimated that more civilians died in 1992 than in the history of the conflict to that date. In this context, and given that UNITA rebel leader Jonas Savimbi was still alive in early 2001, and the potential strength of UNITA was uncertain,[9] talk of democracy would have been premature.[10]

In the case of Botswana, democracy is mentioned only twice. The first is in the following statement: "Botswana has a long history of democratic practices and good governance." The second is in the context of the economic potential unleashed by democracy in South Africa. Conservatism here is unsurprising. Interviews indicated that Botswana's relative economic prosperity, stable political situation, conservative political culture and economic prosperity mean that government sets the parameters and general flavour[11] of political reform, as one informant commented: "The UNDP really only gives support to government programmes. The Botswana government has more say in what programmes it takes onboard than other African governments." Further, while not an unproblematic democracy, (see Good 1999; 2001: Selolwane, 1998), "Botswana is often cited as one of the most satisfactory examples of democracy on the continent."[12]

Still, these materially-linked explanations remain presumptions at best. As discussed later, the omission of democracy from some key texts and not others does not mean that it is not the subject of vigorous debate and/or programming in the ground. Rather, in some respects, it is just another contradiction, just another layer of obfuscation, one among many.[13] Democracy can be absent from one document and all over another, both pertaining to the same context.

The Namibian UNDAF places significant emphasis on the promotion of democracy, despite it having no place in key Mission themes (46). Interestingly, democracy is discussed mainly in the context of education programs targeted at primary and secondary students and curriculum support, under the auspices of UNESCO. However, by and large, the majority of democracy support happens under bilateral arrangements, and the UNDAF names Sweden, Denmark, Finland, Germany and the EU as major donors.

The identification of democracy as a "normative issue" (4) in the Tanzanian CCF also corresponds to the identification of democracy as a question of education. After independence Tanzania emerged as a one-party socialist state under the leadership of the much-admired Julius Nyerere, only to become a multiparty democracy in 1995. Infrastructurally weak in transport and communications, and overwhelmingly rural in the interior, it is widely suggested that many Tanzanians still believe that Nyerere is still president, despite his death in 1997,[14] as one informant noted: "some villages are so remote, that news takes a really long time to get there, and people have no way of telling what is true or not, so they choose to believe that Nyerere is still alive. He is still the big chief." In this context, the CCF's reference to "introducing and sustaining the concept of a participatory, pluralistic and democratic society" (3) is not misplaced. However, note "introducing" not *consulting* or *facilitating*.

Participation is also well-threaded throughout the CCF's discussions on democracy, but its meaning is ambiguous. That is, it refers to "all levels of the electoral systems (parliament, district and village councils)" (4), and to "community-level participation in decision-making" (6), with no elaboration to anchor the rhetoric in specific practices. Yet, the overall sentiment, at times, appears broadly inclusive:

> To provide support for a decision making environment that facilitates participatory, democratic, gender-balanced and transparent decision-making, with communities accessing knowledge, skills and processes that empower them to make decisions about sustainable use of their own resources (9).

Nevertheless, in many respects, the CCF describes a flow of knowledge that is one way and top down, with no references made to processes of cross-pollination between communities and the more technical state-building processes. That is, outputs for democratic support include *putting in place* a "legal and institutional framework . . . so as to enhance democratic and accountable village governance" and the '*systemic dissemination* of information, so as to promote universal understanding of roles and responsibilities in a pluralistic, democratic and rights-based society" [emphasis added] (9).

In sum

Overall then, the Angolan document avoids the question of democracy altogether. While there are good reasons for this, it is also, nevertheless, a troubling omission. That is, no mention at all—not even in the context of recognizing that election talk would be premature—gives one pause in light of charges that the promotion of democracy has often neglected crucial preparatory work and organized elections in climates likely to break out into conflict (Gill *et al.* 1993; Marks 2000; see also Chapter Seven). That is, there is some sense in which the preparatory work should already be underway, even if elections themselves are far off. Further, given the UN's role in the disastrous 1992 elections, the lack of reflexivity is cause for concern.

The Botswana document treats democracy as if the concept were straightforward and unproblematic. In fact, it has been achieved. It is perhaps even one of the 82 *fully* democratic countries referred to in the 2002 *Human Development Report*. Namibia and Tanzania, by contrast, adopt more nuanced, complex and participatory approaches to democracy, yet temper these with a focus on education and, moreover, the *dissemination* of the rules and regulations of a pre-determined form of democracy. Here we also see democracy taking on some of the hallmarks of governance found at the global and regional levels of discourse. That is, democracy is represented as something *disseminated* by the UN and taken onboard by local people—in the absence of substantive opportunities for participation and deliberation or modification. The emphasis on inserting UN ideas right into the psyches of local people of *inculcating* and *systematically disseminating*, specifically school children, is new, however.

HUMAN RIGHTS: STILL MORE VARIATIONS AND NUANCES

Human rights are advanced as the key rationale for the UN mission in Angola, with a large number of references made to "targeting the most vulnerable members of communities through integrated rights-based programming" (1, see also 17, 21, 22, 115), with an emphasis on "rights of displaced populations, in particular, women, children and the elderly" (5, see also

9, 17, 22).[15] Overall, the *Appeal* contains a multi-dimensional approach to rights, conceptualizing their promotion as linked to: 1) strengthening government institutions, justice, and law and order functions as a means to enhance and extend the state's capacity to protect human rights, 2) the provision of humanitarian relief (specifically food, clean water) in order to satisfy "human, social and economic rights" (31), and 3) an emphasis on rights as a normative departure point from which to re-thread community social fabric and support grassroots conflict management and resolution (37). Rights, then, serve as the foundation for a wide and not necessarily substantively similar set of policy directions. In fact they span a number of the different ways of understanding the means and meaning of human rights, as discussed in Chapter Two.

On the one hand, rights are the cornerstone of initiatives to empower the state—a normative position that, given a plethora of ills from elite capture and corruption to violent clashes over state resources, is not unproblematic. Nevertheless, the UN Department of Political Affairs *is* the Human Rights division of the UN Office in Angola (UNOA). Its position is that "[h]uman rights violations generally fall into two categories: those directly related to the conflict and those related to weakness in the institutions required for respect for human rights" (117), although the former might read *conflict between the interests of militarized factions vying for control over the state,* and the latter *the propensity to commit human right abuses.* Public opinion surveys have found, for example, that a key problem is not weakness, *per se,* but rather the predatory nature of these institutions, and the insecurity that government agents, such as police, inflict upon society (Manning 1997). For example, the *Appeal* refers to efforts to enhance capacity of government to register live births. However interviews illuminated those deficits in citizenship and birth registration were not only related to infrastructure weakness, but also to government efforts to manipulate the size and composition of the (future) electorate.[16]

On the other hand, in other contexts, rights are integrated into the *Appeal* in ways that invoke the aspirant dimensions explored in earlier chapters—present in the global discourse, but largely absent from the regional discourse. This includes rights as the basis for interventions designed to enhance the self-sufficiency of individuals and communities and rights-based support as the basis for assisting communities to make use of "traditional and creative ways of reducing daily tension and violence" (119). Here we see the potential for initiatives to enhance the autonomy of individuals and communities in ways that do not necessarily simultaneously enhance the power of the state to act as the central and determining agent of change.

Interviews at the UNDP in Gaborone, Botswana, revealed that the GoB was not in full support of integrating human rights as a central feature of UN governance reform. Nevertheless, the CCF does include human rights, once, as part of a comprehensive approach to addressing gender issues (7). It is noted that, in the past, the UNDP contributed significantly to promoting "the creation of the women's NGO coalition" and supported the "preparation of a National Gender Programme." At the time of interviews, however, the Governance Unit was not pursuing any gender-specific programming and none of the projects had been reviewed through gendered lenses in order to conform to mainstreaming standards.[17] Field staff appeared to be looking forward to a time when funds and capacity would be made available for this critical element of the overall UN commitment, as one informant commented: "We would really like to have someone go over our programmes with gendered lenses." Similarly, in Angola, most staff lamented how women were marginalized. Staff who cared about the issue had to carve resources out of other programmes to include any gender related activities. One informant commented: "We would love to have an organization like the Women's Committee do an evaluation; we really need something like that."

Like the Angolan *Appeal*, the Namibian UNDAF is scripted around the concept of human rights and the "human rights approach to development" (13). It also provides an Annex (1) detailing exactly what this means. Most fundamentally, the rights-based approach correlates to strengthening the architecture associated with the government duty to protect human rights:

> An important element of a human rights approach is the concept of accountability. Human rights have correlative duties or obligations for their realization . . . The ratification of human rights instruments and conventions by the State indicates acceptance of its responsibility. . . . In all cases, the onus is on Government to provide for the conditions and an enabling environment, which may involve the creation of legal and administrative framework and the formulation of supportive policies (83).

This is consistent with a narrow interpretation of human rights as citizen rights and the strengthening of the state apparatus that the UNDP often equates with the "realization and enlargement of human rights":

> Advocacy and capacity-strengthening for the institutions that support the realization **and enlargement of human rights** (legislature, judiciary, central, regional and local authorities) [emphasis in original] (61).

To a limited extent, there are also more radical dimensions to human rights in evidence. For example: "A more equitable distribution of income, the elimination of rural-urban disparities, and variations between regions and language groups, remain Namibia's fundamental human rights challenges" (28). Presumably, these could be tackled through a top-down state centric approach, but also in other ways as well. That is, the desire to use a human rights approach, thereby "empowering the poor to earn their own livelihoods, to control their own destiny and to participate fully in society" (32) is also a consistent theme in the UNDAF. Similarly, special emphasis on issues such as reproductive rights and gender equality may lend themselves to more daring engagements with existing coagulations of power, challenging the necessity of state-centric interventions.

Interestingly, the UNDAF also incorporates human rights in ways that explicitly afford the United Nations a central role in agenda setting within a complex governance agenda:

> The concentration of UN Agency efforts on cross-cutting and multi-sectoral concerns such as the reduction of poverty and the containment of the spread of HIV/AIDS, within a human rights approach and at the highest possible institutional level, will provide an enabling environment for increased co-operation and dialogue between UN Agencies, Ministries, regional structures, communities and international development partners. It is at this level of intervention that the UN Agencies can be most effective and where development co-operation partners converge to discuss policies, strategies and action plans (53–54).

That said, paradoxically, one of the main goals of the inter agency team is "in close co-operation with all stakeholders, to define and reach agreement on, concepts such as poverty, poverty reduction, a human rights approach to programming and good governance" (48: 58: 175).

Similarly, the Tanzanian CCF notes that human rights are a normative rather than a technical or capacity problem (4). Nevertheless, rights are asserted, not as something about which to consult with local groups and reach consensus on emphases, priorities and means, but rather as a pre-set agenda about which awareness "rights and obligations in a pluralistic society" (3) must be disseminated. As such rights are couched in the context of a "civic education programme," compliance with international standards, the promotion of "universal understanding" and the establishment of effective capacity in the central government (9).

In Sum

Overall then, rights find complex expression across the country settings, integrated as the *raison d'être* for intervention and support programmes in Angola and Namibia, and as both top-down state building and bottom-up support for broad-based or popular empowerment. In the case of Namibia, this tense moment is complicated by the central role the UN ascribes itself in agenda setting; in Angola, it is complicated by the lack of clear signal with respect to frictions between citizens and state, and moreover, the sometimes predatory nature of the state apparatus—even where it is strongest (i.e. the coercive apparatus). Rights are more minimally integrated into the Tanzanian CCF, paradoxically as both normative, and therefore in some respects relative, but also as something to be *disseminated* by the UN and taken onboard by Tanzanians. In Botswana, they are less central still, linked only to gender equality but not linked to any gender-base programmig *per se*. Thus, rights are variously the *raison d'être* of UN intervention, part of a package of externally devised reforms, the mechanism of grassroots empowerment and the justification for state building; quite the fungible concept.

PERSPECTIVES FROM THE FIELD—CONTESTED KNOWLEDGE IN MOTION

In this section we carry through our description of the fuzziness of GDH to the impressions of field staff, drawing on semi-structured interviews and participant observation. Not surprisingly, field staffs understand the concept in various and often contradictory ways, while also expressing various degrees of satisfaction with what they perceive as the UN's official approach. Note however, that what follows is not a survey and thus is not a comprehensive or statistically relevant account of how all the various staff members view the various programmes. Rather, here we simply illustrate more generally that tensions and contradictions found in the discourse are further complicated by tensions and contradictions at the implementation level. Additionally, no attempt is made to understand the source of varying and varied perspectives or to map them onto a power grid of the UN bureaucracy, although this would be an important subject to study. Hence, few distinctions are made between country and international staff or the positions of interviewees in the UN hierarchy. Nevertheless, noting that differences and paradoxes are present at the country level remains an important observation because, in the final analysis, field representatives and officers carry out what appears to be quite a tangled and labyrinthine UN policy.

In many respects, however, it is also useful finding that country offices were not broadly comparable. For example, in some countries office and field staffs seemed relatively autonomous to interpret and implement UN goals, while in others their parameters came more directly from New York and/or mandates approved by country governments. For example, in Angola members of the UNHCR team appeared to enjoy a high degree of autonomy within their respective fields of responsibility. In some cases, officers identified needs and designed programmes and interventions to fill that need; in other cases, only general project frameworks were provided while officers had the responsibility of innovating content and implementation. As a result, there were significant provincial differences between how apparently similar projects were viewed and executed (see Chapter Eight).

In Botswana, conversely, field officers expressed frustration at the level of bureaucratic control and the number of inappropriate policy objectives and dictums emanating from New York. To paraphrase[18] one informant:

> Too many decisions are simply handed down from New York with no explanation, giving the distinct impression of a meaningless and arbitrary enforcement of power. For example, we received the new *Human Development Report* this morning, but we were not allowed to open it, to even look at it, to circulate it, until 3 pm.

> The basic framework emanates from New York, and often its stipulations don't have the capacity to enhance welfare in this specific context [Botswana]. So, the framework is just a joke. The UN system as a whole doesn't understand the value of meeting the needs of the host country, specifically.

There were also significant differences in staff composition across the offices. For example, in Botswana, the majority of the Governance Unit was new (less than one year in country); the same was true in Namibia. In Tanzania the majority of the Governance Unit had been in residence for two years or more. In Namibia, there had been almost a complete staff turnover four months before field research (September 2002), and it was difficult to arrange interview times with the new officers.[19]

Bearing these conditions in mind, in all country visits, participants were invited to discuss their respective understandings of the relative importance of governance, democracy and human rights for the country-specific governance agendas.

Angola

In Angola, most informants tended to understand governance as a *de facto*, if laboured, relationship of tutelage between the international donors and government. For example, the government was expected to perform a wide variety of tasks prescribed by various UN Agencies—such as integrate new laws and regulations drafted by OCHA, and prepare strategy papers that indicated that UN norms would be woven into future government programmes. However, it was recounted at the Provincial Working Group that in the wake of the World Bank requesting a Poverty Reduction Strategy Paper in exchange for the dispersal of monies, the GoA subsequently simply contacted the UNDP to prepare it. The government then handed over the very same UNDP-prepared Report back over the World Bank, who then handed over the funding bundle to government. The exercise, it was felt, indicated that the GoA lacked respect for the process, and possibly the UN more generally, while the lack of communication and coordination between UN offices at times like this served to undermine the broader Mission objectives. [20]

The governance agenda exhibited other contradictions as well. For example, in 2001, both the UNHCR and UNDP were pursuing governance projects called "The Human Rights Committee" (HRC)[21] in provinces where they were the Lead Agency. The HRC project was an attempt to build institutional capacity in the provinces by creating committees trained in human rights norms whose members could serve both a quasi-legal-political and conflict mediation role. The HRC comprised mainly provincial government officials appointed from Luanda. It also reserved one place for "traditional authorities" and several for NGOs. A furnished office and a human rights library were in the planning stages. [22]

During Provincial Working Group meetings little consensus was observed on the effectiveness or conceptual appropriateness of the project. Some members felt the key problem was that that the central government was not fully supportive, and thus, was likely to ignore and undermine the Committees. The UNDP representative disclosed that the programme had been put on hold in UNDP-led provinces, as part of an overall tactical retreat from "parallel structure" thinking and movement towards more general constructive engagement with the central government. The UNHCR, in contrast, retained a high level of confidence in the Committee project and was moving forward with devising human-right-based provincial governance structures, hoping to integrate indigenous forms of conflict resolution and political deliberation and foster a new human rights culture.

Thus, the UNDP approach, comparatively, was relatively supportive of building central government capacity. The UNHCR approach, in principle, however, reflected the values and relations of governance expressed in the *Appeal* by attempting to move the political process forward in partnership between government, NGOs, and communities. As is discussed in Chapter Eight however, the preponderance of non-elected government authorities on the Committee as well as the lack of truly consultative preliminary work would prove problematic in the medium term.

With respect to democracy, sympathies appeared to be split. Some felt that a democratic election was imminent and that registration of citizens and voters was a key area of concern; others, however, tended to feel that the registration of voters was a technical impossibility at the moment. They noted that government was selectively stalling the citizen registration process in many areas (including birth registry), and that associated problems linked to IDP and refugee flows presented logistical problems that the UN was not equipped to overcome.[23] In this context, some felt that it was more appropriate to support locally rooted citizen forums and ombuds-person initiatives.[24]

In terms of human rights, "protection" was the central theme of the entire Mission. "Protection" is a euphemism for human rights and a wide spectrum of activities can, in the final analysis, be included under this rubric. To use crude aggregated categories of analysis, Working Group members seemed to hold either political and/or structural sympathies or technical and/or humanitarian relief sympathies. The former tended to understand protection in relation to a broad agenda for political transformation, and included a marked emphasis on drafting rights-based rules for government to sign on to, such as the right to resettlement norms (Regulamento). For example, OCHA expressed the view that despite the government forcing resettlement into insecure areas just after signing the Regulamento, progress was close at hand:

> Government backed down after we applied political pressure. The next key area for Regulamento will be standards ops [operations] for water and sanitation. We are moving forward to identify a government department to partner with.

The latter were more concerned with immediate relief to vulnerable populations, such as stream rehabilitation, building supplies, food stuffs, etc. and wished to avoid entangling humanitarian projects with political objectives generally and state-building initiative specifically.[25] For example one member commented:

> [Working with the GoA] . . . is just guilt and oil interests. The Americans are the only donor Mission who is willing to rock their commercial

interests. The Norwegians and the Swedes just aren"t interested in right to resettlement. We can lobby them, but the emphasis has to be real food, water and shelter today.

This division also seemed to coincide with some inter-agency umbrage. Specifically, one key UN official lamented that the effectiveness of the entire humanitarian operation was compromised by the unrealistic and questionable political goals of the UNDP-World Bank partnership to which it had become subservient: "the UNDP is now just the development arm of the World Bank. It is all about the oil."

Botswana

Members of the Botswana UNDP unit were equally transparent and generous with their time. Circumstance also provided the opportunity to interview each officer (three in total) separately and in-depth. These results provide further interesting glimpses at the subjectivities and complexities upon which a field unit is built. On the question of governance:[26]

> **Informant #1:** Good governance is participatory government, where people can be part and parcel of the decision-making process. It also includes such goods as transparency and accountability. In order to contribute to good governance, our projects make information available to parliamentarians—specifically making incremental information of progress available. It will also include forums—which are a key to enhancing civil society.

> **Informant #2:** Good governance is a whole concept that involves many factors related to the participation of people in decision-making about the policies that affect them. For example, here in Botswana there was never any debate about the constitution; it was just handed down to us from Britain. Law is easier to enforce when people have participated in the law-making process, agree on the general principles, know what the content of the law is, and why it benefits them.

> Moreover, good governance does not involve being paternalistic. How can Botswana be called a democracy when the government structure is so centralized? People need to be informed and educated so that they can exercise their votes. Too often governance is simply equated to the provision of services and goods, such as clinic and medicines—but without understanding and participation, all this amounts to vote buying.

Informant #3: The government does not like the term. They consider it biased; that it represents the UN trying to impose standards. In fact, we tried to change the name of our unit, but headquarters balked. Overall, we don't talk about "good governance" because the term is so problematic.

The government almost didn't participate in the last African Governance Forum [AGF-V]. They didn't feel they had anything to learn.

Thus, we find tensions between the concepts of governance, participation and democracy, and simultaneous tensions between the apportionment of local, national and international decision-making power and authority. On the question of defining democracy and related objectives:

Informant #1: It is a system of government by the people for the people and denotes that they are a part of the decision-making process. This includes free and fair elections.

Informant #2: This is just one element of good governance, which is much more than simply elections. How can we say we have democracy when our parliamentary and constitutional processes are so closed up? The government trades on schools, clinics and ignorance.

Informant #3: Democracy is a pre-condition to good governance. It is when all people have the ability and opportunity to influence political life, and have the freedom to make the decisions that affect them personally.

Interestingly, there are varying degrees of association with elections. Generally, more emphasis is placed on the ability of people to influence decision-making than on a pre-set institutional architecture. This may be, in part, because Botswana's institutional architecture is largely consistent with the UN model, and yet, full participation in the political and legal systems, and in the full benefits of citizenship, remains elusive for many. For example, recently the *Guardian* reported that Kalahari Bushmen[27] targeted for relocation away from diamond mining areas, "had their water supplies cut off before being dumped in bleak settlements with derisory compensation."[28]

On the question of human rights:

Informant #1: Human rights refer to specific rights such as the right to education, right to shelter, to free speech. It also refers to the idea that civil and political and social, cultural and economic rights need to be preserved and that these are inherent and indivisible.

Informant #2: Human Rights: the right to be, such as life, freedom, property, shelter, etc. In Botswana we do not have 3rd generation rights, nor do we have legal aid. 47% of people live below the poverty line and without legal aid, many rights are as good as nothing.

We have good civil and political rights, but the enabling environment is missing. There is a fundamental inability to participate in the policy and law making that affects you. So most people do not have access to human rights because they are not consulted—they are not part of the policy-making process. Lack of consultation is a denial of human rights. There is no enabling environment to participate in policy.

Informant #3: It is sort of taboo in this country to talk about human rights, certainly in the context of the Basarwa [Kalahari Bushmen].

There are a number of approaches to rights being represented here. The first places emphasis on the relativity of rights and values, and mixes this with the UN's emphasis on the indivisibility of rights in interesting ways. In the middle position, we see more frustration with the top-down approach to rights and the structural and institutional barriers to full legal (citizen rights) protections. Finally we have a clear expression of the complicated political environment within which aspirations about human rights float.

Namibia

Arranging interviews with UNDP in Namibia proved more difficult. Here, Governance Unit dealt exclusively with macro-economic questions. Several attempts were made to arrange interviews after an introductory meeting, but these failed. I was ultimately referred to the Poverty Unit, which dealt more specifically with political questions. However, the Poverty Unit had only one member remaining who had been on staff for more than four months. Attempts were made to arrange interviews with new staff members, with whom copies of the questions were left and with whom I went over the questions. New staff members, however, were ultimately unwilling to be interviewed. In the end, I was referred to the only staff member who had been with the Unit for over four months, a Junior Programme Officer, who was finishing her contract imminently. She commented briefly on the substantive issues relating to GDH in contemporary Namibia:

> The civil and political rights that exist on paper are bracketed. Media and freedom of the press are seriously curtailed. For example, *The Namibian* [newspaper] was banned from all government offices when it took a critical stance towards the government. There is also the issue of homosexuality. The state has made it clear that homosexuals are not welcome and do not enjoy equal freedoms.

The participant was clear that no one was currently leading the political side of the governance stream in Namibia. When asked about the *Millennium Development Goals* in specific, she commented:

> Those are really in their infancy stage here. The Poverty Unit isn't doing anything specific. The only thing, really, is that we are coordinating a senir panel for "Talk to the Nation" [a TV programme] for October 17th. It's called "Sustainable Environment and Poverty" and it's about how far Namibia has gone in its global commitments.

When describing the Poverty Unit and its governance activities more specifically, she offered:

> The government is planning to create a parallel Poverty Unit within the NPC [National Planning Committee]. They are short on human resources and funding. We are helping by means of providing a UN volunteer. We are also trying to recruit a senior poverty reduction specialist.

> We are also planning to help Ohangwena[29] add a poverty focus to their development plan. We take our cue from the government and only fund NGOs on agreement with them. We fit poverty programs with gaps that the government has pre-identified. We are committed to our relationship with government.

On gender the informant commented:

> We haven't reached the point of mainstreaming gender. We do not have the capacity. We have a regional gender person and want to organize training, but this hasn't happened yet. Headquarters has funds, in principle, but many people have no idea what gender mainstreaming means. None of our programmes have been gone over with gender lenses.

When asked about human rights and democracy more specifically, the informant could only comment that:

> The Unit deals with everything that is not HIV/AIDS; lots of little
> things. Everything is country driven, and we offer support when
> requested, where we can.

There were clear indications, then, that governance was conceptualized
exclusively as working with government, and that human rights and democracy to the extent that they were important, were subsumed under this relationship. Perhaps the most striking aspect in the Namibian case, however,
was that UNDP governance operations stood at a near standstill, in the
face of the inordinate amount of literature the office had produced over
the recent years, including its own country *Human Development Report*.
That is, while elsewhere, subjectivities and complexities at the field-level
added further texture, in Namibia there was a vacuum, raising questions
about the effect of high and often total staff turn over,and indeed, what un-
staffed and de-activated programming meant when compared to the reams
of glossy reports that might otherwise mask this complete standstill.

Tanzania

In Tanzania, interviews were also difficult to arrange and were ultimately
conducted in group format with all three members of the Governance Unit
present. Consensus converged on the following: Governance was a question of government behaviour and freeing up the flow of information. The
flow of information was seen to be key to the public holding government
accountable (see Chapter Seven for more discussion):

> One of the biggest challenges facing governance in Tanzania is defi-
> nitely corruption. There is no accountability without transparency and
> no transparency without information. Right now, we are in the early
> phases of helping to create a Public Information Department within the
> government. We would also like to get some journalist training up and
> running. It is really important to strengthen the capacity for media to
> monitor government. Here we are working in partnership with the gov-
> ernment, and our programmes are in line with national policies.

The Unit, went on to note, however:

> There are a lot of programs, but they are spread across the differ-
> ent [UN] agencies. So we really need to work on coordination. The
> UNDAF [UN Development Assistance Framework], in practice, is
> really fragmented.

The Unit also noted that it was in the process of collecting data for a "Village Governance Handbook." The Law department at the University of Dar es Salaam had been commissioned to conducts survey and amass quantitative data. When it was offered that REDET, the Institute for Research and Education in Democracy and Technology, in cooperation with the Department of Political Science and Public Administration at the University of Dar es Salaam had already amassed a sizeable amount of base-line data (see Mukandala and Gasarasi (eds) 2000; Mushi *et al.* (eds.) 2001), this was dismissed: "Our study is much more technical than the REDET study."[30] Democracy was conceptualized in a number of ways:

> We have been doing a lot to give a boost to the ideas of participatory democracy. On the mainland, we've supported IT [information technology] capacity building in the National Assembly, and we have some programmes to help strengthen civil society in the planning stages.

> We are also doing a lot of government training, specifically on poverty, HIV/AIDS, and technical staff re-orientation towards multi-partyism. We are working to get a system in place to track resources. There have also been some study tours. Recently, three members of parliament went to the UK, Zambia and South Africa.

> We are also working with the World Bank on creating a database, with all the Bills and Acts, for parliamentarians to refer to. We've just appointed the consultant.

> We have a pilot participatory budgeting project planned for Mwanza. We are sourcing the tendering right now. The hope is to build models that would be democratic at the village level.

There was, then, as in the CCF, a tendency to associate democracy with a wide range of activities, including those consistent with the UNDP's commitment to broad-based participation. At the same time, democracy was most strongly and consistently linked with education and knowledge transfer, particularly to government. Thus, democracy tended to be seen as, simultaneously, a set of universal values, technical skills and institutional forms to be learned by government officials, as well as more participatory processes such as participatory budgeting.

The main human rights issues identified by the Unit clustered around lack of flow in the justice system, echoing the conflation of human rights with state-bound citizen's rights guaranteed by law and order and, ultimately, the coercive machinery of the state:

> There is a slow moving court system here in Tanzania. The flow of justice is a problem. There is an urgent need to improve the human rights stance in the police and prison systems. We are helping to develop a curriculum for human rights training, and to create capacity to strengthen reporting. Here we are working with the ministry of justice, the police and a Professor in the law department [at the University of Dar es Salaam].

Overall, then, the group interview tended to mirror the approaches and values expressed in the CCF, except to the extent that neither rights nor democracy were bracketed by their normative or contextual dimensions. Rather, for example, rights were clearly understood as citizen rights and dependent on the rule of law, and democracy as a more or less known institutional form to be taught *to* government and then implemented *by* government.

In Sum

To iterate, this section on interviews with field staff was not meant to be statistically relevant or to make any inferences about the reasons why country staff, as individuals or in their roles, experience the UN governance agenda the way they do. Rather, the point, as with the previous sections and chapters, has been to highlight the co-existence of various ways of understanding GDH. Exploring this also allows us to glimpse how the social world[31] of the governance agenda dialogues (or fails to dialogue) with the textual. Research into how UN staffs interpret discourse and attempt render it into policy and praxis that suits their own interests and/or world view would be an important area for further study.

For our purposes, however, we note that country implementers can hold very different views from those expressed at any or all levels of discourse. In Angola, for example, tensions between the dominant and minor discourses were manifest in both the *Inter-Agency Appeal* and among implementers. The tensions embodied by the texts engendered no easy solution and field-level struggles also betrayed no easy compromises or standards by which disagreements could be resolved. The result was a number of processes, debates and outcomes that were literally off the discourse map, neither emerging straightforwardly out of the dominant nor minor discourses. In Tanzania and Namibia, the dominant discourse was more or less *dominant* in the texts and among implementers. In Botswana, conversely, there was a high degree of variance between country documents and among the views of country staff.

As a result, the county level can be seen as embodying a wide variety of tensions, many mirroring those in the discourse at large. Governance is seen as being a quality both inherent to and lacking within an apolitical developmental state. Thus, every programme to enhance state capacity is coupled with an artful blindness to the darker potential of state power, even where, in the very next sentence, this darker potential is acknowledged and identified as a key obstacle to UN goals. Governance also tends to be equated with a passing on of information—a relationship a tutelage—yet the plans and stipulations handed down to country offices from New York and Geneva for local implementation were at times a key source of staff frustration. Democracy was also expressed in contradictory terms. Its importance was always linked to the amount of substantive participation it offered, which, in the end, always seemed to be very little, again to the frustration of many staff. Rights, similarly, were caught in the nether land between rule of law and the protections and privileges afforded (or not afforded) by the often corrupt and predatory coercive apparatus of the state. Human dignity and the loftier ideals often associated with rights were, more often than not, not far from the minds of most UN staffers, yet the trend towards moving "upstream" was unmistakeable. Between the lines, then, country staff seemed to be conceding that their tools promised to both deliver and deny the humanitarian project to which they hoped to contribute.

COUNTRY DOCUMENTS IN GLOBAL TO FIELD UNIT PERSPECTIVE

Governance

The previous chapters argued that, seen in the best light, good governance describes a process whereby governments, in cooperation with civil society and in accordance with norms of participation, take on the technical advice of the UN. From global to regional documents, however, the definition becomes progressively more conservative, coming to indicate, moreover, a process whereby experts determine the nature of political transformation and then socialize governing elites to simulate.

In comparison to other levels of discourse and their *Road Maps*, the country documents tend to disrupt the regional discourses and their unambiguous elitism. For example, the balance between support for government and support for civil society seen in the Angolan *Inter-Agency Consolidated Appeal* is completely absent from the regional documents and only very weakly articulated at the global level. Similarly, concessions made in both the Namibian and Tanzanian documents with respect to the normative, unsettled and contextual nature of GDH, are also largely absent from the other levels of analysis. Further, in contradiction to the AGF-V Report and, to some extent the HDRs, the Tanzanian CCF, at times, asserts the centrality and even *necessity* of participatory approaches, if only unevenly. In some important ways, then, very different combinations and balances of emphases are present in the country documents—particularly in comparison with the regional documents.

Preliminary indications suggest that the tensions that characterize the discourses as a whole are, in some respects, reproduced among field staff, where divisions between bottom-up and top down approaches are direct and immediate. At this level, contradictions play themselves out in the inter-agency forums and within the UN hierarchy to uncertain effect, one of which appears to be frustration. Observations here suggest that further study at this nexus would yield important insights.

Democracy

At all levels of discourse, the application of the term democracy is complicated by the failure to include anything particularly *demo*cratic into promotion strategies. Rather UN models and strategies seem designed to pre-determine the institutions and forms of participation that democracy will countenance. Thus, crucial ambiguities about the nature of the state/society relationship are invoked. This trend is carried over into the country documents, with the addition of the central place for media and education as the mechanism through which an *understanding of roles and responsibilities can be systematically disseminated.*

Angolan and Botswana documents omit democracy altogether. This is interesting given the central role the concept of democracy plays when the UN describes what it stands for and to what ends it lends its energies. It raises further questions about what effect the omission of a key component of the GDH bundle would have on intervention more generally. According to the UN, can there be good governance or human rights without democracy? From the analysis in previous chapters, it would seem not. To gesture metaphorically, it would be like baking pie without the sugar, the pie dough, or indeed the apples.

At the field level, glimpses of the tensions between formal or procedural democracy and aspirations for not only popular voice, but also access to the agenda setting process, are evidenced. Expectations that democracy ought not only to be about regulating conflict over who will rule, but also about sharing power more equally across the socio-political field are also seen. That is, minimalist approaches to democracy appeared to square off with more aspirant notions at the level of implementers. Again, this is a nexus that could benefit from further scrutiny.

Human Rights

The global and regional human rights discourses tend to represent human rights as the legal and moral limits to the power of the state and as part of a legitimacy bargain that rests on the state's willingness and ability to *protect* and *extend* human rights, in exchange for submission to its authority. Concessions are made, at times, to more aspirant interpretations of rights, but these seem to dangle detached from any of the expressions of what this *rights-based* programming might actually look like—which is, moreover, advanced by the *Road Maps* as the mere encouragement of states to ratify various rights instruments.

Rights tend to be viewed as more complex and powerful at the country-level than at the regional level. They are important enough to form the bedrock of the *Angolan Inter-Agency Appeal* (under the rubric of "protection") and the Namibian UNDAF, and important enough to be almost totally omitted from the Botswana CCF. Within these accounts, however, familiar tensions obtain. There is significant scope for initiatives and strategies that enhance the autonomy of individuals and communities in ways that don't necessarily empower states. There is also the recognition that rights are multi-dimensional and subjective. Simultaneously, however, rights are couched within a fixed institutional structure based on a *universal understanding* that nevertheless must be *systemically disseminated*. In the case of Namibia, we also find the clear and unambiguous commitment to the state reasserted as central and determinant, above all else.

At the field level, these tensions have the potential to engender frustration, acrimony, and impasse—and intensify the feeling that the political project emanating from the UN hierarchy is falling short of the mark. At the very least, there are indications that gaps between what the UN says and what its staff knows—but cannot feedback effectively into the bureaucratic machine—needs to be taken more seriously (see Righter 1994)—as does the critique of top-down development and the call for substantive improvements in the distribution of power, resources and access.[32]

CONCLUDING REMARKS—POLITICS OR ANTIPOLITICS?[33]

There are a number of ways to view the differences and contradictions, and to assess why it is nearly impossible to guess—at least based on the textual universe the UN has created for our consumption—what composite of GDH will find expression in the lived experience of UN assistance.

From Realpolitik and Marxist perspectives, the different flavour and content of the country documents might be rendered intelligible as the tangled manifestations of political machination—for example, the search for legitimacy by providing a "human face" to the structural adjustment regime—cast over the *more real* and fundamental exigencies of power or international capital (see Cammack 1996; Cox and Jacobsen 1973; Robbins 1994). Similarly, they may reflect competition among various actors, not the least of whom are state and UN elites seeking to enhance or entrench their positions (Galtung 1986: Righter 1995), or merely operationalize what they personally feel is *right*. Conversely, from a technical or problem-solving perspective, they may be viewed as the, perhaps clumsy, expression of the exigencies of different contexts (For in-depth discussion on this point, see Chapters Seven and Eight.). What these approaches to understanding UN dysfunction share is a belief in the somewhere *more real* architectures of power, competition, need, etc, of which the discourses are mere epiphenomenona. That is, they see the discourse as a veil cast over our consciousness of material conditions, rather than as a productive political force itself.

However, such approaches may overstate the role of rationality in the search for causality, as James Ferguson (1994: 14) argues: "political economists are often too quick to impute an economic function to "development" projects," and their structural critiques are often insufficiently nuanced to capture the processes of power embedded in the fabric of knowledge itself. Similarly, political scientists are often too quick to impute a political function or attribute causes to *interests*, as though intentions were straightforwardly apparent to analysts, easily known and moreover easily disentangled from fussier concepts such as identity, perception and misperception (see Black and Wilson 2004; Crais 2001; du Toit 2001; Wilson and Black 2004).[34] Technocratic development specialists, likewise, are often too quick to assume that causality is easily established in complex interwoven tapestries of the social, political, economic, cultural, and historical, etc.[35] Rather, as Pieterse (2001: 137) argues:

> In relation to the complexities of social life, at times development as applied social science gives the impression of navigating the ocean with a rowboat, or a Lego imitation of collective existence, in which mechanistic notions of social dynamics in tandem with political and hegemonic interests push and shove for the driver's seat.

In this light, it may be useful to back away from the search for root causes and drivers (at least in the realist sense) of messy discourse, to de-centre causality, interest and intention, and look instead at the UN discourse, itself, as being constitutive. This provokes us to look for the core that is produced and reconstructed, whether or not there is some *a priori* reason or first cause for such messy discourses. As Foucault urged: the task is to ask what is served *anyway*, independent of all the explanations and legitimacy claims, independent of the development failures and successes? What is served when multiple ways of understanding GDH are all enacted within the same broad band of phenomena—the governance agenda? What is served by the combination of both the dominant and minor discourses finding various homes and expressions at all levels of play?

The following two chapters interrogate the propensities inherent to the dominant discourse. The final and concluding chapter then interrogates the role the co-extant minor discourses play in obfuscating programs that could otherwise be more straightforwardly understood as ill-conceived, or even carrying the clear propensity to be predatory upon the powerless and marginalized in service of the not well understood survival imperatives of the world's pre-eminent international bureaucracy.

Chapter Seven

Wishful Thinking, Willful Blindness and Artful Amnesia in Angola, Botswana, Namibia and Tanzania

This chapter[1] explores the way the Angolan, Botswana, Namibian and Tanzanian governments have expressed their power in the recent past, and in this light, raises a number of red flags about the governance agenda. Specifically, the chapter argues that if we take these states on their own terms, rather than as ideal developmental states, what is illuminated is that the governance agenda risks producing profoundly negative consequences for the distribution of political influence in these four countries. None of the evidence reviewed is necessary or sufficient to undermine optimism about the governance agenda and prove what it will yield.[2] Nevertheless, it is suggested that sufficient evidence exists to suggest that interventions associated with the governance agenda carry the propensity to primarily empower the state apparatus and its elites. At the same time, they are likely to only unevenly and unpredictably contribute to the re-distribution influence across the social spectrum.

INTRODUCTION

Recently, both Thomas Weiss (2000) and Jean Philippe Thérien (1999) encouragingly evaluated recent turns in UN governance thinking, applauding progress towards an inclusive and broadly defensible model. This model includes an ever-widening number of western symbols of rights-friendly democratic governance, including legislative support, judicial reform and electoral assistance (Weiss 2000: 10–11). Further, they argue, new turns in governance thinking deal effectively with the concept of "exclusion" and the relationship of political marginalization to material deprivation (Thérien 1999: 13).

Is their optimism warranted?[3] To answer this question, the following sections draw on in-country interviews with UN country staff and civil society organizations, in-country studies and local grey literatures, and the academic literature more broadly. By illuminating multiple perspectives at multiple levels of analysis, this chapter seeks to bring texture to the relationship between the dominant discourse and the sometimes *darker* dimensions of state power (Pierson 1996; Sorensen 1996), with special reference to the country cases.[4]

Five key themes central to the governance agenda were selected to illustrate this dynamic: 1) rights-based law, 2) media, 3) civil society, 4) elections and 5) state-capacity-building. These themes correlate to the standard components of the UNDP's basic institutional model for democratic governance woven throughout all layers of discourse. They are also central to the 2002 *Human Development Report*'s "Subjective" and "Objective" indicators of governance (UNDP 2002: 37–45), and, finally, they correlate well with the "sensitive governance areas" identified by Weiss (2000: 10). The order in which they are addressed below follows a sequential critique of some of the key assumptions needed for the UN's governance story to *hang together*: 1) claims to objectivity/universality (law), 2) that its model is participatory (*via* media, civil society, elections), and 3) the state as fundamental unit of the good life and thus the most important site of intervention (state-capacity-building).

The five key themes explore the dangers inherent to the dominant discourse as instantiation of rule of law, media, elections, etc. For example, the first section illustrates, by country, that practical dangers lie at the nexus of rights-based law—seen in the dominant discourse as *universally* valid and always good—and states that are assumed to be, but in reality more complicated than, benign developmental states. Similarly, the following sections explore how efforts to promote media, civil society and elections may ultimately fail to establish conditions that check the potential for elite excess (Sorensen 1996). The final section takes a critical look at capacity-building, interrogating the ideal of the developmental state and illustrating that state elites often use state power in ways that create general (human) insecurity, and prevent meaningful or popular participation political decision-making.

By examining each of these themes in turn, the chapter establishes conceptual density around the assessment that the UNDP governance agenda has an overlooked propensity to contribute to the construction and re-construction of spaces where authoritarian practices and elite capture can flourish. It may also, simultaneously, contribute to relative citizen powerlessness. Thus, despite a governance agenda rhetoric that suggests to the casual reader that UNDP praxis can and will "take into account all the complexity of the social environment in which poverty exists" (Thérien 1999: 14), there is room for scepticism. The dominant discourse harbours assumptions and discounts complexities in ways that may ultimately frustrate efforts to enhance life chances across the social spectrum.

RIGHTS-BASED RULE OF LAW: POWER AND THE JURIDICAL APPARATUS

This section takes up the twin concepts of rule of law and rights-based law found in the UNDP's governance agenda and related indicators (2002: 37–45). It describes how UN discourse tends to conflate rule of law with rule guided by the *Universal Declaration of Human Rights*,[5] often using these concepts interchangeably as if one implied the other. In this way, we are invited to interpret human rights—by virtue of being *universal*—and rule of law as synonymous with what rational persons everywhere and always aspire towards.

This section challenges whether this fuzzy conflation justifies ignoring law's more ambivalent dimensions. Specifically, it probes whether the conflation justifies ignoring that law is often the key means through which architectures of power, often pernicious, are maintained and legitimized. For example, Peter Vale (2003) notes that "[t]he construction of southern Africa around the legal claim offered by sovereignty, like much of the knowledge around its security has been incidental, invested, entirely based on imported ideas." (37) "The beneficiaries of this . . . were South Africa's English-speaking settlers. The region's indigenous people (for whom the modernization offered by Colonialism, and the community it promised, were more curse than convenience) were almost entirely excluded." (43) More immediately, just prior to the 1994 Rwandan genocide the Hutu Power passed into law that every Hutu man must kill his Tutsi wife (Baines 2003: 489). Essentially, then, this section asks: is support for a state's rule of law capacity always the same as the extent to which a state protects and extends human rights or affords the structural condition for equality, equity and dignity?

Similarly, this section is also concerned with the extent to which the dominant discourse treats the *universal* architecture of rights as epistomology that, moreover, the public (rather than state) is expected to take on board. Behind this lies the assumption that poverty and powerlessness in developing countries are directly related to widespread ignorance about human rights, and that it is this ignorance that explains why populations have difficulty holding states accountable. But is ignorance about rights and rights-based law where power imbalances between states and society in Africa truly lie?

In Western polities, that the juridical apparatus is liberal reflects the complex working out of layers of historical contingency and struggle. In Africa, the extent that any given juridical apparatus is liberal in character reflects "both the political and economic systems over which it was imposed and the underlying legal and bureaucratic systems that were the legacy of colonialism" (Ghai 1993: 73). The central point is that colonialism brought with it ideas, values and political architectures that were forged in and by the western experiences with the Enlightenment and industrial revolution, and tailored them to the needs of colonial exploitation. Their role in regulating African societies has always been ambivalent, as Timothy M. Shaw (1984: 230) notes: "One of the least helpful vestiges of colonialism in Africa is the legacy of Western values which inhibits radical rethinking of politics and economics."

In this light, "recent studies of the colonial encounter emphasize the penetration of Western law" (Gulbransdsen 1996: 125). Law, both technically and ideologically, was intricately woven into the aspirant agendas of colonialism (see Mamdani 2001) as the *means* through which colonial interests were pursued. Peter Fitzpatrick (1993: 27) cautions, therefore, that that the "blithe advocacy of law in the cause of development is flawed in its very foundation." Specifically, modern law emerges, in part, from the pacification and ordering requirements of the state, and as an institution it carries the propensity to order and pacify populations in ways that serve, primarily, the interests of the state/power nexus (Foucault 1984; Mann 1986: 421–422; Scott 1998; Mackinnon 1989). The history of law is, *inter alia*, the history of elites attempting (and failing) to define, constrain, hierarchically order, shape and erase those parts of civil society that do not suit its purposes. For example:

> It has often been argued that Western legal subjects are founded on an abstract, neutral, gender-blind individual developed from Enlightenment thought (Unger 1977; Smart 1989). Certain categories of people by such criteria are almost *ipso facto* outside the law, and to a certain extent therefore deprived of the status of legal subject: women, homosexuals, the poorly educated (Harris 1996: 2).

While both human rights and law, however, are proven and powerful emancipatory tools in the hands of *the public* (see Brown 1999; Chapter Two), the onus of proof, nevertheless, always lies with the injured party/ies—over whom the law exercises control. That is, law always expresses the mobilization of bias (Bachrach and Baratz 1967), with disadvantaged groups and individuals being saddled with the burden of proof.

This disadvantage is centrally important. For example, one UNDP legal expert in Botswana commented that Botswana's legal system was based on British common law. However, the lack of consultation in law-making, dissemination of information about the content of laws -which are often in structural opposition to alternative social orders (especially in rural areas)—and the complete absence of legal aid legislation, means that many people have few if any tools to mediate an encounter with the state's juridical apparatus.[6]

Human rights embody the means through which power can be wrested from the state. But, human rights-based political orders also re-order the socio-political relations of societies in ways that work to exclude other ways of conceptualizing problems related to human dignity. They work to exclude solutions that do not correspond to the state *extending* and *protecting* rights by means of its juridical and coercive machinery. Further, while human rights can help articulate some assaults on human dignity and security quite well, such as state interference with the right to assembly or free speech, others, such as expropriation in the name of the "right to development," it mediates or illuminates less well. In effect, to date, human rights have an uneven track record automatically balancing power between states and societies (see Desai 2002 in the case of South Africa). Further, it is unclear what rights have to offer in terms of protections against global actors (i.e. multinationals, international financial institutions). In this light, some analysts claim (Brown 1999) that rights in the West simply piggy back on other relations of complex interdependence and the economic prosperity that characterizes developed liberal polities. They are not, in fact, transformative in and of themselves.

Thus, it is also worth noting that both the rule of law and human rights, in contemporary liberal models, route power through the state, increasing the number of social relations controlled, mediated and produced by it (Ferguson 1994; Foucault 1984; MacKinnon 1989). That is, rule of law and human rights bolster the state's position as the central organizing force, which at the same time "organizationally outflanks" all other interests in society (Mann 1985). That is, because human rights are *protected* and *extended* by the state, they don't offer much in terms of protection when the state is not *extending* them. The more dominant the state is the fewer protections rule of law and human rights guarantee. In other words, the less equally influence is distributed across the national landscape (most notably in terms of weak and/or insufficiently diversified economies), the less likely observing rights-based law will be crucial to regime survival (Sorensen 1996). International actors may seek to circumvent this paradox by linking regime legitimacy internationally to the "responsibility to protect" (ICISS 2001), but as yet it remains unclear to what extent such normative shifts rival the structuring power of international commodity chains in oil, diamonds, timber and minerals that can bolster illiberal regimes.

Within the mainstream development literature, however, the rule of law is typically represented instrumentally, as mere adjunct to modernization. The state is an apolitical vehicle for the rational *universal* legal framework for development. Critics argue, however, that "[t]his technocratic approach suit[s] both the new ruling groups in Africa, foreign states, and international political and economic organizations" (Ghai 1993: 51).

Country Caveats

In the dominant discourse, law is taken as more or less self-evidently legitimate—and law's association with human rights further bolsters this legitimacy. Law is not seen to include broad structuring implications associated with the character of the regime or the balance of power between state and society. Ncube (1993: 10), in his discussion on law in Zimbabwe (see also Black and Wilson 2004; Wilson and Black 2004), reveals some of the shortcomings of this approach:

> While the Lancaster House Constitution embodies virtually all the liberal elements of constitutionalism, the same Constitution provides that the Rhodesian legal order was to be continued into independent Zimbabwe and also that those laws which were inconsistent with the Declaration of Rights could not be declared to be invalid by the courts until five years after independence. The fact that the constitution was declared to be the supreme law of the country made little difference since there was available to the independent government a labyrinth of repressive legislation such as the Law and Order Maintenance Act [Chapter 65] and the Emergency Powers Act [Chapter 83], all of which could not be declared invalid until after the expiration of the first five years of independence.

Thus, the application, bias and character of law, as experienced, can depend as much if not more on the character of the regime as expressed in interpretation and application, as on any part of the legal architecture.

Nevertheless, the Tanzanian CCF refers to law only in the context of bringing laws into commensurability with human rights norms, as part of a strategy to create the context for "de-centralized participatory and transparent government" (8):

> The aim is to provide support for a *decision-making environment* that facilitates participatory, democratic, gender-balanced and transparent decision-making with communities accessing knowledge, skills and

processes that empower them to make decisions about sustainable use of their resources [emphasis added] (9).

However, it should be noted that Article 30 of the Tanzanian Constitution declares: "no provision contained in this Part of this Constitution, which stipulates the basic human rights, freedoms and duties, shall be construed as invalidating any existing law or prohibiting the enactment of any law or the doing of any lawful act under such law . . ."(Hellsten 2002: 31). Under these conditions, the transformation of rule of state/ruling party to rule of law will be difficult by means of the introduction of human-rights based legislation alone, as Ncube (1993: 10) notes: "the one party state and former colonial apparatus" tends to offer "unlimited repressive and discretionary powers." For example, visiting professor at the University of Dar es Salaam, Sirrku Hellsten (2002: 27), found that recent developments in the rule of law structure "tend still to be products of the ruling party rather than a fair representation of various views presented by the opposition, legal and political specialists, as well as by the general public."

Additional complications stem from the Tanzanian legal framework's dual emphasis on individual and communitarian rights. That is, in addition to constitutional provisions "that individuals do not exercise their rights and freedom in a manner that causes interference or curtailment of the rights and freedom of other persons" they must also refrain from acting against the "public interest" (Hellsten 2002: 31). Here, the President can still order the indefinite detention without bail of people considered "dangerous to the public order" (*ibid.*: 35). Further:

> The government also has additional detention powers under the Regions and Regional Commissioners Act and the Area Commissioners Act (of 1962), respectively. The Acts permit regional and district commissioners to arrest and detain persons who disturb public tranquility for 48 hours. The category of persons who can be detained range from political troublemakers, *persons who resist self-help projects*, suspected criminals and *witches*. A culprit under these Acts has no right to challenge the legality of an order for arrest/detention in a court of law [emphasis added] (36).

Recently, the US Department of State (2002) reported that: "Arbitrary arrest and detention and prolonged detention remained problems [in Tanzania]." In a particularly troubling example, Leo Lekama, former chairman of the Tanzania Labour Party, spent four years in jail after being charged with the criminal offence of trampling on a copy of the Constitution with seditious intent. He was released in 2001, after the government failed to produce any witnesses (*ibid.*).

Also potentially problematic was that interviews at the UNDP in Dar es Salaam revealed a dual emphasis on re-formulating laws to comply with human rights while also improving the "flow of justice through police and prison reform." On the one hand, improving the efficiency of the police and prison system seems necessary where "[o]bservers have estimated only about 5 percent of persons held in remand ultimately get convicted, and in many cases, those convicted, would already have served their full sentences before their trials are held" (Hellsten 2002: 35). However, improvements in *efficiency* and reach of the state's coercive machinery may be viewed ambivalently in light of Acts such as the Preventative Detention Act, whereby "the president may still order the arrest and indefinite detention without bail of any person considered dangerous to the public order or national security."

The character of the regime suggests the need to proceed with caution. For example, in November 2002 the government took a much criticized decision to table a highly restrictive NGO Bill, widely interpreted as a bid to exercise control over opinion within civil society and muzzle effective dissent. The World Bank commented:[7]

> Unfortunately, we cannot agree that the NGO Act as approved by the Parliament meets this test [of openness and fairness]. We also feel that the process for tabling the Bill in Dodoma did not follow the spirit of openness and consultation. We are concerned about the tone of the debate and the Act and its implications for the NGO sector in Tanzania.

Among certain segments of civil society, the incident was taken as further evidence that government is synonymous with "Kudhibiti, meaning 'thief.'"[8] The controversy surrounding the Bill indicates a more deeply seated systemic problem related to power imbalance between government and society more generally—one that is fostered, if not condoned by, intervention designed primarily to strengthen state capacity, and which may place more faith in the transformational power of the human rights concept than existing legal architectures warrant.

In Namibia's UNDAF rule of law is central. At the same time, however, it notes that: "[i]t was suggested that, because issues such as the rule of law and human rights are very broad, the working group should limit itself to discussing the most important issues in the Namibia context" (253). These issues were not identified, but rather the UNDAF recommended that "[t]he UNDAF process should focus on the follow-up of international conferences and on the implementation of already existing conventions. It should ensure that citizens be educated to be aware of their rights. Education was considered a key focus area to be addressed in order to create a civil society where human rights values and gender equality were rooted" (254).[9] Thus, despite recognizing the need to promote a rule of law approach for the Namibian context, it is not clear to what this might amount other than education campaigns around international norms.

International norms, however, are not unproblematic at the level of implementation. Interviews with legal experts[10] highlighted that one of the most pressing law and order issues was that of traditional courts—and the lack of genuine devolution of juridical power from the old apartheid apparatus, to community centres. Concerns were expressed about imported juridical models—and here much bi-lateral training comes from the Canadian government—which require an intensity of training and institutional capacity that the Namibian state presently cannot sustain, particularly outside the major urban centres. It was argued that currently, externally-devised legal systems that function well under conditions of comparatively abundant wealth and resources were in Namibia easily brought to a standstill by technical minutiae that do not translate well from the Canadian to the Namibian context.

Further, Dianne Hubbard (2000: 1) has also noted a need to move away from the focus on highly abstract and non-specific international principles to rule of law for the specific Namibian context. For women, constitutional protections and Namibia's accession to the UN Convention on the Elimination of All Forms of Discrimination Against Women (CEDAW) are "largely statements of aspiration, rather than principles which govern the daily lives of Namibians in any practical sense." Rather, "under customary law, men and women in many communities patently do *not* have equal rights . . . Until law reform at the behest of either parliament or the judiciary applies these promises to practical issues such as inheritance, they will remain so much useless paper for the average Namibian" (2). Similarly, a gender specialist at the Legal Assistance Centre noted that many apartheid era laws, such as the 1928 Proclamation 15, which "stipulated that all black people living above the 'police zone'[11] are married out of community property still means that women typically lose all inheritance claims in the event of separation or their husband's death. Parliament has yet to do anything to take these laws off the books."

Unsurprisingly, the HDR's (2002: 228) Gender Empowerment Measure notes that women hold 20.4% of the seats in the Namibian parliament. Equally problematic is that the Office of the Ombudsman [sic] expressed, in Dec. 2001, "concern about the "insensitivity, arbitrary and capricious exercise of power, delays, oppressive and unreasonable behaviour, unlawfulness and acts that are generally incompatible with democratic governance and justice" (NSHR 2002: 18).

What can be made of the emphasis on education campaigns in this context?[12] Having lectured for a Human Rights and Politics class at a Canadian university, it is clear to me that Canadian youth are relatively uniformed about the meaning and implication of rights and rights regimes. Similarly, an Institute for Public Policy Research in Namibia Report quotes a recent study: "stop anyone on the streets of any major city around the world and ask, 'What are your human rights?' No matter the age, location or social circumstances—chances are that few people will have a good idea. The sad fact is that most people remain functionally illiterate about human rights" (Keulder 2002a: 22). Under these circumstances the assumption that a rule of law architecture premised on human rights will come to yield higher levels of freedom and prosperity by virtue of public education campaigns fails to bear critical scrutiny. Further, a pilot study conducted by the University of Namibia in 2002 indicated that, in general, people were aware of their rights, while 82 out a 100 respondents felt that "GRN [Government of the Republic of Namibia] had not always complied with its human rights obligations" (NSHR: 18). Thus we return to the question, what protections do rights offer in a political climate where the government controls all the levers of power, but does not *extend* or *protect* rights?

In this vein, recent studies published by the Legal Assistance Centre found that patronage appointments at the level of budgetary control effectively prevent monies getting through for legal reform that would curtail existing government powers. For example, Bukurura (2002: 69) documents that "there is a feeling within the office [the Legal Assistance Centre] that government budgetary control and processes were neither appropriate nor conducive to the independent exercise of audit functions [by the Auditor-General and the Ombudsman]." Government responses to demands for greater autonomy are quoted at length in Bukurura on pages 74–75. Essentially, he concludes: "the desire for autonomy fell on deaf ears and found no favour with the government . . . There is no way, it appears, the executive is going to lift its precious lid, and let either parliament or Ombudsmen and Auditor-General determine independently whom to employ and when" (75–76).

The Institute for Democracy,[13] similarly, expressed concern about the overwhelming strength of SWAPO under then President Sam Nujoma, as well as the lack of viable opposition. In the run up to the fourth national elections in 2004, it remained an open question whether SWAPO might change the constitution in order that President Nujoma could sit for a fourth term or alternatively sit as permanent ceremonial head of state. SWAPO youth and traditional leaders in the northern Oshivambo strong-hold constituencies were mobilizing to agitate for a fourth term.[14] Oshi-vambo (the historical SWAPO stronghold) leaders had much to gain from continued SWAPO dominance. Further, while there is a well-drafted de-centralization policy, implementation has been slow in Namibia. "In practice," it was observed, "the government structure is getting more centralized. The president is increasingly using institutional and organizational powers and installing SWAPO supporters into all key positions."[15]

In Angola, rule of law was also closely linked to human rights. For example, a key area of focus for the Department of Political Affairs in Angola's 2001 *Consolidated Inter-Agency Appeal* was to "strengthen rule of law" (125). "This project is complementary to capacity building activities already underway and is designed to support Government efforts to reform the justice system." Towards this end, the UN system will "conduct municipal seminars on the rule of law with local authorities and civil society" (125). The general social context, however, is one of "profound scepticism about the abilities and intentions of government in general." Carrie Manning (1999: 35, 37), for example, documented some local perceptions:

> We don't believe in extension of the state administration because all of the forces of society are not in agreement that this process should be carried out. So we simply have vandalism by one side against the other.

> In a democracy, the government should listen to the ideas of the people who elected them, but in this democracy [Angola], this provision does not exist in practice.

With respect to law, Manning notes recurring themes among survey respondents: "[O]nly ordinary people were subject to the limitations of the law" (43). Many people believed that the police made the law (43), and this belief dovetailed with high levels of cynicism and frustration: "It is much better to come across a petty criminal than to come across the police" (38). The next chapter takes an in-depth look at the Human Rights Committee initiative in Northern Angola. This case study will serve to further illuminate the tensions discussed in this chapter.

In Botswana, rule of law was not on the governance reform agenda,[16] but at least one Botswana legal expert interviewed felt it should be. Concern was expressed over the lack of consultation and information dissemination, and the lack of mechanisms through which people could participate in the policy and law-making processes. Discrimination on the basis of gender is also recognized as intrinsic to both the constitution and law (Dingake 2000; Obeng 2001; Selowane 1997). UNDP's country legal expert felt that, more generally, many people did not know the laws, or how they personally affected them:

> Botswana has no legal aid. 47% are living below the poverty line. Many rights are as good as nothing . . . We have very good civil and political rights, but the enabling environment is missing. It is the inability to participate in policy and law-making that will affect you.[17]

Juxtaposing Botswana to other countries where rule of law and/or rights based law is afforded a relatively central and uncomplicated status is interesting. It illustrates how plans that integrate rule of law uncritically (as universally rational and therefore inherently unproblematic) can be as problematic as those that leave the issue in silence.[18]

In Sum

Both human rights and rule of law are good examples of how UN thought tends to anchor its approach in rational universalism. To the extent that rule of law and human rights are integrated uncritically, however, can also be the extent to which they are prey to becoming tools for false legitimacy and elite control over an ever more powerful state apparatus. That is, to the extent that support for rule of rights-based law tends to strengthen the monitoring or enforcement capacity of the state *in the absence of rigorous political analysis*, citizens are put at risk. Okafor (2000: 53) argues, for example, that there is strong evidence related to the tendency of African governments:

> to resort to the use of excessive force in order to homogenize the populations of their states, and maintain the territorial integrity of such states. The law has all-too-often provided a ready and powerful justification for such projects, and has thereby contributed to tensions and conflicts that have been produced by efforts to advance these projects (*ibid.*: 92).

As yet however, there is little evidence that the UN has begun to conceptualize the relationship between rights, rule of law and power relations within African states (see Eyoh 1998; Okafor 2000). The previous chapters suggest that this is a function of blindly assigning the state the role of fundamental unit of the good life. As James Der Derian (1989: 5) points out, much of the western theoretical legacy posits that: "where there is no sovereign power, there can be no law—and no absolute means of adjudicating . . . truth claims." Further, conflating rule of law with human rights norms does little to mitigate, as Dembour (1996: 36) notes: "The expression 'human rights' is [generally] used as if it was clear, could stand by itself, and is not in need of substantiation. But it is, for human rights claims can never be divorced from the particular context in which they are raised."

As such, what the UN's focus on "rights-based law" will accomplish, no matter how coherently expressed, remains uncertain. A closer look at state power raises questions. Is a lack of rights-based laws and rights-based education *really* the source of political repression? Where and under what conditions are building state capacity and heightening "awareness of rights, roles and responsibilities in a pluralistic society" (Tanzanian CCF 2001: 9) appropriate ways to enhance human dignity, security and freedom? Is it merely wishful thinking, willful blindness and artful amnesia that ignores the underlying relations of state power and citizen powerlessness?

MEDIA FREEDOM: GOVERNANCE AGENDA INFORMATION WING?

Underlying the UN's emphasis on the media is the liberal theory that well-disseminated and vetted information is crucial to a functioning liberal polity. Actors must have extensive and accurate information to judge what is in their best interests and according to their preferences. As such, liberal approaches to systems-building place emphasis on a strong and independent media, which would have the ability to transmit information, give voice and organizational power to sub-national interests, and deliver them into ever-wider policy debates. In theory, information in the public domain is subjected to the rigours of broad debate. What survives the rigours of such debate is assumed to be consistent with what any rational person would agree is in the general interest, *in theory*. "Critical debate in the public becomes a test of rationality and right." The premise is essentially Kantian (in Chambers 2000: 201):

> "[A]ll action affecting the rights of other human beings are wrong if their maxim is not compatible with being made public." The idea is that the sovereign is the guardian of the general interest and thus should have no fear of public debate on the legitimacy of his [sic] actions. Indeed a sovereign who fears public debate is a sovereign who fears that his [sic] actions are not in the general interest and suspects that that fact will be brought to light within public debate.

The media is also one of the key means through which *the public* is formed. The media provides the space where individual opinions are more than aggregated; it is the space where public opinion, itself, is formed. That is, it is where the public develops a consciousness of its own, separate from and often in opposition to power. As such, political authority and public opinion are held to be distinct, and through the media, "now confront each other as separate political forces."[19] Thus, media is a key technical component of a functioning liberal system—especially one that admits that tensions between state and society exist—challenging the common underlying assumption of Marxist and socialist thought that the state can be a relatively simple *emanation* of society—and systems of accountability are not merely prudent, but fundamental. Essentially, then, media is the central means whereby political power is subjected to public reason and state legitimacy is negotiated (Calabrese 2000: 69).

In the absence of perfect information, media also stands in for the flow of information itself. For example, the *Human Development Report* (2002: 75) argues:

> Perhaps no reform can be as significant for making democratic institutions work as reform of the media: building diverse and pluralistic media that are free and independent, that achieve mass access and diffusion, that present accurate and unbiased information. Informed debate is the lifeblood of democracies. Without it, citizens and decision-makers are disempowered, lacking the basic tools for informed participation and representation.

Yet, at the same time, the HDR also notes that the media industry suffers from a number of structural flaws, such as concentrated ownership, that challenge the proposition that media, when taken as a whole, will represent a sufficiently wide set of viewpoints to be, writ large, unbiased. These biases, critics argue, extend to the sometimes subtle lenses the media uses to make important decisions about framing, themes and subject matter, including biases related to race, class, gender, ethnocentrism, etc. (Herman and Chomsky 2002). These are treated by the UN, however, as mere kinks in the overall theoretical fabric, rather than indications of fundamental flaws in how the media is conceptualized in the governance agenda. The case is made below, however, that the media industry requires more scrutiny, both in terms of the biases it propagates and the power relations it serves.

Further, the analysis observes a seeming slight of hand that raises still more concerns. That is, while the term "media" clearly trades on its liberal credentials, the UN often uses the term interchangeably with state-run media and the use of *multimedia* to *disseminate* information originating from either government or UN sources.

Country Caveats

The "Subjective Indicators of Governance" include "freedom of the press" as a component of "voice and accountability," and as contingent on "media objectivity" and "freedom of expression"—(UNDP 2002: 37). This differs significantly from the way we find the role of the media expressed at the country level. Here media, and moreover publicly owned media, is envisioned to play a key role in "disseminating" information about the "rights and responsibilities" of living in a democratic society (CCF 2001). Thus, we find media playing two very different roles in the governance agenda. In one, it is the key means through which people participate in the liberal model the UN advocates. In another, it is the medium used to transmit the UN's *rational universal* knowledge to the people; media as the information wing for the governance agenda "disseminating" "rights and responsibilities."

For example, the Angolan *Inter-Agency Appeal* (2001: 117) cites a human rights initiative designed to "support government institutions and empower populations." One of the means is to:

> Increase the use of media with emphasis on National Radio and Public television, to promote human rights. Produce accessible and appropriate human rights messages through theatre and other forums.

Thus, the media is not conceptualized as a medium for free and open debate or a forum through which information can be exchanged, but rather as a tool—and moreover a government tool—for promoting a particular agenda, rendered legitimate by its association with human rights. In 2001 MISA (Media Institute for Southern Africa) (16) reported that: "The year 2001 was not a good one for the practice of impartial journalism in terms of major issues of public interest in Angola."[20]

The Namibian UNDAF is threaded with an emphasis on the importance of media, public information and awareness-raising in the fights against HIV-AIDS and violence against women. However, identifiable projects tend to accord with supporting the capacity of the *public* media, which is under the control of ruling the SWAPO regime. While the UNDAF asserts an emphasis on "promoting independent and pluralistic media," this comprises "enhancing the educational and cultural mission of *public* service broadcasting" [emphasis added] (69, 188), and a pilot community radio project in Ohangwena—the SWAPO electoral stronghold. In the meantime, the Namibian Broadcasting Corporation (NBC) is mired in controversy. At the time of research, President Nujoma had recently taken over the key decision-making post at NBC, despite Nujoma's lack of experience and expertise in the media field.[21] More generally, it is not clear that NBC and media more broadly understood bear conflation. Focus groups assembled by the Media Institute of Southern Africa (MISA 2002: 14), for example, revealed widespread dissatisfaction with NBC's pro-government bias:

> TV is not covering diversity, it is pushing political views. It is unbalanced and biased. Speeches by Presidents and Ministers are often the main news. Is that the kind of criteria it lays down? Programmes are shown over and over again, like the speech of a Minister who visited the Kavango region, which was broadcast in three parts for three consecutive evenings.

> A broader view of news lacks. Almost the same kind of news, about speeches and workshops just to mention a few, is broadcasted. Poor production, and picture and sound quality [are] also annoying. Besides that, no investigative reporting due to gate keeping makes the national broadcaster boring.

Further, and more generally, a recent pilot *Media Monitoring Project in Namibia* (MISA 2002: 1–2) found embedded biases in media reporting. Specifically, "[t]he voices that are heard in the media are overwhelmingly male." Further, "media, and especially the Namibian Broadcasting Corporation [public], tends to rely on single sources, particularly government sources, and tends to focus on conferences, workshops, speeches and other high level events; and rarely follows up or provides in-depth investigative reporting." These findings are consistent with the impressions of focus group participants who expressed the view that "media in Namibia were not really independent or objective" (17).

In fact, in all country cases, media sectors suffer from shortcomings that seriously constrain the ideal that media will serve a central role in vetting public policy. In a similar example, MISA (2001:35) reported:

> Botswana shares one of the greatest weaknesses of the African press— that papers publish news in English while the majority of the population, especially in the rural areas, is unable to read this language. Furthermore, the Botswana press is urban-centred, reaching out only to the educated elite while the population in rural areas remains largely cut off.

In Tanzania, the Media Council[22] recorded a "mushrooming of media outlets" (Information Sheet, July 2002) since political and economic liberalization began in the 1990s. The rise in media is seen as a necessary complement to political liberalization in that the opposition is weak, and thus media is often the only place to debate divergent views. Growth of media businesses, however, has been chaotic and in an effort to regulate standards, government has introduced prohibitive taxes and registration fees, which tend to have a debilitating effect on operating costs, maintaining low standards and imposing high survival pressures. Poised on a narrow financial edge, effective freedom is curtailed by the implicit threat posed by an extant arsenal of laws (such as sedition), from which most private media outlets or their independent journalists do not have the resources to defend themselves. The fragile environment has produced a *Catch 22* where local media and journalistic standards suffer (Mauggo 2001), while the use of cheap international media sources has sky rocketed. Further concerns were expressed over the combined effect of the tax and registration regimes and repressive laws constraining media start-ups. This has had the most profound effect on local media, and the Council felt that future trends would see indigenous media under constant threat from foreign competition.

Some implications for the rural and vulnerable, especially women, are asymmetrical access to information as well as the political system. For example Karashani (2001: 14) records that gender analysts in South-Western Tanzania (Sumbawanga) have attributed rural men's monopoly over local politics "to a large extent" to a lack of information that "robbed the women folk of the chance to vie for positions or to make informed choices in the 2000 election." This may overstate the potential role of the media in women's emancipation in rural Tanzania, however, as Sheikh (2001: 11) notes: "In Tanzania as elsewhere in Africa the news is seldom managed or presented by, for or about women. In all forms of media, decisions are most often made by men."[23]

The question of media bias is further complicated by the proliferation of foreign sources—who themselves stand accused of media bias.[24] Over the past few years, for example, East African Muslims have complained about the coverage given to the Muslim faith by western news sources, and question the extent to which the proliferation of these views in East African media is influencing foreign policy decisions and government and community receptiveness to anti-Muslim sentiment.[25] Further, the proliferation of international news and media sources raises additional questions about the role of the media as *local* watchdog.

In Sum

Overall, this brief overview suggests that important limitations to the UN's love affair with the media may stand in the way of vital political transformation. If the media is not up to the task, however, the condition of (widely available and accurate) information that serves to regulate the flow of power is severely compromised. The conditions under which *the public* match and counter the discourse articulation capacity of the state—or indeed of global actors—are revealed as more complicated and fragile than governance models suggest. Weaknesses in the way media is integrated into the governance agenda, then, seriously challenge the model of participation the UN offers.

Further, while the governance agenda depends on a facile cardboard cut out of "the media" to flesh out crucial dimensions of participation, it simultaneously undermines these dimensions by co-opting the power of the media for its own dissemination needs.

CIVIL AND UNCIVIL SOCIETY

The concept of "civil society" is found under the UNDP's "Objective indicators of Governance" (2002: 43) and corresponds specifically to "trade union membership" and "non-governmental organizations." To benchmark *strong* civil society we might look to Norway, the *Human Development Index*'s leading country, where 52% of people belong to trade unions and where there are 2,571 non-governmental organizations. Thus, there seems to be a correlate between *strong* civil society and overall well-being. But we might be confused to find that the US, however, which places 6ᵗʰ overall in the *Human Development Index*, lists only 13 % of citizens as members of trade unions and, comparatively, only 2,685 non-governmental organizations, despite populations of 4.5 and 285 million respectively. In other words, *the US has a comparatively very weak civil society*. In terms of our country cases, Angola's trade union membership is unknown and the country hosts 235 NGOs. Botswana clocks in at 12% and 356, Namibia, 5% and 817, and Tanzania at 17% and 554, respectively, with respective populations of approximately 10, 1.5, 1.5, and 23 million. Thus, all fare well when compared to the US.

It is unclear how to interpret the relationship of civil society to governance, or the relationship between civil society and anything—particularly given the United States' comparatively poor showing. Not surprisingly, the Report makes no reference to the concept in the "Human Development Balance Sheet" (10–11), with its absence most remarkable in the "Democracy and Participation" field.

Nevertheless, the concept is used fairly robustly across the discourse. At times, civil society seems to be a fussy conflation of the word civil meaning civilized or community minded, civil meaning civilian and standing in for the concept of society generally, and civil society in the "pre-modern" sense of "politically organized commonwealth" (Ehrenberg 1999: 235). Few distinctions are drawn and no attempt is made to illuminate the role of external donors in constituting civil society (Bellucci 2002), the various political goals and endogenous organizational imperatives these actors may have (Fowler 1996), or the *darker* side of organized political action, sometimes analyzed under the rubric of *uncivil* society.[26] By leaving these dimensions in silence, civil society as it appears in the discourse is asserted as a rather unproblematic and apolitical intermediary between society in general and the goals of the developmental state. As noted below, more problematic still are the grey areas where the hazy distinction between engagement with civil society actors and communities more generally runs the risk of conflating any number of sub-contracting implementation agents with community participation and consent.

Country Caveats

For example, the *Angolan Inter-Agency Appeal* (2001: 33) characterizes its "protection" strategy as two-pronged: "building capacity and accountability in government structures" and "encouraging communities to participate in safeguarding their rights." One related strategy is to: "Develop and reinforce inter-community protection mechanisms at the provincial and community level by training and supporting provincial and local authorities, civil society actors and community members in protection strategies" (34). Similarly, under the rubric of "capacity-building in re-settlement areas" it is proposed to: "support and strengthen civil society through programmes designed to encourage reconciliation, community building, respect for human rights and conflict resolution" (37). Yet the content and implications of the claims are unclear, simultaneously conflating and delineating civil society and society in general, while leaving silent the question of power and politics within civil society itself. Thus, as Ehrenberg (1999: x) notes: "civil society is often deployed in a thin, under theorized, and confusing fashion."

The Tanzanian CCF by comparison, conflates civil society with general participation and consultative processes. For example, it states: "In partnerships with government, civil society and donors, the UNDP will contribute to the achievement of the seven broad strategic outcomes." One such outcome is that "the budget process should be participatory and transparent, enabling civil society to have an influence on the setting of priorities and allocating resources to them" (6). Similarly, "government technical and organizational capacity to manage the TAS and PRSP processes increased by supporting civil society involvement in planning, implementation and monitoring" (7). "Pro-poor growth strategies" also relied on "[c]apacity building of Government and civil society to identify appropriate and effective pro-poor strategies" (8).

Interviews with members of civil society revealed that while most considered themselves advocates, few made any claims to representativeness.[27] Independent studies also suggested that NGO administered projects were not necessarily more participatory or consultative. For example, an evaluation of the Health Through Sanitation and Water project, funded jointly by the Swedish and Tanzanian governments, found that implementers did not include village recommendations in project design and "that a lack of popular participation in decision-making by the target population at each and every stage of the project cycle contributed to inevitable but predictable negative consequences" (Rugumamu 1999: 49–50). Similarly, R.G. Mutakyahwa, of the Eastern and Southern African Universities' Research Programme, argues that Tanzania's civil society has a propensity to fail to make a visible impact, to take decisions based on reliable data or to monitor or evaluate progress (2002: 78).

Interviews at the ESRF (Economic and Social Research Foundation), a Dar es Salaam think tank, and the Centre for Foreign Relations also indicated that the manifest expression of the NGO presence was the number of fine restaurants and four wheel drives on the road. Both interviewees felt that often, very little was actually accomplished, with NGOs rarely stewarding projects beyond the outfitting (four wheel drives, cell phones, etc.) and planning stages. The representative for the ESRF was particularly sceptical about the role of NGOs in poverty alleviation:

> There are too many NGOs, many of them one-person shows, and all about making money. Tanzanians in general don't drive four-wheel drives. Those cars belong to the aid workers. The classes that drive the NGO business are pretty far removed from regular people. Donors are pouring in excessive funding; the need for an NGO bill arose because there is this widespread feeling that NGO aren't accomplishing anything.[28]

The conceptual and strategic integration of the civil society concept adopted in Namibia tended to be quite similar to that of Tanzania, despite the different contexts. For example, the UNDAF (2002: 10, 19) asserts:

The United Nations (UN) System in Namibia, reflecting on the prospects and in dialogue with Government, civil society associations and donors, have converged upon the following strategic objectives over the near-term, namely to assist the Government and the people of Namibia to . . .

In view of the above target dates, the timing of the formulation of UNDAF allows UN Agencies sufficient time to equip themselves in order to have an even greater influence on the guiding principles of development in Namibia. NDP2 [National Development Plan 2] and Vision 2030 provide an opportunity for UN Agencies to arrange themselves, with the help of a common development assistance framework and in close co-operation with GRN, civil society and the donor community, to face the challenges of assisting in the implementation of a medium-term plan within the guidance of a long-term vision.

Thus, again we find the implicit assumption that dialogue with "civil society" is necessary and sufficient to imbue the intervention process with participatory credentials, and to infuse processes with the benefits of multi-stakeholder views. Yet, civil society is not necessarily representative, which poses significant problems for the implicit claim that consulting civil society experts is the same as holding general consultations. For example, a recent youth survey conducted by Nambia's Institute for Public Policy Research (2001: 38) found that less that 4.3% of respondents felt strongly that experts should make "key economic decisions."

Elsewhere, a recent UNDP study highlighted that differences among gender and class interests of community leaders (civil society?) could tend to frustrate empowerment efforts. For example: "A Herero community leader, who also presides over dispute resolution hearings in the Gobabis area, was quoted as saying that violence repeatedly inflicted on a woman is not a good reason to ask for a divorce."[29] At the same time, interviews with members of Windhoek's NGO community indicated that the processes of NGO consultation were uneven, at best. For example, interviews at the Legal Assistance Centre in Windhoek indicated that donors self-determined what kind of projects they would fund, while "very often we are not invited [to consultations] at all." Similarly, the director for the Namibian Red Cross lamented that they had not received any information about the *Millennium* Declaration, nor had they been invited to the launch of the *Human Development Report*: "We are left out of launches and have not been briefed on the *Millennium Declaration*." The Director for the Institute for Democracy added, "civil society is weak and fragmented, and are not taken seriously." A representative for the Rainbow

Project, an advocacy organization for gays and lesbians, also noted that lobbies were divided along racial lines, with white gays and lesbians drawing funding from the relatively privileged whites of Windhoek, and poorer blacks having little recourse against violence and police harassment, and the compulsions of poverty.

The Botswana CCF doesn't mention civil society, and the observer is left to speculate about the implications of a governance agenda that can exclude the concept altogether. Interviews with the UNDP country representative revealed that NGOs were informally consulted, but that few resources were allotted for either consultations or strengthening any dimension of civil society. At the same time, however, interviews with NGOs also indicated that while their goals may be symbiotic with those of the segments of the population they hope to serve; their mandates are not democratically determined or reviewed.

Further, interviews at BACONGO, Botswana's NGO umbrella organization, suggested that NGO "governance" remained a significant problem in Botswana, with questions of fiscal responsibility and accountability remaining BACONGO's top concern. At the same time, analysts have pointed to the overall weakness of Botswana's civil society as contributing to the democracy's elitist and authoritarian tendencies (Good 1999: Holm 1993).

In Sum

Thus, civil society, typically used to signify some dimension of participatory or consultative process, is both a central and peripheral, yet critically ambiguous component of the overall governance agenda. It tends to be used in ways that implicitly conflate the interests of society in general with those of the NGO community and local leaders. Here, however, we find, *inter alia*, that class and gender issues are denied. The concept of civil society, as seen in the governance agenda, does not leave room to acknowledge that inequities are reproduced in and by civil society. Rather the idea carries with it the implication that power inequities have already been resolved, leaving (only) a representative and concentrated microcosm of the ideal public. Thus, while civil society is clearly a concept that is very important to the participatory claims of the governance agenda, it also obfuscates more than it illuminates. It shadows the dimensions of privilege and underprivileged the donor gaze produces. That is, donors listen to and empower some organizations, imagining that they are representative in order to satisfy their own participation requirements, while empowering certain voices and segments of the population at the expense of others.

ELECTIONS: STILL THE ONLY MEASURE OF PARTICIPATION

Elections appear in the *Human Development Report* (UNDP 2002: 37–45) as the only "objective indicator" of participation, and a "subjective" expression of "political rights" and "voice and accountability." Regionally, they feature centrally as well:

> Elections play a central role in democratization efforts in Africa and elsewhere and this focus must remain strong; but elections must also be part of a long-term undertaking that will lead to a strengthening of national institutions and democratic processes. The real test of a democratization process is not the organization of first elections, but whether those first elections are followed by others in accordance with an agreed electoral timetable (Causes of Conflict 1998: para. 78).

Yet, the ambivalent expression of the key liberal anchors discussed in previous sections might be expected to contribute to trouble and/or voter apathy on Election Day. Approaches to rule of law, human rights, civil society, and media tend to indicate blindness to political competition, while also failing to significantly intervene at the level of real lived exclusion. Election politics have long been recognized as contentious and potentially explosive politics—all the more so when stakes are high and other crucial means of cooperation and accountability are handicapped.

That is, there is a growing awareness that elections do no simply mediate between the ideas of equals, but entail political competition among the vested interests of relatively unequal and sometimes volatile networks of power, and the hopes and expectations of individualized or marginalized publics. Further, it is a competition in which the government of the day or ruling party is privileged by the organizational, financial, regulatory and coercive machinery of the state. Outcomes may appear pre-determined, but stakes for both winners and losers can be extremely high—paving the way for explosive frustrations.

In Africa, elections often take place in the context of historically contingent "chaotic pluralism" or incendiary dualisms (see Eyoh 1998: Mamdani 2001: Snyder 2000), expressing (sometimes desperate) attempts to fundamentally re-configure the relationship between state and sub-state groups, and state and structures of violence and inequality. In this context, at times, "[t]he choice therefore seems to be between two kinds of re-configuration, the one peaceable and the other violent" (Okafor 2000: 127). Similarly, as Monga (1997: 165) notes:

part of the violence is the political game itself, which leaders view as a *winner-takes-all* fight to the finish where defeat means a loss not only of the emoluments and status that office brings, but sometimes of life itself. The game is for keeps. One must win—by any means necessary. The modern state, as Max Weber said, holds a monopoly on the legitimate use of force; the transition, in the eyes of many African politicians, is a battle for control over the state's coercive apparatus.

Micro and inter-personal social cleavages and conflict can also play out on Election Day. In Tanzania, for example, structures of gender inequality continue to form a key basis for social conflict around election time. Karashani (2001: 14) reports that one civic education project in rural Tanzania went:

> well as she [the facilitator] spoke of women's emancipation through economic development . . . but that when she delved into the woman's individual right to choose leaders of her own choice, and to run for office, she was pulled aside by the village heads and asked to end her lesson. "The leaders were unhappy, because they felt threatened. We were disturbing the status quo in this male dominated society."

Alternatively there is also the problem of voter apathy and/or disassociation from the political system. For example, Good (1999: 52–53) argues that Botswana's democracy is characterized by high levels of voter apathy, engendered by, *inter alia*, constitutional structure, "secretive authoritarian tendencies," "the complete absence of right-to-know legislation, and of 'whistle-blower' protections," leading to "[t]he enfeeblement of the mass of the citizenry, in the face of both the quiescence of their elected parliamentary representatives and the domination of the elite" (55). This helps to account for the fact that in 1999, only 41.98% of voting age adults voted, down from 46.63 in 1994.[30]

The broader systemic environment may engender both apathy and conflict on Election Day, especially where the lack of substantive freedom and opportunity truncates participation and the expression of alternative political vision.

Country Caveats

Caveats notwithstanding, and despite being the *only* "Objective" indicator of participation in the HDR, the only country documents that make reference to elections are those of Tanzania and Namibia. Tanzania became a multi-party democracy in 1995, and held its second elections in 2000. In that the UNDP includes elections as the *only* objective measure of participation, one might conclude that it has a stake in seeing high electoral turnouts. According to the US Department of State, voter turn out for Tanzania in 2000 was low.[31] However, according to the UNDP (2002: 45) voter turn out was high: 84%. While it is not stated, this figure must refer to *registered voters*, not *eligible voters*. To get an accurate figure for eligible voters one might first estimate the total population. The UN estimates the 2000 population at 35.1 million. IDEA,[32] estimated the 2000 population at 33, 517,000, for a difference of 1 million 583, 000 people—not insignificant. The UN estimated the population under 15 at 45%. Roughly we might estimate from this that approximately *half* of the eligible voters voted, not 84%. According to IDEA 45.7% of the voting age population voted in 2000. Within these discrepancies lie vastly different pictures of the rate of participation in and citizen satisfaction with the Tanzanian political system.

There are 15 legally registered political parties, six of whom have seats in parliament. Overwhelmingly, mainland support lies with the CCM (Chama Cha Mapinduzi), which holds 198 out of a possible 228 seats. Women hold 47 seats in total; 40 of those are CCM representatives. Recently, SARDC reported that:

> In the rural areas, where 85 per cent of the population lives, the CCM [former one-party state government] structures remain virtually unchallenged even though only the more strident voices in the urban minority are serviced by media and donors. Election results are routinely challenged in the courts as being "rigged" by government and there is an unwillingness to accept defeat which is an inherent component of any democracy.

Irregularities, intimidation and boycotts on the Island of Zanzibar during the 2000 election received widespread attention, and were noted to have been exacerbated by "poor governance, poverty and inequalities" (Tanzanian CCF 2001: 3). The Freidrich Ebert Stiftung (2001: 12) reported:

> A notable incidence in the 2000 general election was the cancellation in 16 constituencies in Zanzibar of election results unfavourable to the ruling party. Subsequently, the Zanzibar Electoral Commission announced results that gave the ruling party a 67% lead as against 33% for the opposition. Peaceful opposition protests of these actions were violently put down.

In this light, Freidrich Ebert Stiftung Foundation (2001: 10–11) has argued that electoral politics in Tanzania are marred by a lack of faith, which is made manifest by partisan appointments to the National Electoral Commission, relatively exorbitant fees to launch an electoral petition, organized youth wings with paramilitary training, and "political repression, harassment and intimidation." The Tanzanian CCF (2001: 3), however, notes that international observers pronounced the elections "free and fair":

> However, it was noted that future elections would benefit from a higher level of civic education, aimed at raising awareness of the electorate of rights and obligations in a pluralistic society.

Namibia compares with Tanzania to the extent that it is a relatively new multiparty democracy dominated by one overwhelmingly powerful party that has used the clout afforded by the state apparatus to further entrench its position and sway election results. It is also similar to the extent that large portions of the population overwhelmingly support the ruling party for ethnic and historical reasons, rather than those typically associated with contemporary and conventional (liberal) policy issues. According to the IPPR (Keulder 2002a: 12), the *de facto* effect has been a "single-dominant-party system, dividing society into a single, strong political majority and a number of powerless political minorities. These two aspects combine to create a zero-sum perception of political rewards in the country, and of the relative permanence of winner/loser status." Henning Melber (2000: 181), well-known Namibian political analyst hypothesizes that growing dissatisfaction, in this case, would manifest in withdrawal from the electoral system, rather than as support for opposition parties. IDEA records that in 1989, close to 100% of the voting age public participated; in 1994, that number fell to 63.78, and in 1999, fell slightly further to 61.71, despite the registration of close to 200,000 more people.[34]

The Namibian UNDAF (2002: 204) gives minimal attention to elections, mentioning them only once in the context of voter registration, despite the last two elections showing a negative correlation between voter registration and voting. Further, a recent study by the IPPR (Keulder 2000: 12) indicated voter apathy rather than ignorance lay at the heart of Namibia's declining electoral turnout. A sample of "focus group participants" responses were used to illustrate the point:

> There are political parties in Namibia, but do you think it helps at all with the fact that you can choose? SWAPO is so big, the party that is in control is so big, it doesn't help if you choose a smaller party. I don't agree that there is political freedom in Namibia, because it is actually a rumour if you are not in SWAPO and you are Owanbo.

I have never voted and I will never vote. Why should I vote? It doesn't help.

In Sum

Elections are the central symbolic act of faith in, and support for, the legitimacy of the national political community. They can also be an indicator of more profound problems in the liberal political transformation agenda. That is, if elections express a number of profound conflicts and ambivalences, none of which are mitigated by the rule of law, human rights norms, civil society or the media, then democratic governance is also bound to be frayed, fragmented, disarticulated and interpenetrated by conflict and ambivalence in ways that elections may be able to reflect, but are not likely to correct.

In the final analysis, however, elections are not only an expression of participation (although not *the* expression), but also a gauge of systemic health. When they become the participatory moment of last resort, when all other forums for deliberation, mediation and self-determination are circumscribed, elections, as well, will inevitably fail to express participation in any meaningful way (Gills *et al* 1993; Marks 2000). Yet, elections are asserted by the UNDP as the *only* objective measure of political participation, behind which a plethora of ills are masked in order to instantiate legitimacy in systems and processes, which in fact, fall short of the mark. It is on the stage of elections where the governance agenda's commitment to participation makes its most artful performance.

CAPACITY-BUILDING: BEWARE THE DEVELOPMENTAL STATE

In UN discourse, governments and states are relatively unproblematic signifiers for benevolent ciphers into which the UN inserts *universal* norms, forms and event. They embody just laws and enforce them in the public good, their media apparatus is synonymous with the free flow of quality information, they receive the wisdom of "civil society" and bend to it, and, ultimately, they willingly subject themselves to fair and periodic review and recall. However, as Ben Turok (1987:94) argues: "Too many critics and opponents have been harassed and imprisoned for us to fail to appreciate that the state is not simply a theoretical construct: it is a *de facto* internal force, an established machine governed by rules and discipline with a powerful capacity for coercion and control." For example, Peter Vale (2003: 171) commenting on the building of the South African state notes:

Prior to the ending of colonialism, minority rule, and apartheid, manifestations of insecurity and war were at the core of the region's discursive formation. Through this, realist security studies was presented as the only means to understand the future social organization in the region; this in turn strengthened the power that this discourse exercised over a political lexicon that used gloomy tropes and hollow patriotism to reinforce the idea that the region belonged not to its people but to its states.

The nexus of state and power in Africa must be understood on its own terms Turok goes on to argue. For example, he posits that "the relation between economic and political power is inverted compared to conventional capitalist states. It is not economic power which yields political power but political power which provides the basis for the formation of an economically powerful class" (71). Or as Vale (2003: 64) notes when describing the apartheid state, it was the coercive apparatus of the state that ordered South and Southern Africa, reserving—by force- places of prosperity and privilege for the white (and male):

> The practice of discrimination and violence along racial divides was to be seen in many places, but if South Africa's was its perfection, the racial politics in the contest over places once called Rhodesia and South West Africa suggests how racial discrimination was regional and how slowly and how violent was its retreat as fears for security—personal, national, even international—deepened.

In this light, humanitarian actors have the added responsibility to recognize the complexities and particularities of the state, as well as their role in state making. Stateness derives from a complex amalgam of internal and external forces (see Shaw and Chasan 1986; McIntosh 1999). Yet disparate analysts agree that juridical statehood, where international sanction is as, if not more, important than domestic legitimacy, is key to understanding the link between contemporary forms of African state power and the personal/elite wealth of state actors. It is juridical statehood that creates for state elites the environment within which it is relatively easy to treat state resources like personal property. Further, as Jackson and Rosberg (1986: 237) note:

> The juridical attributes of statehood can only be conferred upon governments by the "international community" . . . [J]uridical statehood is more important than empirical statehood in accounting for the persistence of states in Black Africa. International organizations have served

as "post-imperial ordering devices" for the new African states, in effect
freezing them in their inherited colonial jurisdictions and blocking any
post-independence movements towards self-determination.

Juridical statehood makes for a mere tangential similarity between African
and Western *nations*, as Mamdani and Eyoh (1998: 9) note, respectively:

> In Africa, more than any part of the world, there is little coincidence
> between the history of nation formation and state formation, between
> social history and political history . . . More than the outcomes of
> internal social histories, they reflect the exigencies of external geopoli-
> tics . . . By and large the states in Africa are not nation states. .

> According to this argument, suppositions that most Africans have come
> to privilege their identities as citizens of national political communi-
> ties over allegiances to subnational groups are unwarranted, or at best,
> open to debate.

Recent studies in South Africa tend to confirm the need for greater attention to this point (du Toit 2001; Wilson and Black 2004). These highlight
the extent to which individuals and communities may not recognize the
legitimacy of the state or its elites—or, indeed, be motivated by stirrings of
patriotism or national community (see Crais 2001).

Yet, tenuous claims to a governing mandate often translate fairly
straightforwardly into control over the proceeds from state resources (i.e.
oil, diamonds, timber, minerals, land and/or expropriation, etc.) and/or
international aid and, during the Cold War, international patronage flows.
Here the resources that flow from international *legitimacy* typically render
all other sub-groups vulnerable to the capriciousness of state elites, who
control state resources and the coercive apparatus. By virtue of its overwhelming resources, the state can be superficial and resilient, imposed and
unopposed, as Mann (1986: 7) argues:

> There is, thus, a simple answer to the question of why the masses do
> not revolt—a perennial problem for social stratification—and it does
> not concern value consensus, or force, or exchange in the usual sense
> of those conventional sociological explanations. The masses comply
> because they lack collective organization to do otherwise, because they
> are embedded within collective and distributive power organization
> controlled by others. They are *organizationally outflanked* [emphasis
> on original].

In this light, the propensity of the dominant discourse to lay multiple forms of power at the feet of stateness, under the guise of "capacity-building" for developmental states is problematic. This holds true even where capacity building is implemented in the context of a broader liberal reform agenda, which inevitably will only be unevenly realized. For example, a strengthening of the institutions and legitimacy of the electoral system may not necessarily be accompanied by gains in access to information, redress of inequities that prevent full political participation or freedom from intimidation. It is, then, at the juncture of capacity-building and unevenly expressed liberal reforms where, many critics have argued, lays Africa's new democratically legitimate authoritarianism/low-intensity democracies (Abrahamsen 2001; Gills *at al.* 1993; Marks 2000).

Country Caveats

The complications and contradictions involved in state-capacity building are well illustrated by the Angolan case. Attendance at Inter-Agency meetings in Luanda revealed that the new central coordinating body, the Office of Coordination and Humanitarian Affairs (OCHA), admittedly did not have the field-level capacity to execute the range of tasks assigned to it. At the same time, it adopted the precept "Do No Harm," while shifting to a strategy of high-level constructive engagement. Most notably this referred to working with and though the government of Angola (GoA), while still hoping to alleviate the worst manifestations of war-related vulnerability. Yet, meeting participants expressed frustration that the GoA was, at times, only cooperative to the extent that specific performances could be linked to the dispersal of monetary "bundles." Further, the GoA routinely played agencies off one another. For example, it was noted that documents the GoA was charged with designing for the World Bank in order to secure the release of Poverty Reduction bundles were typically written by UNDP staff, after government requested their assistance.[35] That is, the Terms of Reference would pass from World Bank, through the GoA to the UNDP, back through the GoA. Ultimately, the UNDP-written documents would make their way back to the Bank. As a result, "bundles" accrued to the GoA for performances carried out by the UNDP for the World Bank.

Similarly, OCHA emphasized the development of *Regulamento*[36] for the eventual adoption by the GoA. The main emphasis of the "Regulamento" was the diffusion of norms, the creation of architectures of competency and political administration, as well as the pairing of government departments with UN/NGO partnerships in areas of intervention, such as water and sanitation, land claims, citizenship registration, etc. Yet, this was not tempered by the knowledge that to date the GoA has *unevenly* pursued development, enfranchisement and the protection and extension of human rights (Hodges 2001; HRW 1999; Wilson 2003; Wilson and Mwaka 2003). Elites have also shown a propensity for wielding state power for self-enrichment (see Global Witness 2001; *ibid.*). For example, the GoA has purportedly been responsible for forced displacements, for both military and narrow economic purposes. In 2001, the government was widely condemned for the forced displacement of slum/barrio residents from the waterfront slum Boavista—and for just one week later calling on the international community to respond to the plight of the homeless.[37] Critics charged that government was making room for luxury accommodation, later confirmed by widely advertised construction plans.[38] Thus, as noted elsewhere, UN strategies were designed not only to enhance the capacities of a benign developmental state, but also the power, reach and control which could be harness towards more sinister state purposes, yet this risk was not consistently acknowledged. *"Political power"* as Mann (1986: 26) notes, "derives from the usefulness of centralized, institutionalized, regulation of many aspects of social relations."

There were also widespread reports of forced displacements in the countryside. The UNHCR recorded the tragic circumstances of a village that had been attacked, allegedly by the FAA (government forces). The leader (termed Sobo) and elders had been shot, and the rest of the village forcibly displaced to the city of Uige, a major humanitarian relief centre. Interviews with the Military Commander confirmed the general thrust of events, but argued that elders were shot in crossfire between UNITA and FAA, and that villagers had been evacuated for their own safety. He also reported that UNITA was in the habit of stealing FAA uniforms and perpetrating atrocities in a battle for the hearts and minds of the rural villagers, UNITA's traditional support base. Interviews with the villagers revealed that they rejected the claim of UNITA presence and insisted they be allowed to return to their tribal lands and subsistence crops. They asserted that they desperately wanted to return to their crops and traditional lands. General Marques confirmed the government would be unable to assist them in this goal in the foreseeable future.[39] Yet, government has been reluctant to guarantee land title or leasing rights in the province of Uige, and all *abandoned* lands have fallen under *government jurisdiction*, raising questions about the stakes that governing and economic elites might have in "unoccupied" resource rich lands (see Chapter Eight for a more thorough discussion).

In Botswana, interviews concerning the nature of projects being implemented revealed special emphasis on deepening information technology capacity of parliamentarians and developing a system for monitoring and evaluating citizen statistics—specifically, the development of a computerized information databank. This project is the result of a partnership and consultation between the UNDP, the World Bank and the GoB. It is important to note, however, that information is not neutral, rather statistics and data matrices:

> have the character of maps. That is, they are designed to summarize precisely those aspects of a complex world that are of immediate interest to the map-maker . . . [It is also important to note] the apparent power of maps to transform as well as merely to summarize the facts that they portray. This transformative power resides not in the map, of course, but rather in the power possessed by those who deploy the perspective of that particular map (Scott 1998: 87).

In this light, one UNDP Programme Officer noted that it was taboo to talk about either human rights or the "Basarwa," and that "gender is not taken into account at all." Similarly a UNECA (UN Economic Commission for Africa) survey and report on governance contained no gender component, while one of the academics charged with analyzing and synthesizing the report felt that while the "sin of omission" might impact negatively on women, it was just as likely that if conditions improved overall, women would simply benefit by extension.

No public, civil society or other consultative meetings had taken place, yet the UN was in the process of empowering the organizational and administrative capacity of the state to effect social engineering with ever more *efficiency* and grander scale. There are, however, caveats to consider. The Botswana polity carries a clear propensity for government hegemony. Civil society is considered weak in Botswana while the political elite strong and entrenched. As one local academic—since expelled from the country—argued: "civil society is weak, accountability is low, equality is lacking, secrecy is high and formal opposition, at least since 1999, is non-existent." Further, a number of people interviewed from the academic community and NGO sectors expressed the concern that government lacked direction, yet seemed unwilling to consult more broadly with society or to allow criticism to air out the "settled conservatism and complacency."[40]

Africa's shining light of democracy, Botswana has also been characterized as an elite democracy and/or authoritarian liberal regime (Good 1999), which "often shows tendencies toward an authoritarianism more reminiscent of apartheid engineering than openness, accountability and respect for human rights," argues Larry Swatuk, from the University of Botswana (UB). This state, Swatuk argues, is geared towards "the continuing intersection of interests between large cattle ranchers, mining capital and the State of Botswana" (1999: 7). Similarly, Good, recently deported Professor of Political Science at UB, argued previously (2002: 18) that hierarchies of wealth and status have helped to "entrench a culture of passivity and deference where the elite refuses to explain and account for its actions . . . The 'real losers' within an elite-promoted obscurity and silence are probably the 'poor and voiceless.'"

With respect to other "crosscutting" issues to which the UN has made clear commitments, Selolwane (1997: 30) has noted the dialectical relationships between women's limited political power in Botswana and the gendered face of poverty. "In the context of the postcolonial state, where the state is the chief distributor of economic opportunities and development resources, women's capacity to influence distributional decision-making is critical to the enhancement of their development status." Yet interviews reveal that the UNDP's current governance and data generating agenda had no gender component, and had not been reviewed through gendered lenses.

In Namibia, governance programming was stalled and few capacity-building efforts not covered in previous sections were either planned or running. Despite having produced more documents than any of the other Country Offices visited, the UNDP (governance/poverty unit) was in transition and had no programmes—except a TV debate on *Talk to the Nation* in the planning stage. UNDP Namibia had, however, made a clear commitment to "moving upstream." This strategy was described thus: "we fit poverty programmes with gaps the government has pre-identified. We are committed to a relationship with government."[41] The only project in the recent past was in Ohangwena, the poverty stricken and densely populated Swapo electoral stronghold. Yet, evidence of what Namibian Scholar Henning Melber (2000: 183) describes as "[a]n increasing tendency towards totalitarian methods of political rule," was widely available. "Our political rulers," he argued, "foster a culture of fear, a culture of silence." At the time of research, for example, the independent newspaper, *The Namibian,* reported Prime Minister Theo-Ben Gurirab "proposed that the Swapo strongholds of Rundu Rural, Hakahana and Ohangwena be split into two to create three more constituencies under the ruling party."[42]

The UNDP governance unit in Tanzania placed its emphasis on strengthening the capacity of the National Assembly, "staff-reorientation towards multipartyism" and a pilot de-centralization project in four wards—*all through existing government channels.* It was also, reportedly, moving forward on an information database—similar to that underway in Botswana—and a pilot project in participatory budgeting in Mwanza (in the west, flanking lake Victoria).[43] Activities were modest when compared to the "examples of activities" cited on the "UNDP-Tanzania" website, especially with respect to gender mainstreaming, which was, as elsewhere, not as yet operationalized. Similarly, efforts to refine government capacity were ongoing, while civil society support was, reportedly, "in the planning stage." As in Botswana, a central anchor of the governance support agenda was the creation and segmentation of information whereby complex social structures and conditions could be rendered intelligible for government purposes. The process was still in the data collection phase in late 2002.

Interestingly, interviews at the UNDP revealed that instead of using a massive database amassed by the University of Dar es Salaam think tank REDET (Research and Education for Democracy in Tanzania), the UNDP had commissioned a completely new data set from the Law Department, arguing that the data collected by REDET would not be appropriate for the "technical" intervention that was planned. In response, one academic interviewed observed that the marginalization of existing data in favour of new data collection projects is a common practice among donors in Tanzania. Given the short funding life spans of many projects, however, most never get past the data collection phase.[44] Nevertheless, the UNDP planned (CCF 2001: 8):

> A *master plan* for a holistic and effective poverty monitoring system, including the establishment of a long term survey programme, sectoral data collection, Participatory Poverty Assessments (PRAs) and independent studies and dissemination plans [emphasis added].

To the former subjects of Ujamaa,[45] the idea of a *master plan* may, indeed, resonate. For example, Scott (1998: 224) details how aesthetics, miniaturization and simplification were the means for implementing Nyerere's great socialist villagization experiment (1973–1976):

> [T]he existing patterns of settlement and social life in Tanzania were illegible and resistant to the narrow purposes of the state. Only by radically simplifying the settlement pattern was it possible for the state to efficiently deliver such development services as schools, clinics, and clean water. Mere administrative convenience was hardly the only objective of state officials . . . The thinly veiled subtext of villagization was also to reorganize human communities in order to make them better objects of political control and to facilitate the new forms of communal farming favoured by state policy.

The UNDP was also undertaking a pilot de-centralization project that relied on participatory rural appraisal methods, but also worked exclusively through government channels and official headmen. Gender was not mainstreamed into project design, despite UNDP staff noting during the interview that women tended to be absent from, or silent within, meetings. One observer of the aid community commented that PRA invitees were rarely given any preparatory workshops or materials, leaving them sceptical and confused about the overall exercise.[46] Further, the explicit goal was to render information to Tanzanian state officials. In light of the character of state/society relations discussed earlier, James Scott (1990: 2) draws our attention to the existence of "public transcripts" and "hidden transcripts. The former is "a shorthand way of describing the open interaction between subordinates and those who dominate." The latter is the "discourse that takes place "offstage," beyond direct observation by powerholders." Given the UN's unambiguous (and largely uncritical) support for government and state structures, PRA researchers are likely to be considered powerholders, and thus the information they receive would be part of the public transcript. This could differ significantly from what participants might say privately, outside of the view state agents, or indeed what they might do, if they were empowered to act in their own interests rather than encouraged to work through the state to see their basic needs satisfied. A recent study (Karashani 2001: 15), for example, noted that political meetings tended to embody a range of challenges and threats for women:

> "When you raise the hand to ask a question, they first ask you for your name and where you live. This means they may follow you, and who knows, pick you up from home," said Ms Elisa Saini, the [church group] vice secretary. And in the rural setting where they might victimize you for what they think you think, her fears are not without justification.

In this context, gathering information is both highly politicized and highly vulnerable to biases and misinformation. Additionally, one interviewee noted that the concept of "decentralization" already had a long and troubled history in Tanzania, a country which has gone through a number of de-centralization and re-centralization rounds since independence. As a result of these experiments, both the local and centralized government are linked in the popular imaginary with the imposition of illegitimate and often chaotic political interventions, as well the creation of new strata of unaccountable and often inept political elites. Since independence, for example, a number of layers of local government have been created, imposed and disbanded.[47]

Overall, UNDP-Tanzania's governance focus on government capacity occurs in a context where "undoing the state monopoly in economic and political affairs has been especially difficult" and "[a]ssociational life . . . is quite weak, even by African standards" (Hyden 1999; 143, 148). Corruption and neopatrimonialism are widely acknowledged as well-entrenched, while public service operations remain opaque in the hands of "corrupt officials [who] are motivated to create disorganization and intransparency" (Kobb 2000). Yet, these problems seem have had little effect on the strategy of working though, empowering and socializing state officials (Hyden 1999; Kobb 2000).

In Sum

In sum, this brief sample has sought to illuminate the nexus of UN governance and the state, where, as Good (1999: 62) argues in the case of Botswana, "[p]opular non-participation and elite predominance persist in close, mutually supportive circularity." While the countries surveyed all have widely varying democratic deficits, the UN model persists in imagining these states as ideal developmental states and not as the political complexes they really are. This facilitates interventions that seek to build capacity, but which may also have the consequence of merely empowering a state apparatus (especially in relation to other social forces) with which elites can entrench their position. There is little reason to be optimistic about the effect of UN presence on women's opportunity landscape, or the distribution of power across the political spectrum more generally.

CONCLUDING REMARKS

Previous chapters highlighted the extent to which the dominant GDH discourses tend to coalesce and become coherent around, ostensibly, *universal* knowledge inserted from the top-down into states. Simultaneously, it provides few reasons to be optimistic about the authenticity of the participatory practices to which the governance agenda alludes. In the preceding sections, we see this same pattern conditioning the expression of some of the UN model's most valued symbols of democratic governance. That is, the concept of universality under girds approaches to rights-based rule of law; participatory credentials are claimed by virtue of thin versions of the media, civil society and elections; and the state is rendered as an apolitical cipher, a benign developmental state where the only thing that stands in the way of development is knowledge and capacity. The preceding sections also highlight that, given the mismatch between the state the UN imagines and the state as lived experience, at the level of praxis there is a propensity for governance-related support programs to translate into support programmes for authoritarian and elitist regimes. Together, these sections speak to a density of evidence coalescing around the propensity of the dominant discourse to instantiate institutions and social practices that are unlikely to have direct or causal links to empowerment, and which conversely carry the propensity to contribute to the political powerlessness often identified as the underlying cause of material deprivation (Ferguson 1994: Parpart 1995; Reason 1994). This chapter also speaks to the necessity for further study comparing architectures of development intervention with local political landscapes. The next chapter compares one specific project—the Human Rights Committee—with the specific political landscapes with which it was meant to interact and *fix*—the province of Uige, Angola.

Chapter Eight

Paradoxes and Dilemmas of Institutional Change: Human Rights and Livelihoods in Rural War-Torn Angola

This case study¹ critiques the conceptual architecture of a United Nations peace-building project called the Human Rights Committee (HRC). Committees were designed for implementation in Angola's war-torn provinces as peace loomed uncertainly in early 2001. The case study assesses the information available in April 2001,² and on this basis forecasts how the Committee was set to affect lives and livelihoods, if it were to operate as planned. In the sections below, the study compares three "snapshots" of the small semi-urban city of Uige, capital of Angola's Northern Uige province. These "snapshots" are: the formal political institutions; the informal landscapes; and how these were imagined in the documents and processes of the Human Rights Committee.

The case study proceeds in six parts: First is a brief description of the HRC and how various implementers imagined it. Second, is a portrait of the capital city of Uige set in the context of Angola's 30-year civil war and the massive displacement of its citizens that followed. Third, is a sketch of the formal and informal political and civic landscapes of Uige. The fourth section describes how the HRC valued and sought to interact with both the formal and informal dimensions of Uige's socialscapes. The fifth section examines the finding that the Committee resembled a top-down, externally driven, state-building project premised on values that were ostensibly universal rather than on vetted knowledge. The article concludes by suggesting areas for further research in order to identify mismatches between local context and institution-building efforts, and to forestall the creation of disempowering government structures.

INTRODUCTION

The peace-building operation in Angola—and the Human Rights Committee (HRC) specifically—took its cue from the merger of security and development that characterized the development landscape in the aftermath of the Cold War (Duffield 2001). Here, the prevention and resolution of conflict are married to developmental concepts such as liberal governance, democracy and human rights. Both security and development, however, remain unsettled practices of global relations, and the focus of intense scrutiny. Many related critiques pertain in one way or another to the charge that mainstream security and development studies tend to operate on the basis of problematic assumptions about the way the world *really* is and how it *really* operates. A key feature of these assumptions is the way traditional paradigms of security and development favour elite and expert knowledge, while excluding and marginalizing the opinions and preferences of those whose poverty has become the *raison d'être* of the humanitarian industries (Abrahamsen 2001; Ferguson 1990; Parpart 1995). To the extent that this is true, peace-building efforts may, in fact, hinder the efforts of recipients to manage their own resources and enrich their local socialscapes. This is especially true for Africa. No other region has seen UN discourses of conflict and development as explicitly married. [3]

Angola is a textbook example. The country has always been at war. It endured one of the most pernicious colonial histories on record, was subject to the bloodiest colonial anti-independence insurgency south of the Sahara, and became one of the worst casualties of South African expansionist policies and covert United States Cold War destabilization policies. Then, in the early 1990s Angola was the site of arguably the poorest example of "experimental" peacekeeping. Today Angola and its geopolitical baggage are no less complex and controversial. Sceptical observers contend that the MPLA,[4] long considered the legitimate government, is gatekeeper to a parasitic and predatory system in which a small number of national and international interests, reaching to the highest level of the most powerful administrations in the world, profit grossly on the back of humanitarian catastrophe. To say that Angola's relationship with the international community is complex is to belabor the obvious. In this polarized context, constructive relationship building among local, national and international stakeholders have been slow while efforts to build coalitions for sustainable, equity-based reconstruction and development remain fraught and complicated. With the 2002 military defeat of the rebel group UNITA[5] and the battle death of its leader, Jonas Savimbi, Angola finally came to stand on the brink of long-awaited development and prosperity. Despite the presence of a sizeable UN humanitarian mission, the people of Angola have suffered tremendously from an uneasy and complicated relationship with international forces. Their future will be scripted by the institutions and policies that international actors bring with their peace-building efforts.

Relying on field research carried out in Luanda and the Northern Angolan province of Uige in April 2001,[6] this article explores a UN initiative called the Human Rights Committee. This case study illuminates the tensions and contradictions invoked by attempts to thread a rights-based governance architecture into communities faced with a weak and predatory state apparatus. It is important to note that at the time of research, however, the HRC was embryonic. Thus, this article cannot comment at length on how the project played out.[7] Rather, the research interrogates the assumptions within the HRC's conceptual architecture and "regulatory norms" with a view to illuminating how well they fit or failed to fit with Angola's complicated landscapes. The article concludes by identifying crucial areas of further peace-building and development research.

WHAT IS THE HUMAN RIGHTS COMMITTEE?

Human Rights Committees were initiated by the United Nations Observer Mission in Angola (MONUA) in 1997, and officially created in the northern province of Uige on November 9, 2000. Conceptually, the Human Rights Committee was designed to serve a non-coercive law-and-order function and to help bridge the gap left by weak or non-functioning government institutions, partly the result of more than 30 years of war. That is, it sought to create a framework that individuals could use to mediate and minimize interpersonal and state/society conflict, notably abuse, violence and disputed claims to resources. To accomplish this, it sought to build institutional capacity for government and civil society to monitor communal relations, document abuses, and finally consider petitions for redress. The ultimate aim was to create a social climate in which respect for human rights would become the norm. It was envisaged that each of Angola's provinces would have an HRC as part of its provincial government system. In most provinces the committees were the responsibility of the UN Development Programme (UNDP). In Uige, however, the HRC was a UN High Commission for Refugees (UNHCR) project. The UNHCR was the lead agency for Uige owing to the high number of internally displaced persons (IDPs) and extensive humanitarian relief operation.

Provincial HRCs typically included eight government officials, one representative of traditional authority and several members of civil organizations, especially religious institutions and NGOs promoting human rights.[8] Committees were designed to operate in conjunction with local volunteer monitors who were elected at community meetings. It was envisaged that the Committee would meet regularly and hear complaints and reports from the volunteer community activists, and otherwise co-ordinate human rights awareness activities, such as a local weekly radio show that broadcast information about human rights. In the longer term, the Committee was meant to provide the roots for a social and political culture based on human rights, which could keep political reforms *on track* once peace-building and reconstruction had begun in earnest.

Discussion at the Provincial Working Groups meetings in Luanda revealed that the HRC project was not uncontroversial. For example, the UNHCR staff and NGO partners remained committed to the instantiation of a quasi-political body. In provinces where UNDP led the process, however, both the project and the underlying thinking were being set aside. The Office for the Coordination of Humanitarian Affairs (OCHA) representative commented: "Initially, OCHA was supportive of the parallel structure approach [to institution building], but now we are going in a different direction, towards constructive engagement; we may be going in a horribly wrong direction; if so, we will move back to the first strategy. We are still relying on informal chats with key informants in various organizations to keep us up to date." The UNHCR staff, however, expressed a strong commitment to the grassroots credentials of the HRC, with the field officer in charge arguing that HRC had the potential to mimic the elder council structure common at the village level. That is, it was envisaged that the credibility and utility of the HRC would be enhanced by structural similarities between decisions rendered by a council of governmental and non-governmental notables at the municipal and provincial levels, and decisions rendered by a council of elders at the village level. This contrasted significantly with the perspective of OCHA and the UNDP, who had begun to see the community-level component of the HCR as something that the central and provincial governments might view as an attempt by the UN to create a parallel UN-sponsored government body. In this light, one high level UNHCR official commented to the researcher that the UNDP "was now just the development arm of the World Bank."

At the time of field research in April 2001, the Human Rights Committee project remained both conceptually and operationally embryonic. The Committee had been established, a number of community-level meetings had taken place and volunteers selected. UNHCR in Luanda was in the process of putting together a library of human rights related resource materials. The Committee still lacked permanent office space, and government officials only haphazardly attended meetings. Nevertheless, from the steps that had already been undertaken it remained possible to look at the project's conceptual architecture, and identify some potential implications. That is, it is possible to make some tentative extrapolations that point to areas in need of further research before implementation.

A PORTRAIT OF UIGE

The provincial capital of Uige was a Safe Area protected by the MPLA army, as well by the United Nations humanitarian presence. Since UNITA rebels were active in the province, most people living in the countryside had either gravitated to the city for safety, or had been "relocated"[9] there by government forces. In the final years of the war, government forces adopted an aggressive military strategy to force UNITA supporters and civilians alike out of the countryside and into internally displaced persons (IDP) centres such as Uige. This was part of a strategy to flush UNITA out of the bush by leaving it no rural support base for food and other needs, and no non-partisan civilians upon which to prey. At the same time, UNITA was stepping up raids against villages. One of its more pernicious practices was the abduction of women and children, who often suffered sexual abuse and were forced into relations of servitude.

The city itself was largely destroyed in the war of 1992, and had not been rebuilt. Most of the buildings were uninhabitable. The city lacked basic civic infrastructure, including water, electricity and phones, except in the case of humanitarian offices and military offices, for which special connection provisions had been made. By and large, basic water and electricity were supplied by generators. Power from the thermal electric plant was erratic, usually "a few hours in the evenings, with frequent power cuts, unstable current and days without any power whatsoever" (OCHA 2000:9). Municipal buildings, such as the Ministry of Justice, had no access to electricity or water. All the windows were broken, and electrical and plumbing fixtures had been stripped. Few residents had electricity, and the primary source of water was rivers, creeks, unprotected shallow wells, and a dozen rehabilitated streams. The city had two small bars, one of which doubled as a restaurant, and no stores. All basic necessities available in Uige were to be found at the central outdoor market, which had an odd variety of wares and manufactured goods, as well as produce grown mainly in the Uige area or imported by the World Food Programme. The roads to Uige were impassable at the time, and air transport infrequent, which meant that prices and availability of basic foodstuffs, especially sugar, could vary widely. According to a Médecins sans Frontières (MSF) representative, malnutrition affected a large percentage of the population, especially children, which was manifestly obvious.

In 2001 the city of Uige was reportedly home to 50,000 people living in over 100 villages. UN officials estimated that 39,000 of these people were IDPs, but the definition is fungible; given Angola's long history of war, most people are at some stage of displacement. Villages filled the bucolic green spaces that surround the former city of Uige, and, in 2001, new IDP settlements were being formalized on the outskirts of existing villages. A notable aspect of these villages, from the perspective of governance, was the extent to which they existed independently of any state regulation of social, economic or political life.

POWER AND THE FORMAL AND INFORMAL POLITICAL STRUCTURES IN UIGE

Based on information provided by the UNHCR in Luanda and other UN agencies in Uige, it is possible to discern at least six striking features of the provincial political system: 1) All key members of the provincial political structure were appointed by the highly centralized presidential system in Luanda—the rest were appointed by the provincial administration; 2) the provincial government had essentially no independent decision-making authority, and answered in all things to Luanda; 3) the provincial government received no guaranteed budget from Luanda and had no discretionary funding capacity or authority, nor did the province itself have any wealth-generating capacity; 4) the court- and prison- based justice system was essentially not functional; 5) the traditional elder/Sobo-based decision-making and conflict resolution systems were largely intact (but unstudied) and governed village and inter-village life, and; 6) a significant portion of the population had no citizenship or identity papers or status.

These features combined to make up a political architecture in which the provincial government was accountable only to Luanda and existed in Uige mainly as a conduit for presidential objectives. Provincial political positions were not elected, and the provincial political system had no institutional mechanisms for deliberative democracy or popular accountability. To the extent that the provincial government functioned at all, then, it boasted meagre democratic credentials and could be considered authoritarian, top-down and highly centralized. At its disposal was a large number of paramilitary forces that policed law and order in the city and its core of international non-governmental organizations (INGO), but not the surrounding village areas. Police and paramilitary forces tended to have an uneasy relationship with the local population, many of whom saw them as a threatening or illegitimate authority.

At the time of independence in 1974, all of Angola's resources were handed over by the Portuguese to "the people of Angola," and under the Constitution continue to belong to "the people of Angola." This ambiguity left key resources, such as oil and diamonds, mainly in the hands of the state elite, while few institutional mechanisms exist to police resource use or mediate resource disputes. The government retains for itself the ultimate title to land. Elsewhere in the country, informal guarantees of land use have been secured, but this was not the case in Uige. Agricultural land was at a premium in the Uige Safe Area. The established members of the larger loose confederation of communities had reportedly worked out a seniority plan of land use where subsistence crops are grown, but according to government officials, neither individuals nor villages own this land; this informal tenure remained at the discretion of the local administration and could not be secured by guarantees or legal title.

The formal justice system barely functioned. It consisted of one functioning court in a building without lights, running water, windows or permanent offices. In April 2001, the prison housed 86 inmates, 68 of whom were awaiting trial. The city had a military and police presence responsible for general order and military functions, but they operated only in the urban core comprising the airport, military and municipal offices, and UN and NGO offices. Officers had limited capacity to function in the villages where most people lived, and thus provided little by way of civil protections. Reports of police abuse of power were common and confidence levels in the police among the general population were extremely low, as was the case in other areas of Angola (Manning 1999). The relationship between paramilitary forces and the population in general was manifestly tense.

The vast majority of people were self-organized into village communities. These communities adhered to their own internal political logic reportedly governed by the Sobo—a male elder and traditional chief—in concert with a council of elders. Political life was similarly structured among the internally displaced, the majority of whom tended to integrate into existing communities upon arrival. Where whole IDP communities were relocated or where the UNHCR and its partners had constructed IDP villages, the Sobo systems tended to remain intact or re-emerge

To date, having some knowledge of the Sobo system had proven key to mobilizing communities toward common goals. For example, YME, a stream rehabilitation NGO that relied on community labour organized by the Sobo to make use of new technologies and provide clean water, reported that co-operation from the Sobo was the key determinant of swift project success and community support. Traditional systems also played an important role in dispute resolution. Both the YME and local UNHCR representatives confirmed that the Sobo, in co-operation with a council of elders, acted as community ombudsman by mediating resolutions when inter- and intra-community disputes arose. Thus, the vast majority of political and law—and-order functions in Uige were organized at the village level.

It is important to note, however, that these operated mainly within a framework of traditional forms of privilege and responsibility. For example, the YME representative noted that because women had primary responsibility for water provisioning, it could be difficult (but not impossible) to persuade the Sobo of the importance of stream rehabilitation, especially when it brought clean water closer to the village and reduced the women's workload and time commitment.

Yet, it was at the village level, then, where most of the people living in Uige mediated crosscutting social struggles associated with access to productive resources and social freedoms—bounded by issues of class, gender, age, and ethnicity. This is in contrast to the formal state sector, which lacked the legitimacy, the coercive capacity, the pluralist deliberative institutions and structures of accountability to respond to people's preferences. That is, in Uige the state was clearly a "distinct and discrete organization of power" (Mohamed Salih 2002:27). As noted, the state did not and could not operate in or police village areas, and its capacity to extend even the most basic services and thereby justify its existence was extremely limited. This meant that while, in theory, the power of the state confers "fixity to otherwise unstable power blocks in society, the social order is constituted through the state and exists within the parameters laid down by the state" (*ibid.*:28), this was not the case in Uige. Here the state was manifestly separate and distinct. Its interests did not map well onto those of the population at large. It was not an emanation of the collective will and no checks and balances existed to mediate its authoritarian or harmful tendencies, should they become manifest (Manning 1999).

THE HUMAN RIGHTS COMMITTEE AND UIGE'S FORMAL AND INFORMAL POLITICAL STRUCTURES

Notwithstanding the potential for any intervention to have accidental but liberating effects, the design of the HRC introduced the risk of undermining existing social and political forms while re-apportioning political power to unaccountable state elites. Four areas of particular concern will be discussed:

1. The HRC failed to engage with local landscapes and indigenous ways of being and knowing, and did not attempt to include the perspectives of the local communities about where they were going or how the various partners wanted to get there;

2. it relied, essentially, on moral and ideological foundations rather than substantive assessments of the political and material constraints, and thereby overlooked important structural constraints such as the lack of shared liberal social context, a common citizenship status, and a functioning law-and-order capacity;

3. it relied on "thin descriptions" of both the identities of local peoples and human rights in order to make the context seem more amenable to a the Human Rights Committee initiative;

4. Finally, it ignored the potential for current and future structural oppositions of interests between rural subsistence farmers and state elites.

To explain: first, then, the Committee was established by the UN—which was the main driver of the project—and only marginally incorporated local perspectives, both in the planning stage and in organizational design. For example, the Committee reserved only one seat for a representative of traditional authorities, despite the fact that there are over 100 villages nestled in the hills surrounding Uige. Most members of the Committee were state officials appointed from Luanda. The rest represented religious organizations and human rights-oriented NGOs. Thus, the Committee was premised on assumptions that undervalued the contributions of local and indigenous political forms, while it simultaneously ordered them out of the emerging formal political structure. From the onset, then, the Committee was top-down, highly centralized and disempowering for the people it was meant to serve.

Second, the HRC's attempt to bring certain modes of engagement and certain social identities into being for which human rights was the proper solution lacked any material base. As noted, the formal justice and legal system in Uige was essentially non-functional, and police and military personnel were often seen as predators. Thus, human rights could not be addressed—at least not in the traditional political and civil understanding of the term, which as earlier chapters have noted, tends to conflate *human* rights with *civil* and *political* rights extended and protected by the state. This lack of material basis was underscored by confusion among the local community *volunteers* who had been trained in human rights awareness and who were scripted to perform a human rights monitoring function. According to one UN representative, most expressed confusion at their voluntary—and therefore unpaid—status, unsure why they were being expected to enforce human rights norms in their villages if it wasn't a desperately needed remunerative position. Many also noted that enforcement could not be carried out without weapons and police powers, especially if they were being asked act in a quasi-state-like capacity in communities whose relationship with the state was ambivalent at best. At best, volunteers seemed to be saying that they expected to be targets for retribution should they report community-level human rights abuses (accurately or not) to the state-representative-heavy Human Rights Committees.

The lack of legal infrastructure and shared liberal social context was further complicated by the fact that many people in Uige lacked citizenship papers, and at the time of research, the central government was refusing to initiate or consent to a process of recognizing citizenship and providing formal legal papers. In this context, it was problematic to assume that a government body could protect or recognize the rights of non-citizens, since it would establish a precedent upon which citizenship rights could later be claimed. This dilemma raised related questions about how people might claim rights, and the divisions and asymmetries a rights-based system might leave in its wake if some members of the community could legitimately claim rights (as citizens), while others could not (as stateless or displaced people). Thus, the HRC had no real legal or normative justification, and it lacked crucial elements such as popular legitimacy and possibility of equality of application.

Mark Duffield (2001:221–222) has identified a logic behind these non-legal human rights initiatives: "Essentially, a distinction [is being] made between human rights interpreted in legal terms and associated with monitoring and enforcement, and human rights understood as a moral force derived from the *universality* of their application [emphasis added]." However, to the extent that the HRC approach relied on the ideal of simply bringing the *truth* of human rights, as a pre-determined package, to *unknowledged* peoples, human rights initiatives rely on "thin descriptions" that, as Clifford Geertz has argued:

> model social phenomena in minimal measurable terms. They give a comforting appearance of objectivity and seem to travel with ease across cultural and historical boundaries . . . [and] often assume a taken-for-grantedness that escapes critical scrutiny . . . Such thin descriptions and images have a tendency to turn into very thick,

politicized, and controversial ones the moment they move out of global speech-space and become localized and situated in social reality (in Broch-Due 2000:49).

Third, then, the HRC used thin descriptions of both local peoples and human rights in order to create an alien space where the claims of local people could be neutralized and squeezed through liberal moral discourses. This is consistent with Duffield's (2001: 212–213) findings in his Sudanese case study where aid agencies consistently failed to engage with local landscapes and indigenous ways of being and knowing, instead embarking on political development using a badly matched "neoliberal" model. This model, he argues, substitutes universalistic and atomistic liberal rational actors for distinctive social relations. That is, the model "overcomes the problem of complexity by understanding [local peoples] through pre-existing categories of developmental studies"—as isolated individuals and archetypical free economic actors. These "generic indigenous" are more attractive subjects of development work because they make an enormously promising case for the sort of intervention a Western development agency is capable of launching—a universalistic one (see Ferguson 1994). Lip service is paid to culture and traditions, but in reality local people are emptied of history and cultural specificity and reinterpreted as caricatures from modernization mythology.

For displaced people (IDPs) the process is compounded (see Duffield 2001) by the assumption that they live in the *state of nature*. In this case, the model proposes to simply transform the rational actor in the state of nature into the liberal citizen. Framed in this way, the most complex dilemmas and vexing paradoxes can be resolved by the mere substitution of *the state of nature* (read: empty space) for a rights-based regime. Thus, where we ought to find some evidence of local consultations and sensitivity to local processes, we find only that: "All activities of the committee shall be conducted in accordance with the spirit of the Universal Declaration of Human Rights, the African Human and People's Rights Charter, other international conventions and the Angolan Constitutional Law" (Republic of Angola 2001:4) . The values expressed in these documents are taken as universal, and thus the peoples of Uige, who have had even fewer opportunities than most Africans to participate in the rule-making and agenda-setting processes, need not be consulted (see Chapters Two-Six for further examples of this dynamic). That is, the norms and principles used are the same as the ones the people living in Uige *would* choose, if they had the opportunity. We know this, because the norms and principles are *universal*.

Thus, by side-stepping both legal and culturally relevant questions and substituting thin descriptions of the local peoples and human rights, the HRC attempts to pre-determine the trajectory of some of the most important aspects of the emerging political system without even attempting to get some perspective on "a shared community of discourse and argument, consisting essentially of a sense of direction about where the society is headed and how its various partners want to get there" (Bustello 2001:10). The HRC in many respects, then, resembled a top-down project of transformation and consolidation. Specifically, the HRC was designed to legitimize human rights as the platform from which people understand their place in Angola's emerging political structures. As enticement it held up rights, which ironically, the state cannot protect, but which nevertheless confer upon citizens the duty to recognize that the state is invested with the authority to make binding decisions on their behalf in the interests of those rights (see Chapter Three, final section, for further discussion).

Fourth and finally, the promulgation of the myth that non-democratically installed state elites are in fact invested with the authority and legitimacy to act on behalf of peoples within the boundaries of the states they claim to control has tended, as in Sudan and elsewhere, to have negative implications for rural smallholders. One reason for this is that the levers of power in states characterized by low-intensity or non-democratic political economies tend to be dominated by political elites whose interests are often in structural opposition to other national groups. Here, Angola is no exception. In the current global climate, national elite interests and strategies readily dovetail with those of foreign investors whose interests in exploiting natural resources and cash crop opportunities are often in contention with interests of rural smallholders. Rural smallholders may or may not have legal title to land and other resources; nor do they have access to a sufficiently robust legal system to protect their title. Yet, the right to development has often meant that the indigenous rural population is expected to sacrifice access to resources vital to their survival, such as land, water, and forests, for the *greater good*. "These [the resources of the poor] are the very resources that authoritarian development appropriates as an exclusive domain for its destructive interventions" (Mohamed Salih 2001:58). For example, in Sudan, the "appropriation of Nuba land by a privileged political and business elite in the name of development" has resulted in over "100,000 people being forcibly evicted or displaced by . . . private agricultural schemes" (*ibid.*:48). Thus, as indigenous rights activist, Luis Hernandez Navarro (2001:117–118), points out: the threat development poses "is attributable, in part, to the lack of recognition of indigenous political institutions and to their lack of political representation in institutions which wield power at the municipal, state and federal levels."

The HRC, then, despite its laudable focus on the values and principles associated with rights, was not designed to challenge the architectures of power that can negatively affect the livelihoods of rural peoples. In which case, to the extent that the HRC typifies the deep structure of the security and development nexus—and the UN's governance agenda more generally—there is reason to be concerned about the legacy it will leave for the peoples of Uige, now living on some of the richest agricultural lands in Africa.

CONCLUSIONS

> *What keeps a place alive is not the preservation of its past per se, but the continual weaving of the past into the present (Marks 1991:9).*

Often, governance support projects attempt to effect radical transformation in the structures of a society, from structures that contribute to poverty and powerlessness to those which sustain the political and economic fabric of peace and prosperity. This case study has challenged the HRC on the basis of a growing body of evidence suggesting that the pursuit of top-down processes of state capacity building premised on claims to *universal* knowledge may be implicated in the most negative outcomes of development (see for example Rihani 2002). Some of these problems lie with the watering down of concepts such as human rights and democracy in order to make the context out as one that seems promising for a more general state-restoration project. Others lie where the imaginary and real contexts meet. That is, failure to factor in real cultural differences, low-intensity democratic and authoritarian structures, the voices and interests of local peoples, and the failure to make inroads into understanding what kind of political structures would most appropriately address local conflicts between resource users or the structural opposition between elite/state (domestic and foreign) interests and rural smallholders, may be to lay the foundation for greater harm. Specifically, more research needs to be done in Uige proper before peacebuilding tries its hand at institution-building. As a consequence of the war and Uige's isolation, very little is known about the structure of interest that operates there, or how inappropriate institutions might harden them, sealing off avenues to an authentic transformation to post-war order.

One reason why the HRC is an important and telling case is because in Angola, as elsewhere across Africa, the UN has linked the rule of law with human rights, conflating governmental authority with the satisfaction of basic needs and dignity—even in the face of widespread evidence to the contrary. As such, rule of law has come to be seen as a straightforward, uncomplicated, and unambiguous good. For example, one of the key areas of focus for the Department of Political Affairs in Angola's 2001 *Consolidated Inter-Agency Appeal* is to "strengthen rule of law." It notes: "This project is complementary to capacity building activities already under way and is designed to support Government efforts to reform the justice system." To this end, the UN system will "conduct municipal seminars on the rule of law with local authorities and civil society" (125).

This idealism, however, unwittingly confronts a general social context of "profound scepticism about the abilities and intentions of government in general." Carrie Manning (1999:35, 37), for example, documented some local perceptions: "We don't believe in extension of the state administration because all of the forces of society are not in agreement that this process should be carried out. So we simply have vandalism by one side against the other. In a democracy, the government should listen to the ideas of the people who elected them, but in this democracy [Angola], this provision does not exist in practice." With respect to law, Manning also noted "recurring" themes among survey respondents, such as only "ordinary people were subject to the limitations of the law" (43). Many people also believed that the police made the law (43), and this belief dovetailed with high levels of cynicism and frustration: "It is much better to come across a petty criminal than to come across the police" (38). Similarly in Uige, residents were clearly sceptical and uneasy about the perceived imposition of the new normative and legal standards represented by the HRC.

More research needs to be done in order to better understand these tensions and the dynamics underlying them before institution building starts. Part of such research would be a mapping of the structure of interests that characterize state/society relations in order to challenge illusions that elites can and ought to speak for people and communities in general. Even the most cursory review of Angola's history and contemporary political architecture makes clear that the routine conflation of the ruling elite with society in general—and in this case rural smallholders—is wholly unwarranted. As such, the Angolan case illustrates well the complications and contradictions involved in the UN's approach to building "good governance, democracy and human rights."

This case study should be seen as a supplement to the plethora of evidence presented elsewhere in the book making the case that more research is urgently needed to systematically document and synthesize these types of dilemmas and the ways they suggest we need to complicate UN policy. The finding here is that the HRC was not poised to effectively navigate the treacherous post-conflict landscape. Rather, it posed unacknowledged risks to those it, ostensibly, sought to help. First, it failed to engage with local landscapes and indigenous ways of being and knowing, and did not attempt to include the perspectives of the local community on where it was going or how its various partners wanted to get there. Second, it overlooked important structural constraints such as the lack of a shared social and political context and the absence of common citizenship status. Third, it relied on "thin descriptions" of both the identities of local peoples and human rights in order to make the context seem, in effect, more amenable to the HRC *solution*. Finally, while it is unlikely that it will address the structural opposition of interests between rural subsistence farmers and state elites or to go much distance towards creating an impartial and ordered tribunal for the resolution of local disputes, it is likely to contribute towards the further empowerment of political elites—who at least at the time of research remained essentially unaccountable.

That is, in a very real sense, rights, *at least in the UN universe*, are conferred on individuals by states (see Chapters Two–Six). In the absence of governments that are accountable to the people, "not only for the resources they receive and spend, but for the very policies they formulate and execute" (Mamdani 1995:22), a human rights paradigm asks peoples to accept and legitimize a fundamental re-orientation of the power architecture that further empowers unaccountable elites. From here it may be a slippery slope to the appropriation of lands and resources by a privileged state elite in the name of the "right to development." As the victims are often the first to find out, access to resources vital to survival and self-determination and freedom, such as land, water and forests, "are the very resources that authoritarian development appropriates as an exclusive domain for its destructive interventions" (Mohamed Salih 2002:58).

Chapter Nine

Disorganized Deception and the Performance of Irony

Chapter One described the core purpose of the study as: a) the illumination and interrogation of the implications associated with the UNDP's dominant governance discourse, and b) the illumination and interrogation of the interplay between the dominant and minor discourses. Chapters Three though Six describe these two discourses in great detail and at various levels and scales, from global to regional to country. Chapters Seven and Eight, however, were primarily concerned with the potential for the dominant discourse to result in a praxis that creates space for authoritarian and elitist tendencies to flourish. In this final chapter, we ask: Where does this leave the minor discourses? What do they serve?

INTRODUCTION

The chapter proceeds in two major sections. The first section situates the main findings of the book within the critical scholarship that has emerged in response to 50 years of uneven development. Here, much evidence exists to support the finding that deep assumptions embedded in mainstream development thinking are implicated in, often catastrophic, development dysfunction. It is important to stress, however, that this is not to suggest that the UNDP's governance agenda is the driving force behind development dysfunction, *writ large*. Further, nothing in the book, more generally, denies or is inconsistent with the notion that UNDP praxis is enmeshed within a web of actors and material interests involving major states, corporate actors and other international organizations and bodies, such as the World Bank and World Trade Organization. Rather, as noted in the introductory chapter, all of that notwithstanding, there is good reason to emphasize the UNDP's discourses of development. Discourses have potential effects of their own— particularly key agenda setting documents such as the *Human Development*

Report and *Millennium Declaration*. What development players *say* about development *matters* because, among other reasons, the work they undertake to enact their *representation* of reality has material effects. In this light, we can see the UNDP's governance agenda competing with other ways of understanding development and its context; other ways of envisioning the surface conditions and deep structure of the future. We can also start to assess implications associated with how the development problematic is understood. That is, for example, what are the implications of understanding a development context as more or less apolitical versus highly diverse and contested? Chapters One through Eight suggest that among the key implications of the how the UNDP's dominant governance discourse understands the development problematic may be the refining of elite hegemony and subversion of more broadly-based empowerment processes.

Yet, what role do the minor, more aspirant and sometimes even radically participatory, discourses play in light of 50 years of ever-evolving, yet patchy and even systematically dysfunctional, development? It is in light of this question that the first section of this conclusion weaves together elements of the critical literatures to suggest, ultimately, that the ambiguity introduced by the minor discourses is central to the systemic failures of the development machinery to *imagine what is, in fact, real* (Gourevitch 1999). That is, mountains of paper, endless meetings, and system-wide ambiguities about key terms, values, principles and processes may be critical constitutive elements of the propensity of UN social practice to misperceive and ignore the possibility that, as in the past, current practice carries substantive risk of harm to those whose powerlessness has become the *raison d'être* of the UN bureaucracy.

The second major section of this conclusion then takes this point one step further. Chapters Three through Six illustrated that the governance agenda, *writ large*, weaves and tangles both the minor and dominant discourses. This tangled weave is evident wherever one cuts in. Thus, at every point, the governance agenda is labyrinthine and jagged, ambiguous and circuitous. Everywhere and simultaneously the discourses of the UN governance agenda exhibit organizational bias in favour of state restoration and top-down (non-participatory) intervention at the level of the apolitical developmental state, but this always co-exists, however uneasily (in discourses and the people who implement them), with polycentric meanings, objectives, subjectivities and methods. This is, in fact, *inter alia*, what the governance agenda appears to *be*; a sum of fragments inhabiting tensions between structured totalities and splintered pieces.

Illuminated as such, the GDH script is rendered intelligible as, at once, a political exercise meant to appeal with equal ease to multiple contexts and social settings—including the private world of implementers—as well as an expression of *how* the UN systematically fails to imagine what is, in fact, real. The GDH discourse is a labyrinthine tale that suppresses the immanent realization of irony, re-inscribing repeated patterns of failure into the ordinary, unproblematic, and nonexistent:

> A performer may be taken in by his own act, convinced at the moment that the impression of reality which he [sic] fosters is the one and only reality. In such cases the performer comes to be his own audience; he comes to be performer and observer of the same show . . . It will have been necessary for the individual in his performing capacity to conceal from himself in his audience capacity the discreditable facts he has had to learn about his performance; in everyday terms, there will be things he knows, or has known, that he will not be able to tell himself (Goffman in Gordon (2002: 80).[1]

FITNESS, DENSITY AND THE BROADER CRITICAL LITERATURES

This section revisits four well-established critical approaches to understanding the UN's role in development dysfunction more generally, and relates them to the conclusion offered in the previous chapters: that the governance agenda *is* both its propensity to construct and reconstruct authoritarian and elitist polities *and* messy and incomplete, patterned by interruptions and contradictions; there are multiple and unpredictable readings and emphases driving UN praxis. In this view, the seeds of dysfunction reside, not always in technical glitches or well-laid plans gone awry, but also in ambiguous principles and strategies *and the function they play in bureaucratizing failure*. Thus, the following critical approaches contribute to understanding the discourses and "development bureaucracy *between* intentions and outcomes" [emphasis added] (van Ufford 1988: 12). The studies drawn upon here roughly correspond to four ways of understanding UN dysfunction:

1) Challenges to the UN's definitions of powerfully emotive and essentially contested concepts such as democracy and human rights—and what gets organized into and out of agendas on the basis of these definitions (Abrahamsen 2001: Marks 2000; Moore and Schmitz 1995).

2) Critiques that juxtapose mountains of paper, endless meetings, junkets, executive summits and international bureaucratic elite

excess with slow or negligible progress in global goals and commitments (Hancock 1989; Righter 1995).

3) Critiques that understand the UN as lumbering in the "wake of
   rapid evolutions of power" that have dramatically altered the face
   of the "body politic of contemporary societies" (Righter 1995: 7;
   Rosenau 1992), both local and global.

4) More trenchant critiques that challenge the bureaucratic and
   organizational capacity of mainstream development to "imagine
   what is in fact real" (Gourevitch 1999), and related to this, its
   tendency to participate (however unintentionally) in the poverty,
   powerlessness and underdevelopment it claims to merely describe
   (Abrahamsen 2001; Ferguson 1994; Snyder 2000).

The following paragraphs, then, review some of the ways in which the analysis of the previous chapters is consistent with broader literatures, and the
extent to which these, taken together, suggest that conceptual and practical
messiness *serves* the survival needs of UN development as global ordering
norm. That is, messiness provides the space within which responsiveness
to criticism and the attenuation of the gross oversights of the past seems to
take place, while simultaneously *smudging* the dominant discourse and its
more obvious implications. By itself, the dominant discourse and its related
praxis, as argued in earlier chapters (see especially Seven and Eight), indicates that very little progress has been made towards conceptualizing the
relations of power and powerlessness mainstream development interventions have contributed to in the past. *The minor discourses work to disrupt,
to smudge this.*

CHALLENGES TO UN DEFINITIONS

In Moore and Schmitz's (1995: xxi) important collection *Debating Development Discourse*, the editors identify a key source of malaise for liberal
internationalism: "Half a century after the first promise of modernization
was held out for the "third world," it is obvious that very little of that
ambition has been realized." While many critiques have argued that inef-
fectiveness is the price of multilateralism, the articles in their collection
"demonstrate that there is indeed a crisis within development discourse
which seeks to be all things to all people" (xxii). In a related analysis, Rita
Abrahamsen's (2001: 139) recent study *Disciplining Democracy* illustrates
the manner in which thin discourses transform the meaning of commonly

used concepts, such as democracy, in ways that serve narrow interests and ideological perspectives. With respect to World Bank discourses, Abrahamsen finds that:

> Essentially, the discourse blurs the distinction between democratization and the retreat of the state from the social and economic field. Democracy is tacked on to the promotion of economic liberalism, which is accorded primacy in discourse and practice. Democracy emerges as the necessary political framework for successful economic reforms, as there is concern that the latter will be "wasted if the political context is not favourable" (World Bank 1989: 192).

Thus, Abrahamsen finds that "democracy" means something rather specific within the World Bank discourse—a meaning that is not necessarily widely shared. Given the diverse associations invoked by democracy in other contexts, the specific meaning adopted by the World Bank may, in fact, mislead. For example, Abrahamsen finds that "[o]ne of the consequences of constructing democracy and good governance in this way has been the emergence of unstable, exclusionary democracies" (140). Elsewhere, Gills *et al.* (1993) termed these political Frankensteins low-intensity democracies or neoauthoritarian regimes (see also Marks 2000). While such democracies may have little in common with their western cousins, they (or rather their elites) do enjoy rights and privileges within the international system, including the *legitimate* sale of state resources, World Bank and IMF loans, etc. for which *citizens* can ultimately be held responsible.[2] In this way, *mere* words are revealed as having the capacity to structure knowledge, which in turn plays a central role in constructing or enacting social life, and determining life chances (Gill 2000).

At the level of the development organization or bureaucracy itself, van Ufford (1988: 22) has argued that "[d]evelopment policy is . . . constructed and reconstructed within the organization . . . [about which we] should as a matter of fact start to speak in the plural. There is more than one set of goals and priorities in the development organization." Intra-organizationally, then, there are dynamics of intellectual convergence and divergence at play, leading van Ufford and others to argue that this dynamic should be considered as a part of the development problematic itself. Barnett and Finnemore (2001: 428) argue similarly and more recently, for example:

> Different segments of the organization may develop different ways of making sense of the world, experience different local environments, and receive different stimuli from outside; they may be populated by

different mixes of professions are shaped by different historical experiences. All of these would contribute to the development of different local cultures within the organization and different ways of perceiving the environment and the organization's overall mission.

Thus, the temptation to see development categories, such as democracy or governance, as settled and monolithic should yield to, among other things, the recognition of intra-organizational contests and processes out of which any given project is—perhaps inevitably—forged. That is, the resort to hierarchies and discretely segmented technical components designed to rationalize, control outcomes and eliminate fuzzy conceptual spaces is in itself, the authors argue, limited: "[T]o the extent that hierarchy resolves conflict by squelching input from some sub-units in favour of others, the organization loses the benefits of a division of labour that it was supposed to provide" (*ibid.*).

The deeper point is that, while Abrahamsen (and the previous chapters) laboriously deconstruct democracy in order to gain insight into how, specifically, the word hangs together for the World Bank or, in this case, the UNDP, it is unlikely that the numbers of bureaucrats and practitioners have done the same. Each is just as likely to support democratic reform based on private rather than institutional understandings, if only for the simple fact that institutional understandings are elusive. Yet, within a certain range, each would likely find satisfactory support for their aspirations in the UN's broader literatures, even where these aspirations are contradictory. That is, the previous chapters have illuminated the extent to which contradictions, fuzzy connections and idealized constructions bolstered by stealthy claims to universality breathe life into the various dimensions of GDH uneasily welded together within and among the levels of discourse. Indeed, there any number of philosophies and epistemologies in evidence, which in their totality address many of the concerns and criticisms of good governance, democracy and human rights in the broader literatures. They come together, not as a comprehensive approach, but rather as a number of contradictory and competing approaches, each more or less strongly iterated at different levels, in different documents, at different moments. At the same time, some of the strongest recurring themes are the privileging of the de-politicized state, the top-down insertion of UN expertise at the level of the state, a jigsaw of forms and events such as political parties and rule of law, and circumscribed forms of participation. But even these elements are attenuated and smudged.

Thus we find that UN discourses tend to concede the legitimacy of a wide range of critiques made of multilateral development generally, from the lack of democratic structures at the UN to the need to play closer attention to the systemic "subversion of institutions by corruption or moneyed interests" (UNDP 2002: 65). At the same time, however, few of the implications of these critiques are integrated into specific programs or the overall strategic approach. Rather, overall, *Road Maps* and country strategy papers tend to iterate and reiterate the intent to empower a benign developmental state with an apparatus of liberal power—blind to both widespread and context specific problems documented in the HDR itself. The effect is a subtle—if unintentional—deception, wherein concerns about the basic model are acknowledged, even legitimized, but rarely and unevenly woven into the fabric of the general problematic or the activities proposed in the *Road Maps* and country documents.

In other words, at one level, the UN acknowledges and accepts that its definitions and processes of GDH beg re-conceptualization, as do the channels and processes through which definitions and strategies get scripted (*ibid.*: 101–122). At another level, however, it deploys admission as a decoy behind which an elitist and top-down approach to agenda setting is iterated and reiterated. Paradoxically, then, it consumes and embodies challenges to its agenda-setting process (most notably in the *Human Development Report*), without actually being transformed by them (most notably in the *Road Maps*)—except in, perhaps, relatively isolated spaces forced open in the field.

For example, as noted in the previous chapters, while participation is an often-advanced component of the democratic and governance agendas, what it means and how important it is shifts and changes. At times, participation is the key mechanism through which the worst excesses and failures of development thinking can be mitigated and corrected (Tanzania CCF 2001; UNDP 2002: 53). At others, and sometimes simultaneously, the emphasis is upon democratic decision-making producing *wrong* outcomes (UNDP 2002: 53; AGF-V 2002). Moreover, UN discourses of participation tend not to describe actual processes of participation, but rather are used to make platitudinous legitimacy claims on behalf of UN-devised political architectures that seek, rather, to define the limits of *legitimate* participation in political processes. Often the definition of participation explicitly *orders participation out* of the agenda-setting process, while privileging the voices of elites and experts (see AGF—V, for example). More troubling, however, is that the small number of exceptional cases of participatory processes are found few and far between in the UN documents, indicating that participatory processes will remain peripheral to the mainstream of the agenda for some time to come. That is, despite a few isolated claims, there is, in fact, very little to suggest that the UN has cracked the code for continually accessing and integrating knowledge from diverse local (non-elite) actors. There is much to suggest that its methodology contributes to confining local autonomy to the margins while refining elite hegemony in the societies with which it engages. Specifically, it manifests a preference for engaging with state elites (or selecting new state elites) in ways that empower and legitimize stateness, while far fewer attentions are paid to troublesome power asymmetries between state elites and vulnerable populations.

More generally, participation is a model contested term and stands at the centre of debates about to what democracy, human rights and governance amount. That is, all of these terms are multi-dimensional, and depending on how they are framed and constellated, work in service of any number of theories and functions of development. "Broadly speaking each development theory can be read as a hegemony or a challenge to hegemony. Explanation is not always the most important function of theory—agenda setting, mobilization and coalition building are others." (Pieterse 2002: 8). Thus, by constellating and re-constellating various and contradictory meanings of powerful and powerfully contested terms such as governance, democracy, human rights and participation, the discourse attempts to be all things to all people, thereby affording *development* legitimacy well past its sell-by date.

In another light, imprecision allows people to believe what they want to believe; what they must believe in order to lend their support. Fuzzy definitions do not only reflect the UN's position between the interests of various powerful states and actors, they not only serve to bridge these divides, but they also perform for an intra-UN audience, and ultimately perform for the UN itself, concealing from itself what it knows, but cannot tell itself.

MOUNTAINS OF PAPER AND ENDLESS MEETINGS

The UN's reputation suffers from the ambiguous contributions it has made to international development. As noted in Chapter One, there have been a number of important studies suggesting a need to place bureaucratic pathologies and the lifestyle interests of its international bureaucratic elite closer to the centre of related analyses. For example, in 1989, Graham Hancock's critically acclaimed *Lords of Poverty* (1991) exposed the "free-wheeling lifestyles, power, prestige, and corruption of the multibillion dollar aid business"—specifically the UN. In 1995, Rosemary Righter (1995: 177) chronicled the "debilitating impact of managerial drift, ill-conceived programs, inter-agency rivalries, and inept or corrupt personnel policies." More recently, even Kofi Annan joined the fray, acknowledging the need for far-reaching reforms in the UN bureaucracy. [3] The implication is that in many respects the UN has become an organization that mainly serves the personal and professional goals of its bureaucratic employee base, thereby reflecting intra-organizational goals and political contests, which may "override the official goals of the organization as a whole" (Mills and Simmons 1999: 57).

> One of the most famous critics of bureaucracy was the popular author, C. Northcote Parkinson, who argued that bureaucrats have a vested interest in making work for themselves in order to justify hiring assistants and, thereby increase their own statuses. He believed that the tendency towards empire building was endemic to all bureaucracies (*ibid.*: 58).

Max Weber (Barnett and Finnemore 2001: 413) commented similarly, lamenting that bureaucracies select and reward careerist professionals who follow and enforce general rules rather than interpret and innovate. Righter and others contend that the organizational culture (*ibid.*: 2001: 428: Hatch 1997: 210) at the UN is such that the core beliefs, assumptions and practices contribute significantly to conditions where the production of reports, attendance at meetings and summits, the completion of checklists, etc. become the means through which individual career and social goals are satisfied, thereby becoming the *raison d'être* of the organization more generally.

> Two features of the modern bureaucratic form are particularly important in this regard. The first is the simple fact that bureaucracies are organized around rules, routines and standard operating procedures designed to trigger and standardize predictable response to environmental stimuli . . . This kind of routinization is, after all, precisely what bureaucracies are supposed to exhibit . . . However, the presence of such rules also compromises the extent to which means-ends rationality drives organizational behaviour. Rules and routines may come to obscure overall missions and larger social goals (Barnett and Finnemore 2001: 422).

Righter and others, however, go further arguing that the tangible accomplishments of meetings, summits, and conferences, in terms of development and social welfare in the South, are only dimly intelligible; leaving labyrinthine paper trails and fragmented laundry lists that tend to obfuscate rather than illuminate. For example, as noted in Chapter One, the *Human Development Reports* come with the caveat: "The analysis and policy recommendations of this Report do not necessarily reflect the views of the

United Nations Development Programme, its Executive Board or its Member States." Yet the introduction by Mark Malloch Brown (2002) asserts that: "Nevertheless, I believe that its central message is very relevant for the broader work of the UNDP and its partners." It is hardly to the credit of the UN as an organization that it simultaneously asserts and denies ownership of, perhaps, the most widely recognized UN publication in the world. In this context, one can only speculate as to the *Report's* relationship to practice *or accountability*. Yet it is important to underline that the research presented here suggests that, indeed, the bureaucratic and cognitive labyrinth of the governance agenda serves a more sophisticated function than mere contribution to bureaucratic excess and ineptitude.

The previous chapters have documented so many and such striking differences existing between aspirant global discourses and their correlate *Road Maps*, and between and among the layers of discourse—global, regional and country—that this messiness should be understood as a core feature of the UN's philosophical space. In this light, mountains of paper, aimless flurries of meetings, etc., add material texture to the fuzziness. Yet, it is important not to lose sight of the interplay between dominant and minor discourses when taking stock of intellectual and organizational messiness. At least three things are going on. The general thrust of reports, workshops, summits and meetings matches the UN's paradigmatic tendencies towards non-participatory, top-down, state capacity-building projects. Simultaneously minor discourses create the impression of substantive attenuation of the sources of past development dysfunction, thereby inoculating the UN against criticism. At this interface, various fuzzy and contradictory frameworks of development (most notably bottom up versus top down) work to disrupt and smudge the fact that the minor discourses have had no deep effect on the bedrock epistemological structure or related practices of development intervention.

We know this because the actual *Road Maps* tend to endorse a relatively one-note state restoration project punctuated by a plethora of exclusive, high-level meetings and workshops, while evidencing much less progress towards other aspirations, such as participatory forums and/or explicit links among civil society and between society and state. [4] Routine bureaucratic practices would appear to mirror rather than attenuate these tendencies.

NEW ARCHITECTURES OF POWER AND POWERLESSNESS

On the heels of the Cold War, James Rosenau (1992: 79) predicted that a changing world would have profound and contradictory implications for the UN's capacity to act as an agent of progress:

Change and transformation, some will surely contend, ought not to be allowed to deflect the UN from its historic role as simply a forum in which the state-centric world can contain or resolve its conflicts. These voices will have to contend with the processes of maturation whereby the UN becomes ever more fully woven into the fabric of world politics.

More critical scholars of International Organization (IO), however, challenge the assumption that the UN is becoming more relevant and more able to solve serious international problems. Rather, they charge that IOs do not just occasionally fail, but "fail systematically" (Martin and Simmons 2001: 338). From this view, the UN is not poised on the brink of "maturation," but rather on the precipice of a willful blindness that inches it towards the edge of relevance, if not most certainly helpfulness. That is, in response to predictions that IOs will inevitably become more central to global processes, others assess their future potential as residing in how well IOs navigate their comparative advantage as deliberative institutions for knowledge sharing:

> In the international arena, neither the processes whereby knowledge becomes more extensive nor the means whereby reflection on knowledge deepens are passive and automatic. They are intensely political. And for better or for worse, international organizations have manoeuvred themselves into the position of being the vehicle through which both types of knowledge enter into the international agenda (Kratochwil and Ruggie 2001: 361).

Yet, while IO power resides, *inter alia*, in the power to structure knowledge, "there is nothing about social construction that necessitates good outcomes." "Bureaucracies are infamous for creating and implementing policies that defy rational logic, for acting in ways that are at odds with their stated mission, and for refusing requests of and turning their back on those to whom they are officially responsible." Barnett and Finnemore (2001: 431, 419), for example, argue that the tendency is for IOs to "flatten diversity" and generalize across widely divergent contexts in the quest for universalisms and generalized knowledge. In other words, as the previous section also indicates, the knowledge ordering function of IOs is not (necessarily) one that effectively mediates the complexities of knowledge or world politics, at local or global levels.

At the same time, there are emerging webs of global power forging new norms, forums and processes described by some as the "new multilateralism." Robert Cox (1992: 161), for example, observed that multiple forces have the capacity to affect "structural change at the close of the twentieth century":

> An enlarged conception of global society would include economic and social forces, more or less institutionalized, that cut across state boundaries—forces of international production and global finance that operate with great autonomy outside state regulation, and other forces concerned with ecology, peace, gender, ethnicities, human rights, the defence of the dispossessed and the advancement of the advantaged that also act independently of states.

That is, if IOs are to be helpful to the relatively powerless who have become their moral justification, they must do so in the context of proliferating social, economic and political organizations (including the state) on either side of the public, private, national and international divides, which are "either unanswerable or only weakly accountable to citizens" (Hirst 2000: 20). They cannot blindly empower states while ignoring the real "anatomy of influence" (Jacobsen and Cox 1973)—including multination corporations and transnational advocates (Archibugi et al. (eds.) 1998; Bohman and Rehg (eds.) 1997).

In this light, previous chapters have illustrated that while there is an abundance of rhetorical moments at which an attenuation of the state-centric, top-down development model of the past seem to take place, these translate unevenly throughout the multiple layers of aspirant texts and implementation *Road Maps*. Rather more clearly articulated, in principle and practice, is the dominant discourse, characterized by UN claims to rational *universal* knowledge and state-capacity-building efforts with very limited room for participatory input. This paradigm, however, is smudged and softened by its association with the contradictory minor discourses, which promise commitments to (substantively elusive) participatory practices, and other radical freedoms. That state and development-elite expertise is routinely experienced in counter-intentional ways, is of course, the untreated fetid core of multilateral development in Africa more generally, and one that will resist serious healing until questions of exclusion and voicelessness are rendered in ways that touch the real lived experiences of "the victims of progress" (Bodely 1999). Jochnich (2001: 160) underscores his concern by reference to Texaco in the Amazon:

> For decades, the affected Amazon communities had suffered Texaco's abuses largely in silence, having been repeatedly told, both explicitly and implicitly, that they had no rights against the oil company and that

the damage was a natural and inevitable price to pay for the country's development . . . Texaco has operated for years in the Amazon as practically a state unto itself, with annual global earnings four times the size of Ecuador's GNP, and with the active support of the US government. Even if the Ecuadorian government had been disposed to control the company, few believed it could.

Concomitantly, James Ferguson (1994: 186) documents the voices of villagers subjected to a conflation of international and/or state interests with their *right to development* (see also Mohamed Salih 2002). In the following quote a village man in Lesotho explains why he simply tells public officials what they want to hear:

> If you don't do this, it is taken as proof that you don't understand. You may not like to do it, but you are forced by the government.

A second man adds this rejoinder:

> I don't like to do it, but out of fear, I will do it, falsely . . . if I don't agree, I am afraid to say to you: "No! I for one will not do this thing." We understand very well what they are saying; we simply do not agree.

In this light, as Chapter Eight details through in-depth case study, an international agenda constructed around the principle that substantive participation is unnecessary because *universal* knowledge has been adequately apprehended by experts is highly problematic. When that *universal knowledge* includes problematic foundational templates such as the de-politicized state, it almost necessarily ignores the real "anatomy of influence," thereby facilitating the ability of those with real power to act unfettered by the nuisances of substantive monitoring, accountability, and meaningful participation.

In this light, and on the basis of the evidence presented in the previous chapters, the governance agenda may well continue to fail systematically, which might ultimately rip open the leaking reservoir of faith in and good will for the United Nations.

FAILURE OF THE IMAGINATION AND THE INSTANTIATION OF HARM

In his seminal book *the Anti-Politics Machine* (1990, 1994), James Ferguson provides a detailed account of the inaccuracies, tales and total fabrications that characterize the World Bank's and the Canadian International

Development Agency's *description* of Lesotho. So glaring are the inaccuracies, so imaginary the data, so sweeping the claims, Ferguson goes on to conclude that the most plausible explanation is that in order to insert the kind of development project the World Bank is capable of launching, it must first *imagine* Lesotho as it is not: an enormously promising candidate for its kind of intervention:

> The premise of all "development" analysis of Lesotho is that it is a stagnated agricultural peasant economy which requires only the correct technical inputs to become "developed." It has been shown that the World Bank Report systematically exaggerates the importance of agriculture and ignored the role of Lesotho as Labour reserve [to apartheid South Africa]. But this is not unusual; "development" reports regularly twist their words, and often their numbers as well, to make Lesotho fit the picture of the "peasant society." This means not only that the importance of wage labour is understated, but that a particular image of "peasant agriculture" is systematically promoted.

In a related analysis, Abrahamsen (2001:138) remarks on the irony of development failures continually reinterpreted as the rationale behind each subsequent intervention.

> [D]evelopment is commonly perceived both by its practitioners and by its critics to have failed in achieving its stated aims and objectives, and has reproduced poverty and encouraged aid dependency. Nevertheless, the development effort continues and is constantly reinvented and formulated in order finally to arrive at a solution to the problems of underdevelopment.

Both authors highlight that there is an element of delusion marked by the disinclination to imagine the more pernicious outcomes of development lurking between the lines of the public transcript of development discourse.[5] For example, in 1989, UNICEF published Adjustment with a Human Face (Cornia *et al.*), which documented escalating levels of real poverty and vulnerability, especially among women and children,[6] associated with IMF "shock therapy" and World Bank Structural Adjustment. This study was sandwiched between a plethora of independent studies and analyses that pointed to Adjustment's deleterious effects and attributed them to short sighted and wrong-headed models of economic reform (see Wilson 1998 for a review). Nevertheless, modifications to these models have been slow and grudging. Still today, widespread academic concern continues that "neo-liberal policies imperatives and structural adjustment programmes conditionalities [are] leading to exponential inequalities entailing intensified impoverishment for the majority" (Shaw 2002: 450).

Similarly, seminal studies amassed by Gills *et al.* in 1993 pointed to the dangers associated with the promulgation of thin and impracticable versions of democracy. The potential for conflict is inherent to development intervention that brings radical reforms legitimized only by the hasty orchestration of elections, especially in elite controlled societies with few institutions for deliberation or authentic participation. In the absence of more substantive democratic change, elections are likely to be perceived by various sub-national groups as zero-sum. Yet in the face of countless election debacles, the UN system has been slow to learn critical lessons (see Chapter Eight). In 2000, Jack Snyder's seminal *Voting to Violence* implicated very similar UN policy prescriptions in both the Rwandan Genocide and the Burundi Genocide, which erupted *less than one year earlier*. That is, Snyder argued that the Bank and its partners (most notably the UNDP) simply could not integrate the knowledge that their policy prescriptions, in fact, expedited genocide in Burundi. So deep was the self-delusion, that the UN went on to prescribe a strikingly similar package of prescriptions and conditionalities in Rwanda less than one year later,[7] with strikingly similar, yet even more catastrophic, results.

In response to global horror at the UN's decision to evacuate the peacekeeping force that was on the ground at the time of the genocide—in place to oversee transitions associated with the package of UN-led reforms-Gourevitch (1999:7) described international gridlock as the inability, on the part of international bodies, *to imagine what was in fact real*:

> All at once, as it seemed, something we could only have imagined was upon us—and we could still only imagine it. This is what fascinated me most in existence: the peculiar necessity of imagining what is, in fact real. During the months of the killing in 1994 . . . I was repeatedly reminded of the moment, near the end of Conrad's *Heart of Darkness,* when the narrator Marlow is back in Europe, and his aunt, finding him depleted, fusses over his health. "It was not my strength that needed nursing" Marlow says, "it was my imagination that wanted soothing."

Similarly, Barnett and Finnemore (2001: 424) argue that bureaucratic procedures also play important roles in explaining how the multiple individuals who know a genocide is, in fact, taking place, are silenced or encouraged to discipline what they know into conforming with what the organization is prepared to know—to imagine (see Off 2001; Powers 1999). Checklists,

meetings, and stultifying procedures come to embody dangerous "irratio-
nalities," while "means (rules and procedures) may become so embedded
and powerful that they determine ends and the way the organization defines
it goals." In part this process reads off the claims that bureaucracies make
to efficiency and universal rationalities. That is, bureaucracies aim to think
on behalf of their more partial, subjective and located members:

> The power of IOs and bureaucracies generally, is that they present
> themselves as impersonal, technocratic and neutral—not exercising
> power but instead as serving others; the presentation and acceptance
> of these claims is critical to their legitimacy and authority . . . [How-
> ever], [b]ureaucracies always serve some social purpose or set of cul-
> tural values (Barnett and Finnemore 2001: 412).

Barnett and Finnemore caution, however, that there is no *a priori* reason to
assume that the ends served or achieved by bureaucracies will be better or
worse than alternatives.

James Ferguson's (1990: 1994) study cuts in at a deeper level still,
illuminating how the tendency for development bureaucracies to *imagineer* both the problem and the solution has both deeply political but also
profoundly messy implications, aptly naming the process *The Anti-Politics
Machine*. In Lesotho, he finds that the *Machine* has little to no mitigating effects on poverty, while its mystification of politics—however unintentional—empowers the tangled clots of petty powers which feed off the
spoils of developmental intervention.

At the moment the imagination fails, the dark and unforeseen organizational and political spaces operating to facilitate a genocide planned
and executed under the nose of the *international community* (Gourvevitch
1999) are born; food aid disbursed to male heads of household by-passes
the women and children en route to urban markets;[8] refugees sell sex to
UN workers for biscuits; belligerents re-arm under cover of elections;[9] field
staff grow disillusioned, disinterested and disconnected.[10]

Yet, these are also, equally, the product of organizational imperatives,
checklists,[11] hierarchies and processes of self-referential knowledge, thriv-
ing in ambiguity, such that "[a]rguably a number of the more spectacular
debacles in recent UN peacekeeping operations might be interpreted as the
product of these contradictions" (Barnett and Finnemore 2001: 428). That
is, as van Ufford (1988: 20, 21) argues:

> Looking back on the history of development cooperation, the stron-
> gest trait of "development" is clearly its flexible nature (Goulet 1971).

The concept has been used to advocate conflicting and rapidly changing definitions of problems in the Third World. At issue is not which
definition is the best, or whether a new one can be added to the long
list. On the contrary we should ask ourselves how this veritable jungle
of analysis and therapies can be explained . . . The ambiguity greatly
affects the ways development organizations operate; one might say that
it is reproduced in the workings of developmental bureaucracies, and
must be regarded as a basic characteristic.

Seminal studies by James Ferguson (1990), Gran (1986), Weiss and Pasic
(1997), Goodwin-Gill (1996) and Anonymous (1997)[12] all further suggest
that pre-existing categories, assumptions and patterns of behaviour powerfully shape not only UN responses, but even whether organizational actors
will be able to *see* or render intelligible what is, in fact, real. Thus, as discussed later, what is being proposed is that the politics around definitions,
the labyrinthine bureaucratic processes and the imperatives of interest and
power all help to explain development dysfunction. *However it is the poly-
centrism-the interplay between the dominant and minor discourses—that
creates space within which responsiveness to criticism and the attenuation of the gross oversights of the past seems to take place.* This is where
longstanding practices that displace situated knowledge to the margins are
smudged. At its most basic, grand delusions on the scale of those preceding the Rwandan Genocide happen when the voices of the people who
know, who live the consequences, don't matter. Tutsi women prostitutes
don't decide on the governance agenda, they don't decide on the means to
implement it, and they are most certainly not *sitting Sundays by the pool in
Kigali,*[13] they just live and die the consequences.

A NOTE ON INVISIBLE ALTERNATIVES

How does systematic disassociation from the lived consequences of delu-
sional social engineering find fertile space to flourish? Insight is well
expressed by James Ferguson in the epilogue of *The Anti-Politics Machine*
(1994: 279–280):

The question "what is to be done about all the poverty, sickness and
hunger in the Third World" immediately identifies the undoubtedly
worthy goal of alleviating or eliminating poverty and its suffering. A
first step, many would agree, towards clarifying that goal and the tac-
tics appropriate to achieving it is to reformulate the question somewhat
more politically: since it is powerlessness that ultimately underlies the

surface conditions of poverty, ill-health, and hunger, the larger goal ought therefore to be empowerment.

Ferguson then goes on to ask, "What is to be done?" to which he replies: "it seems clear that the most important transformations, the changes that really matter, are not simply 'introduced' by benevolent technocrats" (281). Yet to suggest that state elites, multilateral organizations or admitted self-interested bi-lateral organizations such as USAID "are not really the sort of actors that are very likely to advance the empowerment of the exploited poor . . . seems . . . to imply hopelessness; as if to suggest that the answer to the question 'what is to be done' is: 'Nothing' (285). The absence of substantive alternative thinking that takes seriously the propensity for top-down expertise to be part of the problem, rather than the solution, helps to render fundamentally different approaches unthinkable. Yet, a look at recent UN discourses suggests that something else is going on. That is, some of the alternative thinking has taken place. *But the weave of alternative and top-down thinking works to pass the former off as the latter.*

MINOR DISCOURSES AND THE ART OF ILLUSION

In contradiction to the findings presented here, both Thomas Weiss (2000: 9) and Jean-Philippe Thérien (1999: 14) recently applauded evolutions in the UNDP's governance agenda governance, arguing respectively that it represents an "incipient heresy against conventional wisdom" and that "the UN paradigm seeks to take into account all the complexity of the social environment in which poverty exists." Previous chapters have attempted to show that these perspectives are prey to a number of important oversights. Perhaps the most significant relates to the governance agenda's failure to deal honestly with the state—as a source of power over which actors compete, and an apparatus that is frequently deployed towards ignoble ends. Rather, the governance agenda is designed to engage with a wholly benign developmental state, whose interests are imagined to be synonymous with those of the UNDP and citizens everywhere, and whose past failures are attributable almost entirely to some fundamental local ignorance about how liberal democratic polities are supposed to behave. Thus governance reform is heavy on "civil service reform, which assumes that training Africans into better bureaucrats and isolating some key government agencies for social pressures for redistribution will solve Africa's capacity problem" (Englebert 2000: 11).

At the same time, evidence of the anti-developmental tendencies rooted in the relationship between African states (Eyoh 1999; Okafor 2000) and the aid industry is becoming widespread (Chabal and Daloz 1999: Evans 1989: Ferguson 1994; Reno 1998). Thérien claims that the UN has transcended pathologies and dysfunction associated with state restoration, asserting that "the UN paradigm proposes a vision of the world which is less and less centred on the nation-state . . . Today the UN tends to regard poverty affecting individuals rather than states" (1999: 130). However, the evidence presented in the preceding chapters suggests that this is *not true*. Rather, the UNDP remains wedded to the sanctification of the state, and the idea that societies carry the inevitable burden of adjusting to the prerogatives of the state system, not the other way around. The governance agenda is an "upstream" agenda and where it describes engagement, it is almost exclusively with or at the behest of government (see Chapters Three–Six).

Weiss and Thérien also emphasize the ways that the UNDP agenda has responded to criticism. Thérien claims that the UNDP has wrestled effectively with the concept of exclusion, coming to incorporate an integrated view of "material deprivation, employment situation and social relatedness (formal and informal) as major components of people's disadvantage" (ILO-UNDP in Thérien 1999: 13–14). Weiss, more modestly, settles for the promise that "leaders" are now being held to "higher standards" (2000: 10). Similarly, Ruggie (2003) emphasized recently the transformative potential of what he calls the Millennium Development Goals "Network"—"an unprecedented . . . unifying substantive framework," and argues that we have entered something of a new era in country coordination with the *Common Country Assessments* and *Frameworks*. However, in the previous chapters, we have seen that in many cases these are only minor discourses given uneven expression at multiple levels of praxis. Rather, the evidence suggests that a transformation in the agenda has not taken place. The minor discourses provide space within which responsiveness to criticism and the attenuation of gross oversights can be seen to have happened, while simultaneously smudging the dominant discourse where it has not. Practices congruent with the dominant discourse, as argued in the last two chapters, would indicate that very little progress has been made towards addressing the relations of powerlessness UN intervention has contributed to in the past. Further, both Weiss and Thérien tend to minimize the tangled bureaucratic context through which these lofty goals are filtered.

Weiss and Thérien also tend to ignore the ambiguities and contractions that pervade the development discourse from which they choose to draw their optimistic conclusions. Quarles van Ufford (1988: 21), however, basing his arguments on those of Lissner (1977), Nuscheler (1986) and Koucher (1986) argues, "[t]he ambiguity greatly affects the ways development organizations operate; one might say that it is reproduced in the workings of developmental bureaucracies *and must be regarded as a basic characteristic*" [emphasis added]. From this perspective, development bureaucracies are understood as "arenas" in which different "constructions of reality" interact. Even if we are impressed with the UN's introduction of the minor discourses, as Weiss and Thérien clearly are, we are still confronted with the question: "[w]hat explains the rapid change of development goals and fashions, so much more spectacular than development change as such" (*ibid.*)?

Thus, in place of a coherent improvement in the quality of UNDP discourse (which Thérien and Weiss both imply correlates to improvement in praxis; see also Ruggie 2003), here the multiple discourses that conflict and contradict each other are given centre stage. There are state centric paradigms of development interacting and intersecting with UN-led paradigms, which interact and intersect with participatory or civil society centric paradigms, and so on. At the same time, amorphous organizational and conceptual hierarchies collide with polycentric approaches, which are nevertheless free to be re-configured and reinterpreted in ways that accord with multiple world views of multiple actors—*including the academics who analyse and endorse them*. In this context, "[d]evelopmental goals, then, must relate with equal ease to quite different social worlds" (van Ufford.: 20). Ruggie, Thérien and Weiss prove that they do, but not that they hold greater promise for the marginalized than their cousins did a year, two, five, ten, and so on, years ago.

DARK SYNERGIES AND ABSOLUTION

The previous chapters introduced but only obliquely responded to questions relating to the *function* of the co-extant but often contradictory minor and dominant discourses of GDH. Rather, they attempted to provide a thick description of the tensions inhabiting the unevenly structured splintered pieces of the governance totality. With the material implications in full view, this is the right time to reprise the Foucauldian question: "what is served anyway?" I would like to conclude this book by hypothesizing that messy discourses satisfy the intra and extra-organizational needs of the UN to conceal knowledge of core ironies from itself, its members, and its supporters—to provide, at least, plausible deniability for ineptitude and/or gross indifference.

The marriage of the dominant discourse to the minor polycentric and participatory discourses has a dark synergy that, *inter alia*, allows the UN to reinvent itself—despite the evidence of its contribution to substantive harm—without actually having to undertake a major overhaul of the bedrock assumptions that structure patterns of systemic failure. That is, UN discourse must do what a substantive subset of the academic work on development and the African state inevitably does not; it must imagine a new future from the same problematic assumptions of the past. The minor discourses facilitate, replicate, implicate and complicate the dominant discourse, re-inscribing it as chameleon-like, as other than it is. They obfuscate and grant the absolution of uncertainty. They allow us to think UN programming is now participatory, *if we want to*; that UN programming is no longer about states, but people, *if we want to*.

Thus we can understand the critical approaches to understanding development dysfunction surveyed earlier in the chapter as signposting patterns of systemic failure that not only originate in technical glitches or funding constraints, but also in general dispositions inherent in, and enacted by, the storytelling and fairytales themselves. The development story continues because we can continue to imagine that it works, that it is other than it is. In terms of the governance agenda, stories tend to advocate top-down strategies of state restoration, as evidenced by a preponderance of these types of activities documented in the *Road Maps* and country documents, while denying local, regional and global politics. At the same time, discourses assert a number of competing interpretations of key terms and values, simultaneously validating disparate understandings and dimensions; suggesting that participatory processes are central; suggesting that money, perks and other resources are not flowing to unaccountable elites; suggesting that democracy, not government will be stronger as a result of UN intervention.

Praxis, predictably, shows signs of being equally messy. However, where this messiness is disciplined, it seems to be by organizational hierarchies and imperatives that frustrate the ability of knowledge to pass from the local to the global, while preventing alternatives to the global to local flow of information from gaining significant footholds. These tendencies are punctuated by a propensity for failure to imagine where intervention collides with local conditions to create new insecurities for the very people whose misery has become the *raison d'être* of the global humanitarian machinery. This failure of the imagination *depends* on the exclusion of those who speak different stories; hence participation is everywhere so unevenly endorsed and expressed. Delusion depends on the marginalization of the voices of different *truths*. It also depends, sometimes, on the simplest of hooks.

In this light, this re-synthesis of UN discourse offers itself as evidence towards a theory of the UNDP's governance agenda as a barely repressed chain of negation that smudges core ironies, concealing the knowledge of them from the UN and its proponents. In everyday terms, there are things the UN corporate body knows—things that are part of its core philosophy—that it is not able to tell itself. At this juncture, it becomes its own audience, "performer and observer of the same show" (Goffman in Gordon 2002: 79). Its messy discourse performs for a pro-UN audience; it admits, constructs and absorbs the development past in order to smudge how similar it is to the development future on offer. "Everyday life is ideological in an ontological sense; that which we know and which seems true depends on our sense of what is real" (Gregory 1989: xx).

I like to say that I never travel without a map, but then none of us do. (Hall 2004: 15)

Appendix
List of Interviews and Special Libraries

(Names of representatives withheld, as per university ethics process determination.)

ANGOLA: 2001

Uige: Interviews

AngoTrip (NGO supporting victims of African Trypanosomiasis)
The Catholic Agency for Overseas Development (CARITAS)
Association for Cooperation, Interchange and Culture (CIC)
Delegate of Justice
Director of Prisons
Governor
Education for Development (Ibis)
International Medical Corp (IMC)
Angolan Ministry for Social Assistance and Reinsertion (MINARS)
Northern Front Commander, Angolan Armed Forced (FAA)
Office of the coordinator for Humanitarian Affairs (OCHA)
United Nations Security Coordinator, Uige (UNESECCORD)
UN High Commission for Refugees (UNHCR)
UN International Children's Education Fund (UNICEF)
Vice Governor
World Food Programme (WFP)
Yme

Luanda: Informal Interviews and Participant Observation

Provincial Working Group (observer)
United Nations Development Programme (UNDP) briefings (observer)
United Nations High Commission for Refugees (UNHCR)

BOTSWANA: 2002

Gaborone Interviews

Botswana Coalition for Non-Governmental Organizations (BACONGO)
United Nations Development Programme (UNDP)
University of Botswana, Department of Political and Administrative Studies

NAMIBIA: 2002

Windhoek Interviews

Human Rights Documentation Centre, University of Namibia
Institute for Democracy
Law Reform and Development Commission, Chairperson
Legal Assistance Centre (LAC)
Media Institute for Southern Africa (MISA)
Minister of Justice
Ministry of Women Affairs and Child Welfare
Rainbow Project
Red Cross (focus group)
United Nations Development Programme

TANZANIA: 2002

Dar es Salaam Interviews

Canadian International Development Agency (CIDA)
Centre for Foreign Relations
Economic and Social Research Foundation (ESRF)
Equal Opportunity for All Trust (EOT)
Law Reform Commission
Media Council
Research on Poverty Alleviation (REPOA)
Tanzanian Council of Social Development (TACOSODE)

SPECIAL LIBRARIES AND PUBLISHERS: 2001–2003

Africa University, Mutare, Zimbabwe
Botswana Institute for Development Policy Analysis (Bidpa), Gaborone, Botswana,
Centre for Conflict Resolution (CCR), Cape Town South Africa
Economic and Social Research Foundation (ESRF), Dar es Salaam, Tanzania

Emang Basadi, Gaborone, Bostwana
Freidrich Ebert Stiftung, Dar es Salaam, Tanzania
Government Printer, Gaborone, Botswana
Institute for Public Policy Research (IPPR), Windhoek, Namibia
Legal and Human Rights Centre, Dar es salaam, Tanzania
Legal Assistance Centre (LAC), Windhoek Namibia
Namibian Economic Policy Research Unit (NEPRU), Windhoek, Namibia
National Bureau of Statistics, Dar es Salaam, Tanzania
Namibian Society for Human Rights, Windhoek, Namibia
Research and Education on Poverty Alleviation (REPOA), Dar es Salaam, Tanzania.
Research and Education for Democracy (REDET), University of Tanzania, Dar es Salaam, Tanzania
Southern Africa Documentation Centre (SARDC), Harare, Zimbabwe
The World Bank, Dar es Salaam, Tanzania
United Nations Education and Social and Cultural Organisation (UNESCO), Windhoek, Namibia
University of Botswana, Gaborone, Botswana
University of Cape Town, Cape Town South Africa
University of Dar es Salaam, Dar es salaam, Tanzania
University of Stellenbosch, Stellenbosch, South Africa
University of Zimbabwe, Harare

Notes

NOTES TO CHAPTER ONE

1. *New York Times*, November 12, 2003, see: http://www.nytimes.com/2003/
   11/12/nyregion/12COLL.html.2.   Online journal database version, no
   page numbers provided.
3. Here, "thick description" refers to a dense, detailed and multi-layered
   description of the policy discourse. The concept is taken from the work of
   Clifford Geertz, an anthropologist, who uses the term to refer to dense and
   detailed ethnographic data. It is useful in this context because the underlying motive is the same—to subvert knowledge that is based on superficial
   understanding. The following interpretation of Geetz's work is useful:

   > Geertz presents this ethnographic approach as predicated on a vision
   > of "man as an animal suspended in webs of significance he himself
   > has spun," a vision that he traces back to Max Weber, one of the
   > founders of the discipline of sociology. Those committed to thick
   > description, a term Geertz attributes to philosopher Gilbert Ryle,
   > take for granted that even the simplest act can mean different things
   > depending on the cultural codes at work. Borrowing an illustration
   > first used by Ryle, Geertz demonstrates what he means via reference
   > to the many things that a person rapidly opening and closing an eye
   > can signify. It can be an involuntary twitch, a conspiratorial wink, or
   > even a parody of such a conspiratorial wink. A "thin description"
   > that just says that an eye opened and closed is not enough; assuming
   > that every twitch is just a twitch will lead us astray in cultural anal-
   > ysis; what we need is a "thick description" that separates twitches
   > from winks and one sort of wink from another (http://www.ssrc.org/
   > sept11/essays/wasserstrom_text_only.htm).

   In this spirit, thick descriptions in the following analysis attempt to separate
   the various different claims being made about good governance, democracy, and human rights—highlighting how it is never quite clear what they
   mean—or may come to mean—in any specific instance.

4. Throughout the following chapters, the term "governance agenda" is used interchangeably with "good governance, democracy and human rights" (GDH). It signifies the UN's political reform agenda.

5. It was hypothesized that outcomes would be partially affected by understandings, misunderstandings and contending interpretations of key terms and processes integral to the execution of the plan or strategy. That is, that the failure to insert institutional procedures to insure that all relevant actors had adopted the officially sanctioned definition of key concepts such as human rights amounted to the failure to control a crucial intervening factor/variable. Kratochwil and Ruggie (2001: 352–353) comment on the importance of integrating this insight into methodology:

> In many . . . puzzling instances, actor *behaviour* has failed adequately to convey intersubjective *meaning*. And, intersubjective meaning, in turn, seems to have had considerable influence on actor behaviour. It is precisely this factor that limits the practical utility of the otherwise fascinating insights into collaborative potential of rational egoists which are derived from laboratory or game-theoretic situations [emphasis in original].

Thus, I hoped to observe and document anomalous incidences where a given program strategy was vague and/or differentially understood by implementers, contributing to uneven or inconsistent application. Identification would signpost key areas where *objective* standards and robust regulations were absent.

6. A re-organized and re-directed OCHA replaced the Department of Humanitarian Affairs.

7. An in-depth case study of the Human Rights Committee is found in Chapter Eight.

8. Paraphrased from field notes, interviews, Luanda, April 2001.

9. "Minor discourse" is the term used throughout the book to describe streams within the discourse that tend to *hang loose* from the discourse as a whole. For example, feminists have often argued that gender considerations, when they appear at all, tend to hang loose or be tacked on at the end of chapters, without being well integrated into the overall analysis ("and women add stir")

10. This is well-covered elsewhere (see Financial Times 2002), is not the subject of academic controversy, and thus in the interests of parsimony, will not be discussed further here.

11. See Wilson 1998 for a review of previous analyzes of the World Bank and IMF in Africa, especially gender dimensions.

12. An important area of study, however, would be a comprehensive mapping of the links between the UNDP and other agencies and organizations. For example, relationships between the UNDP and World Bank were clear and present in some cases, but not in others. Further, this close relationship was more evident from interviews than from official documents.

13. "Annan calls for UN reform," *The Namibian*, Tuesday September 24, 2002, p.7.

14. See Chapter Nine for a more in-depth discussion of the various critiques of UN organization, and how they relate to the central themes of this book and the conceptual density of the conclusions drawn.

15. See Chapter Seven for a critique of this concept.

16. In September 2002, the UN adopted NEPAD (the *New Partnership for Africa's Development*) as its guiding principled approach to development in Africa. Presumably, this will supplant the *New Agenda for Development*, the *Causes of Conflict* report, the *International Development Goals* (IDGs) and the section on "the special needs of Africa" in the *Millennium Declaration Goals* (MDGs) and related *Road Maps*. Interviews in the field, however, indicated that the diffusion of another new mandate throughout the system could be slow. For example, interviews at the UNDP in Namibia in 2003 revealed that the Unit had not yet received any special training on the 2000 *Millennium Declaration*, and that its adoption had not altered the direction of policy and projects. Similarly, group interviews at the Red Cross in Windhoek revealed that no one had even heard of the MDGs. In 2004/2005, the UNDP, stated, that "within the context of the Governance, Peace and Security Cluster, UNDP has been actively supporting the NEPAD and APRM, both institutionally as well as in terms of programmes." Yet, while the UN states, "The United Nations is committed to supporting the New Partnership for Africa's Development (NEPAD) as the framework for addressing poverty and underdevelopment throughout the African continent," it is worth noting that the UNDP statement falls significantly short of pledging to abide by NEPAD. Further, all key agencies of the UN have released their *own* individual commitments to NEPAD. (see: http://www.un.org/africa/osaa/systemsupport.html; and http://www.un.org/africa/osaa/2005%20UN%20System%20support%20for%20NEPAD/UNDP.pdf).

17. http://www.undp.org/rba/docs/CP-BOT%2003–07%20-%20E.pdf

18. Gill (2002) describes "prescriptive descriptives" as descriptions that imply a particular kind of solution.

19. Rather than express findings in terms of "validity," research approached knowledge from the perspective that there are "multiple, often conflicting, constructions, and all, (at least potentially) are meaningful" (Schwandt 1994: 128). Thus, the goal of research and interpretation was not validity, but rather to construct a view that fits otherwise disparate phenomena together, that works, that has reach and conceptual density.

20. Recent studies in discourse analysis suggest that "utterances do not simply mean one thing and . . . cannot therefore be interpreted from the standpoint of the speaker or hearer alone; there is a sense in which utterances are ambivalent and are interpreted by participants according to hypotheses and working models they develop . . ." (Mills 1997: 142).

21. Steve Smith opts for the term reflectivist to describe non-foundationalist theories, such as post-positivist, critical, feminist, post-modern (including discourse) and normative theories.

22. "UNDP says Urgent Action Needed to Meet Poverty Reduction Goals," Gustavo Capedevila, July 09, 2003. Inter Press Service. See: http://story.

news.yahoo.com/news?tmpl=story&cid=655&ncid=655&e=3&u=/one-world/20030708/wl_oneworld/4536631141057696399.

NOTES TO CHAPTER TWO

1. "Democratic deficit" is a term used by the UNDP in the 2002 *Human Development Report* to signify democratic shortcomings (i.e. growing monopolies in media ownership) within otherwise or nominally democratic contexts.
2. For critique of this position see: Chabal 1997.
3. To the extent that these disagreements represent alternative or differently nuanced conceptions of human dignity, "our list of authoritatively recognized human rights may change" (Donnelly 1999: 84). In many respects, each additional covenant, protocol and instrument is evidence that this process is already well underway.
4. Such claims are qualified, however, as seen in the following quote: "Rights to housing, health care and the like do not mean a claim to free services or a state handout. Instead they are claims to social arrangements and policies that promote access to these rights through both the market (housing) and the state (free primary education)" (UNDP 2000: 8–9).

NOTES TO CHAPTER THREE

1. This chapter is the result of a process of coding and discourse analysis, which illuminated some aspects of the rhetoric as more centrally important to the overall thrust of the text, and some as mere footnotes, sidebars, and marginal remarks. I have focused on the former and not the latter, in that this is where we find the meaning of GDH most coherently expressed.
2. Date: 15th century
   1 : to involve as a consequence, corollary, or natural inference 2 *archaic* : to fold or twist together 3 a : to bring into intimate or incriminating connection b : to involve in the nature or operation of something (Merriam-Webster Online, www.m-w.com).
3. These four characteristics are referred to in the remainder of the thesis as the dominant discourse. The inexplicit and contradictory features of the texts are referred to in the remainder of the thesis as the minor discourses.
4. Approximate, accounting for human error.
5. I am indebted to Patrick Bond for this reference.
6. Legitimacy is taken to mean a socio-political phenomenon linked to plausibly democratic participation in constituting the state, as well as in government decision-making. Thus the conditions for legitimacy are not satisfied by international recognition alone.
7. The World Bank (2002: 99) also noted recently: "Good governance requires the power to carry out policies and to develop institutions that may be unpopular among some -or even a majority—of the population."

8. Most recently, the role the transitional administration in Iraq has played in privatizing the Iraqi state resources (now the most privatised economy in the Middle East) leads to speculation about its utility rather than legitimacy.

9. See "Africa won't back apartheid lawsuits" by Elliott Sylvester, *Associated Press*, April 18, 2003 and "US 'Jihad' for Human Rights Immunity Advances" by Jim Lobe, *OneWorld US*, June 25, 2003.

10. Jeffery Herbst, notes: "A paradox central to the nature of political boundaries in Africa: there is widespread agreement that the boundaries are arbitrary, yet the vast majority of them have remained virtually untouched since the late 1800s, when they were first demarcated." The reasons, Herbst argues, for the continued sanctification of the colonial inheritance is partly practical, partly ideological. "the ideological reason was the desire of relatively weak new leaders to protect their territorial domains from the constant threat of the many centrifugal forces that the deeply divided new states had inherited at independence." Nevertheless, "despite [a] remarkable record in the area of inter-state conflicts, the post-colonial African state has been crisis ridden virtually since the very moment of its independence." This crisis results in large part by from the propensity of state elites (typically linked to one sub-state nation) to "assert suzerainty over their sub-state groups largely by military force" (Okafor 2000: 34, 35).

11. While at the present moment, "[t]here is no corresponding and general right to take up residence anywhere else. The threat of becoming a 'stateless" person in a world exclusively divided up between nation-states may well make one's present citizen status always the lesser of two evils" (Pierson 1996: 134). However, if duty were no longer wedded to states, the international political and legal landscape would start to look very different, as Stephen Lewis forewarns with respect to the AIDS pandemic in Africa: "there may yet come a day when we have peace time tribunals to deal with this particular version ["mass murder by complacency"] of crimes against humanity" (*The Sunday Independent*, SA, Dec. 2003: 7). In part, the approach to rights embedded in the Reports can be read as a denial of the appropriateness of this direction. It other words, we can read a firm commitment to constructing and reconstructing the inevitability of the relationship between state and citizen.

NOTES TO CHAPTER FOUR

1. See specifically: www.undp.org

2. This is a question to which we will return in later chapters, specifically because interviews with the UNDP and UNHCR staff in all case countries lamented that their programmes did not have any gender component, nor had they been reviewed through gendered lenses.

3. The section on Africa will be taken up in Chapter Five, where regional questions are addressed more explicitly.

4. "Democracy in area an unlikely result of war, report says." *Globe and Mail,* Saturday, March 15, 2003.
5. *ibid.*
6. See: Global Witness 1999; 2001; Wheeler et al. 2001.
7. The *International Convention on Cultural, Social and Economic Rights* places a duty to protect rights only in so far as signatories feel their resources are sufficient. Thus, African states, *de facto*, are not legally bound to their obligations. I am indebted to Susan Thomson for this point.
8. The *Map* mainly includes human rights with respect to promotion during democratic elections, within transitional administrations, and "human rights assistance in such areas as holding elections, law reform, the administration of justice and training for law enforcement" (38).

NOTES TO CHAPTER FIVE

1. Similarly, as will be discussed in the next chapter, democracy is sometimes omitted from country documents, as well.
2. As noted in Chapter One, the UNDP was appointed lead agency for governance in Africa at the *Fifth African Governance Forum* in Maputo (AGF-V), May, 2002. This paper is the foundational concept paper for that Forum.
3. For Susan Marks (2000: 52), such unresolved tensions suggest that "some kind of "ideological agenda" seems to be at play. The drive to promote democracy is also a drive to constrain democracy, against the efforts of those seeking to transform relations of domination by insisting on the link between democratization and change in the structures of wealth and power."
4. This corresponds with what Mamdani (2001: 24) has identified as a central feature of western internationalism: "The architecture of the modern state was inscribed in modern law, Western law. And rule of law was in turn central to the construction of civilized society, in short, civil society."
5. Interviews, UNDP.
6. *Ibid.*
7. Interview, Human Rights Documentation Center, Windhoek, 2002.
8. Not all African countries are participating in this initiative, and not all participants participate with equal interest and resources.
9. It is also significant that empowering states to gather and systemically index data about citizen demographics is one of the few initiatives that can be traced to its actual implementation. For a more in-depth discussion, see Chapter Eight.
10. Such initiatives, however, are called into question by allegations in 2002 of widespread sexual exploitation of refugee girl children by relief workers in West and Central Africa–often in exchange for food and basic necessities such as tarpaulin. "Aid-for-sex children speak out," BBC News, Wed., 27 Feb. 2002 (www.news.bbc.co.uk/i/hi/world/africa/1843930.htm.).
11. In *Leviathan,* Order must be maintained by a strong and all-powerful state. It is not democratic, except to the extent that Hobbes posited that the need for an all-powerful force would be self-evident to all.

12. The *Map* includes "human rights assistance in such areas as holding elections, law reform, the administration of justice and training for law enforcement" (38).
13. I wonder if peoples clamouring for their rights have in mind that the UN should empower their often corrupt and rights-abusing governments with a legal and coercive apparatus strong enough to protect and extend rights, and by extension, strong enough for other enterprises, as well?

NOTES TO CHAPTER SIX

1. It is important to note at the onset that this chapter does not compare text or interview discourse with the contemporary political architecture of the case countries, and makes few comments on veracity of claims made or potential implications for real life. These questions are taken up in-depth in Chapter Seven. Rather, this chapter concludes by merely introducing the *potential* political implications of a governance agenda that contains both a dominant discourse and polycentric discourses, which are fragmented along various axes, internally contradictory and often incoherent, while also simultaneously advocating manifestly top-down processes with few participatory credentials.
2. I use the world "art," in order to capture the processes of engaging with a labyrinth of texts, for which the UN has not provided a *Road Map* or schema by which the bulk can be prioritized or set in relation to each other.
3. Designed to span 1997–2002.
4. Interview, UNDP, Windhoek, 2002.
5. An interesting question here might be to ask whether shifting country approaches mirror the movement of particular staff members, who typically move post every two years, or so.
6. United Nations Angola Verification Mission
7. União Nacional para a Independência Total de Angola
8. Movimento Popular de Libertação de Angola
9. UNDP briefing, Luanda, April 2001.
10. However, by 2005/06 speculation about the next elections is widespread and international pressure is mounting.
11. Ruggie (1998) uses the word flavour to help illuminate the difference between *American* hegemony and American *hegemony.*
12. Southern AFrica Research and Documentation Centre (SARDC), (Feb. 2000) *Democracy Factfile: Botswana*, Hararre: SARDC. This perception has started to shift with the 2005 government decision to deport University of Botswana political science professor and long time resident Kenneth Good for expressing critical views about the government. Good has long advanced the thesis that Botswana's *democracy* is both elitist and authoritarian.
13. That is, the chapters, as they unfold ever more complexity and contradiction, indicate that the governance agenda, is not ultimately quantifiable, but

inchoate. The agenda exhibits more or less dominant tendencies, but these, always and everywhere are tangled and smudged by other tendencies.

14. Interviews, Dar es Salaam, 2002.
15. The focus on women was not well integrated into planning. The UNHCR, for example, had no funding for a gender desk, and none of its projects had been reviewed through gendered lenses. There was also a deficit of gender expertise in the Province of Uige, and across the entire UN mission (source: interviews, Luanda, 2001)
16. Interviews, Luanda, 2001.
17. Interviews, Gaborone, 2002.
18. All quotes are paraphrased from hand written notes, and may not be exact quotes.
19. Interviews subsequently revealed, however, that UNDP had no governance programs or initiatives on-going, had received no special training on the *Millennium Development Goals* (MDGs), and had not begun to integrate them into policy approaches. The main concrete policy directions identified were that the UNDP had moved upstream, in both theory and methodology, which meant focusing on gaps that government had pre-identified. As one informant noted: "We are committed to a relationship with government."
20. Paradoxically, the OCHA (Office of the Coordinator Humanitarian Affairs) representative urged everyone present not to expect much progress or change in the overall humanitarian situation in the coming year, noting that despite being named the mission's Lead Agency, it had neither the capacity nor expertise to manage the mission and was refocusing the lens to "do no harm" and "upstream" constructive engagement with the GoA.
21. See Chapter Eight for an in-depth case study, and related end notes for a full list of its members.
22. Interviews with the Delegate of Justice in the province of Uige revealed that he had already prepared a list of needed resources several times for various UN employees, but had yet to see the library materialize. I was also asked to solicit this list while in Uige, which the Delegate of Justice sent to me later in the month. At the next Provincial Working Group meeting , I brought the list forward, only to be dismissed as naïve, and told that this list has been submitted numerous times already.
23. These questions also underscore the complicated climate in which elections were orchestrated in 1992, leading to the most destructive war of Angola's post-colonial history (Anstee 1999; Heywood 2000).
24. Comments of the Uige Roving Field Officer, country of origin, Zimbabwe.
25. The above findings are distilled from attendance at a number of inter-agency meetings in April 2001, Luanda, Angola.
26. Paraphrased from notes.
27. There is widespread disagreement over what constitutes a politically correct term for this group, indigenous to the area and long thought to be the original inhabitants of Southern Africa, preceding the Bantu migrations.
28. *Guardian*, 20 February 2003. I am indebted to Patrick Bond for this example.

29. Ohangwena is a Northern province and ruling party (SWAPO) electoral stronghold (see Chapter Seven).
30. Interviews with an independent party at the Centre for Foreign Relations in Dar es Salaam suggested that there was some frustration related to the propensity of aid projects to collect data, rather than use existing data and get on with operationalizing projects (see also Chapter Seven).
31. Here, a contrast is being drawn between how implementers receive and reflect upon UN theory, and the theory itself.
32. This also raises the possibility that aspirant documents are not designed to have resonance at the level of implementation, but rather to satisfy inter- and intra-organizational political dynamics. I am indebted to Dr. David Black for this point.
33. This term is taken from the title of James Ferguson's seminal *The Antipolitics Machine* (1990).
34. This year's Nobel prize honoured the work of economists Kaheman and Tversky detailing "that people look mostly to information that surrounds them to understand how the world works, rather than having the unlimited knowledge hitherto assumed by ivory-tower economists. They also proved that people have a hard time working out the probability of future events" (The Economist, October 12–18, 2000: 82).
35. For example, separation of powers causes, *inter alia*, accountability.

NOTES TO CHAPTER SEVEN

1. This chapter is re-printed with the permission of the Centre for Civil Society, University of KwaZulu Natal Durban South Africa, where it appears, in part, as Wishful Thinking, Wilful Blindness and Artful Amnesia: Power and the UNDP's Promotion of Democracy in Botswana, Namibia and Tanzania. *Centre for Civil Society Research Reports*: Vol. 1, # 31, 2005.
2. It is not the position here that the governance agenda has the power to be determinant in the face of other development actors and programs.
3. As noted earlier, Chapter Eight compares the architecture of one specific governance project—the Human Rights Committee—with the specific local political landscape to which it was meant to be applied—the city of Uige, in northern Angola. Here the dangers associated with investing decision-making power with a nominally legitimate provincial administrative apparatus are explored in-depth. Chapter Nine then elucidates the role of the minor discourses play in diffusing criticisms aimed at the dominant discourse. How has UN thinking escaped fundamental transformation in the face of overwhelming evidence of persistent development dysfunction? Chapter Nine implicates the minor discourses.
4. With respect to African states more generally, see Clapham (1993), Chabal and Daloz (1999), and Reno (1998).
5. Developing countries have been cooperative, at least nominally, with over 150 of the world's 191 states recognizing the UDHR in the preamble of their constitutions.

6. Interview, UNDP, Gaborone, 2002. This does not take into account the mitigating effects of the customary legal system.
7. See: www.worldbank.org/afr/ts/reports/2002_CG_governance.pdf.
8. NGO interview, Dar es Salaam, Nov. 2002.
9. With respect to rule of law specifically, however, the Framework notes that during a session on UN competency:

    One of UNICEF's representatives continued by arguing that if any members of the working group felt that no UN agencies had a comparative advantage in focusing on the rule of law for example, then within the UNDAF discussions this should be stated and recorded in the UNDAF document to prevent the UN operating in this area in the future. The working group should focus on delimiting the areas in which the UN agencies should be involved in the future (255).

10. Interviews, legal Assistance Centre, Human Rights Documentation Centre and Media Institute of Southern Africa, Windhoek, 2002.
11. The "police zone" is a legal boundary separating the bottom two thirds (approx.) of Namibia from the top third, which borders on Angola. It was designed to act as a *cordon sanitaire*, containing both undesirable people and livestock.
12. The Institute for Public Policy Research (IPPR) in Windhoek argued that "it is clear that much more education on human rights is needed. Not only should awareness be raised about such rights, there is also a need to explain the very notion of *rights*. In addition, there is a need to explain how rights relate to duties, liberties and obligations, and where rights originate" [emphasis in original].
13. Interview, Windhoek, 2002.
14. See also: www.thenamibian.com.na.
15. Paraphrased from field notes.
16. Some developing countries are freer than others. Botswana is a case in point. The least externally-dependent of the countries explored here, and fully paid-up member of the IMF, the GoB has opted to severely circumscribe the latitude it gives to the UN to include rights-based programming.
17. Interviews, UNDP, Gaborone, 2002.
18. That Botswana has rejected the UN's focus on human rights need not be viewed too pessimistically, but rather as an invitation to the underlying organization power, as well as the imbalances between state power and other groups. For example, Swatuk (1999: 7) has argued that the relocation of the Kalahari Desert San people to bleak settlements is illustrative of more than the abrogation of human rights; it expresses the intersection of "interests between large cattle ranchers, mining capital and the state of Botswana" (see also Good 1999). Similarly, a rights-based approach may not see the complex extra-legal sources of vulnerability, or how the legal architecture produces existing power relations rather than disarticulates them (see also Selolwane 1997 on status of women).
19. In the following section on civil society, we take up the question of whether it is useful to conflate all the positions and interests that exist among "the public," and if so, what it is useful for, and to whom?

20. The Tanzanian CCF (2001: 8) similarly envisions media as part a "master plan for a holistic and effective poverty monitoring system."
21. Interview, Namibian Institute for Democracy, Windhoek, 2002.
22. Interviews, Dar es Salaam, Nov. 2002.
23. See the Tanzania Media Women Association website for more information on this issue: http://www.tamwa.or.tz/.
24. See: www.commondreams.org.
25. See: http://www.africaonline.com/site/Articles/1,3,47429.jsp.
26. I am indebted to Sandra J. MacLean for this insight.
27. Interviews, Dar es Salaam, Nov. 2002.
28. Paraphrased from field notes.
29. "Male leaders giving nod to marital rape, says UN report." *The Namibian*, August 31, 2001. See: www.namibian.com.na/2001/August/news/01E7BD169.html.
30. See: http://www.idea.int/vt/country_view.cfm.
31. A study conducted in 1995 revealed that voter turn out was low for the first election, while the average voter was "in the main: a male (concept of head of family) between 36 and 55 years of age; with below primary education level; dependant on farming as a occupation; living outside Dar es Salaam with previous voting experience (Maliyamkono 1995: 48).
32. Institute for Democracy and Electoral Assistance. http://www.idea.int/vt/region_view.cfm?CountryCode=TS.
33. Southern African Research and Documentation Centre.
34. See: http://www.idea.int/vt/country_view.cfm. IDEA has not updated their website for the 2004 elections. The National Democratic Institute, however, reported voter turn out as close to 86%. See: http://www.usaid.gov/locations/sub-saharan_africa/features/namibia_elections.html
35. A similar pattern is reported to have developed in Botswana. Interviews with the UNDP revealed that while the GoB had committed to a poverty reduction and development plan (Vision 2016), it relied on the UNDP to draft the particulars, coordinate activities and provide funding.
36. Regulations for Resettlement.
37. See also: www. Reliefweb.int; http://www.cpj.org/attacks01/africa01/angola.html.
38. See also: www.boavista.cc.
39. Within the span of eight months, the entire UNHCR staff had been rotated and it proved impossible to obtain information about the status of this village and their plight.
40. Interviews, BACONGO and University of Botswana 2002, Gaborone, 2003.
41. Interview, UNDP, Windhoek, 2002.
42. See: http://www.namibian.com.na/Focus/Elections/results.html; http://allafrica.com/stories/200211220206.html
43. Interviews, UNDP in Dar es Salaam, 2002.
44. Interview, Centre for Foreign Relations, Dar es Salaam, 2002
45. Ujamaa was a government-led and enforced "villagization" programme that sought to carve collectivized farms out of the social, political and geographical landscape.

46. Interview, Centre for Foreign Relations, Dar es Salaam, 2002.
47. *Ibid.*

NOTES TO CHAPTER EIGHT

1. This chapter is reproduced with the permission of the *Journal of Peace-keeping and Development*, where it originally appeared in Vol. 2, No.1. Dec, 2004, pp 37–50.
2. At the time of research, the only document which related specifically to the HRC was the Republic of Angola's *Internal Regulations of the Provincial Comitee* [sic] *on Human Rights: Uige Province (2001).* It provides information about the HRC's creation and application, and notes that "five other committees were also created" on November 9, 2000. It gives a skeletal overview of the scope and operational procedures and notes: "Having taken note of the lack of a document that regulates the operation of this committee, there is an urgent need to establish regulatory norms that will enhance its effectiveness and orderly operation." At the time of research, this had yet to take place. It also notes that: "All activities of the committee shall be conducted in accordance with the spirit of the Universal Declaration of Human Rights, the African Human and Peoples Rights Charter, other international conventions and the Angolan Constitutional Law."
3. For an example see *Roadmap towards the Implementation of the United Nations Millennium Declaration* (2001) and Report of the Secretary General, *The Causes of Conflict and the Promotion of Durable Peace and Sustainable Development in Africa* (1998).
4. Movimento Popular de Libertação de Angola.
5. União Nacional para a Independência Total de Angola.
6. For a description of the methodology used for this case study see: Wilson, J. Zoë (2005). "Truth, Certainty and Subjectivity: the ethics of war-time research in contested spaces." *Researching Violently Divided Societies.* Marie Smyth and Gillian Robinson (eds.). United Nation University Press and Pluto Press.
7. Given high staff turnover, it was difficult to track the evolution of the HRC. There are strong indications that the project was ultimately abandoned, as it had been in Angola's other provinces, but this is yet to be confirmed.
8. Positions Reserved on the Uige Human Rights Committee: Provincial Justice Delegate, Provincial Attorney General, Chief Justice of the Provincial Court, Provincial Police Commandant, Provincial Director of Angola's Ministry for Social Assistance and Reinsertion (MINARS), Provincial Director of The Minister of Public Administration, Employment and Social Security (MAPESS), Provincial Director of the Ministry of Family and Woman Protection, Provincial Director of Angola's National Institute for Children (INAC), Representative of the traditional authorities, Representative of religious institutions, Representatives of the NGOs working in the areas of human rights.

9. While in Uige, I recorded a tragic account of a village that had been attacked, allegedly by the FAA (government troops). The leader and elders were shot, and the villagers were forcibly moved to Uige. The military commander claimed in an interview that the elders were shot in crossfire between FAA and UNITA troops and that villagers had been evacuated for their own safety. The villagers disputed the claim of a UNITA presence and insisted they be allowed to return to their tribal lands.

NOTES TO CHAPTER NINE

1. Former UNDP staff member commented at the recent "Enhancing Human Security" workshop at Dalhousie University, August 8–9th 2003, that no external studies and literatures were circulated during his tenure. Rather, in their professional capacity, all UN staff were immersed in UN produced documents only.
2. Many states elites who have not worn the legitimating cloak of low-intensity democracy have also been afforded the rights and privileges to treat state resources as private property while incurring massive debt loads for future generations. Nevertheless, this is less and less acceptable. I am indebted to Dr. David Black for this point.
3. "Annan calls for UN reform," The Namibian, Tuesday September 24, 2002, p.7.
4. As noted in Chapter Three, where participation is emphasized it is integrated, moreover, as a regulative rather than constitutive norm, and thus *intrinsically* open to prescriptions about where and under what conditions participation is valuable or warranted (i.e. warranted on Election Day, not warranted at World Forums).
5. Drawing on similar evidence, Cooper and Packard (1997: 4) revisit some of the complications that arise from the assumption that locating power (whether in discourse or practice) is synonymous with its being determinant. Rather, the absence of a clear signified for terms such as human rights and democracy may make the ideas amenable to becoming tools of power, while also becoming sites of political struggle. "What at one level appears like a discourse of control is at another a discourse of entitlement, a way of capturing the imagination of a cross-national public around demands for decency and equity." In other words, the World Bank's adoption of a rather narrow and low-intensity definition of democracy does not mean that its commitment to "democracy" cannot be used against it by more radical groups.
6. In 2002, 100% and 92% of the Members of the Boards of the IMF and World Bank, respectively, were male (UNDP 2002: 115).
7. By 2002, it is unclear how much these events have penetrated policy making at the Bank, whose recent World Development Report argues: "Good governance requires the power to carry out policies and to develop institutions that may be unpopular among some—or even a majority—of the population" (99).

8. Interviews, World Food Programme, Uige 2001.
9. UN orchestrated elections in Angola in 1992.
10. Visits to the homes of UNHCR workers in Luanda revealed a fondness for Angolan art, particularly fruit bowls filled with carved apples and bananas of ivory and finely carved ivory statuettes. In the markets of Luanda, stalls could be found piled high with elephant tusks ready to meet aid/oil worker demand.
11. During an interview with former UNDP staff stationed in Rwanda as the genocide was unfolding the observation was made that one of the reasons why the UN was caught unaware was the self-referential nature of programs, and staff incentives to complete bureaucratic procedures, such as checklists, rather than seek meaningful solutions.
12. Aggregated by Barnett and Finnemore (2001: 415).
13. The Title of Gil Courtemanche's (2003) award winning fictional indictment of the aid industry's complicity in the fate of over one million Rwandans.

Bibliography

Abrahamsen, Rita. (2001). *Disciplining Democracy*, London & New York: Zed Books.

Adejumobi, Said. (2001). "Citizenship, Rights, and the Problem of Conflicts and Civil Wars in Africa," *Human Rights Quarterly*, 23:1.

Adekeye, Adebajo and Chris Landsberg. (2000). "Back to the Future: UN Peacekeeping in Africa," *International Peacekeeping*, 7:4.

Anstee, Margaret. (1999). 'The United Nations in Angola,' *Herding Cats*, Washington: United States Institute of Peace Press.

Archibugi, Daniele, David Held and Martin Kohler (eds.). (1998). *Re-imagining Political Community*, Stanford, CA: Stanford University Press.

Bachrach, Peter and Morton Baratz. (1969). "Decisions and Nondecisions: An Analytical Framework," Rodrick Bell, David V. Edwards, R. Harrison Wagner (eds.), *Political Power: A Reader in Theory and Research*, New York: The Free Press. London: Collier-Macmillan Limited.

Badie, Bertrand. (2000). *The Imported State*, Stanford, California: Stanford University Press.

Baines, Erin K. (2003). "Body Politics and the Rwandan Crisis," *Third World Quarterly*, 24:3.

Baines, Erin K. (2004). "*Les Femmes aux Milles Bras*: Building Peace in Rwanda," Jane Parpart, Angela Raven-Roberts and Dyan Mazurana (eds.), *Gender, Complex Emergencies and Peacekeeping: National and International Feminist Perspectives*, Lanham, Boulder, New York & Oxford: Rowman & Littlefield Publishers, Inc.

Barnett, Michael and Martha Finnemore. (2001). "The Politics of Power and Pathologies of International Organizations," Lisa L. Martin and Beth A. Simmons. (eds.), *International Institutions*, Cambridge, MA & London: The MIT Press.

Barnett, Michael. (2002). "Radical Chic? Subaltern Realism," *International Studies Review*, 4:3.

Bartelson, Jens. (2001). *The Critique of the State*, Cambridge: Cambridge University Press.

Bauer, Martin W. (2002). "Classical Content Analysis," Martin W. Bauer and George Gaskell (eds.), *Qualitative Researching with Text, Image and Sound*, London, Thousand Oaks, & New Dehli: Sage Publications.

Bellucci, Stephano. (2002). "Governance, Civil Society and NGOs in Mozambique," *Management of Social Transformation*, Most: UNESCO.

Bernault, Florence. (2000). "What Absence is Made Of: Human Rights in Africa," Jeffrey N. Wasserstrom, Lynn Hunt and Marilyn B. Young (eds.), *Human Rights and Revolutions*, Lanham, Boulder, New York & Oxford: Rowman and Littlefield Publishers, Inc.

Black, David and J. Zoë Wilson. (2004). "Rights, Region and Identity: exploring the ambiguities of South Africa's human rights role," *Politikon, ,* Vol 31, No. 1, May 2004.

Black, David. (1999). "The long and winding road: international norms and domestic political change in South Africa,"Thomas Risse, Stephen C. Roppe and Kathleen Sikkink (eds.), *The Power of Human Rights*, New York: Cambridge University Press.

Bodely, John. (1999). *Cultural Anthropology: Tribes. States and the Global System*, London, Toronto & California: Mayfield Publishing Company.

Booth, Ken. (1999). "Three Tyrannies," Tim Dunne and Nicholas Wheeler (eds.), *Human Rights in Global Politics*, Cambridge: Cambridge University Press.

Brahimi Report—United Nations General Assembly. (2000). "Report of the Panel on United Nations Peace Operations," A/55/305-S/2000/809, 21 August 2000.

Bratton, Michael and Nicholas van de Walle. (1997). *Democratic Experiments in Africa*, Cambridge: Cambridge University Press.

Broch-Due, Vigdis. (2000). "Producing Nature and Poverty in Africa: An Introduction," Vigdis Broch-Due and Richard A. Schroeder (eds.), *Producing Nature and Poverty in Africa*, Oslo: Nordiska Afrikainstitutet.

Bond, Patrick. (2006), *Looting Africa: The Economics of Exploitation*, London, Zed Books, Pietermaritzburg: UKZN Press.

Bond, Patrick (2005), Talk Left, Right Walk: South Africa's Frustrated Reforms: Durban, South Africa: University of Natal Press.

Brown, Chris. (1999). "Universal Human Rights: A Critique," Tim Dunne and Nicholas Wheeler (eds.), *Human Rights in Global Politics*, Cambridge: Cambridge University Press.

Bukurura, Sufian Hemed. (2002). *Essays in Constitutionalism and the Administration of Justice in Namibia*, Windhoek, Namibia: Out of Africa Publishers.

Bustello, Eduardo. (2001). "Expansion of Citizenship and Democratic Construction," Willem van Genugten and Camilo Perez-Bustillo (eds.), *The Poverty of Rights*, London & New York: Zed Books.

Butler, Judith. (1990). *Gender Trouble: Feminism and the Subversion of Identity*, New York: Routledge.

Buzan, Barry (1983). *People, States and Fear: The National Security Problem in International Relations*, Brighton: Wheatsheaf Books.

Calabrese, Andrew. (2000). "The Means of Communication and the Discourse on Sovereignty," Simone Chambers and Anne Costain (eds.), *Deliberation, Democracy and the Media*, Lanham, Boulder, New York & Oxford: Rowman and Littlefield Publishers, Inc.

Cammack, Paul. (1997). *Capitalism and Democracy in the Third World: The Doctrine for Political Development,* London & Washington: Leicester University Press.

Chabal, Patrick. (1997). *Apocalypse Now? A postcolonial journey into Africa,* available at: http://www.kcl.ac.uk/deptsta/humanities/pobrst/pcpapers.htm; accessed 24 April 1999.

Chabal, Patrick and Jean-Pascal Daloz. (1999). *Africa Works: Disorder as Political Instrument,* Indiana: Indiana University Press.

Chambers, Simone. (2000). "A Culture of Publicity," Simone Chambers and Anne Costain (eds.), *Deliberation, Democracy and the Media,* Lanham, Boulder, New York & Oxford: Rowman and Littlefield Publishers, Inc.

Clapham, Christopher. (1996). *Africa and the International System: The Politics of State Survival,* Cambridge, New York: Cambridge University Press.

Cohen, Ronald, Goran Hyden, and Winston P. Nagan (eds.). (1993). *Human Rights and Governance in Africa,* Gainesville: University Press of Florida.

Connolly, William. (1984). "The Dilemma of Legitimacy," William Connolly (ed.), *Legitimacy and the State,* New York: New York University Press.

Cooper, Fredrick and Randall Packard (eds.). (1996). *International Development and the Social Sciences,* Berkley: University of California Press.

Cornia, Giovanni Andrea, Richard Jolly, and Frances Stewart. (1989). *Adjustment with a Human Face,* Oxford & New York: Clarendon Press.

Cox, Robert W. (with Timothy J. Sinclair). (1996). *Approaches to World Order,* Cambridge: Cambridge University Press.

Cox, Robert W. (1987). *Production, Power and World Order: Social Forces in the Making of History,* New York: Columbia University Press.

Cox, Robert W. and Harold K. Jacobsen (eds.). (1973). *The Anatomy of Influence: Decision Making in International Organization,* New Haven & London: Yale University Press.

Crais, Clifton. (2001). *The Politics of Evil,* Cambridge: Cambridge University Press.

Danaher, Kevin (ed.). (1994). *Fifty Years is Enough: The Case Against the World Bank and IMF,* Boston, MA: South End Press.

Davidson, Basil. (1975). *In the Eye of the Storm: Angola's People,* Middlesex, England: Penguin Books.

De Rivera, Oswaldo. (2001). *The Myth of Development: the non-viable economies of the 21st century,* New York: Zed Books; Halifax, N.S.: Fernwood Publishers.

Dembour, Marie Benedicte. (1996). "Human rights talk and anthropological ambivalence," Olivia Harris (ed.), *Inside and Outside the Law,* London & New York: Routledge.

Denham, Mark E. and Mark Owen Lombardi. (1996). *Perspectives on Third-World Sovereignty: The Postmodern Paradox,* New York: St. Martin's Press.

Denzin, Norman and Yvonna Lincoln. (1994). "Introduction: entering the field of qualitative research," Norman Denzin and Yvonna Lincoln (eds.), *Handbook of Qualitative Research,* Thousand Oaks, London & New Dehli: Sage Publications.

Der Derian, James. (1989). "The Boundaries of Knowledge and Power in International Relations, " James Der Derian and Michael J. Shapiro (eds.), *International and Intertexual Relations: Postmodern Readings of World Politics.*

New York: Lexington Books: Toronto: Maxwell Macmillan Canada: New York: Oxford: Singapore: Sydney: Maxwell MacMillan International.

Desai, Ashwin. (2002). *We are the Poors*. New York: Monthly Review Press.

Diamond, Larry. (1999). *Developing Democracy: Towards Consolidation*, Baltimore: Johns Hopkins University Press.

Diamond, Larry and Mark Plattner. (1996). *The Global Resurgence of Democracy*, Baltimore: Johns Hopkins University Press.

Dingake, Oagile Key. (2000). *Key Aspects of the Constitutional Law of Botswana*, Botswana: Pula Press.

Donini, Antonio. (1996). "The Bureaucracy and the Free Spirits: Stagnation and Innovation in the Relationship between the UN and NGOs," Thomas G. Weiss and Leon Gordenker (eds.), *NGOs, the UN and Global Governance*, Boulder: London: Lynne Reinner Publishers.

Donnelly, Jack. (1999). "The Social Construction of International Human Rights" Tim Dunne and Nicholas Wheeler (eds.), *Human Rights in Global Politics*, Cambridge: Cambridge University Press.

Du Toit, Pierre (2001). *South Africa's Brittle Peace: The Problem of Post-Settlement Violence*, New York: Palgrave.

Duffield, Mark. (2001). *Global Governance and the New Wars*, London &New York: Zed Books.

Dunne, Tim and Nicholas Wheeler. (1999). "Human Rights and the Fifty Years' Crisis," Tim Dunne and Nicholas Wheeler (eds), *Human Rights in Global Politics*, Cambridge: Cambridge University Press.

Dunn, Kevin C. and Timothy M. Shaw (eds.). (2003). *Africa's Challenge to International Relations Theory*, London: Palgrave.

Ellis, Stephen. (2001). *The Mask of Anarchy: The Destruction of Liberia and the Religious Dimension of an African War*, New York: New York University Press.

Englebert, Pierre. (2000). *State Legitimacy and Development in Africa*, Boulder: London: Lynne Rienner Publishers.

Enloe, Cynthia. (1989). *Bananas, Beaches and Bases: Making Feminist Sense of International Politics*, Berkeley: University of California Press.

Eyoh, Dickson. (1998). "African perspectives on democracy and the dilemmas of postcolonial intellectuals," *Africa Today*, July-December, 45:3–4.

Ferguson, James. (1990; 1994). *The Anti-Politics Machine*, Cambridge, New York, Port Chester, Melbourne & Sydney: Cambridge University Press.

Field, Richard H. G. and Robert J. House. (1996). *Human Behaviour in Organization*, Scarborough, ON: Prentice Hall Canada Inc.

Financial Times. (2002). *World Desk Reference*, London, New York, Munich, Melbourne & Delhi: Dorling Kindersley Publishing, Inc.

Fitzpatrick, Peter. (1993). "Law's Infamy," Sammy Adelman and Adbul Paliwala (eds.), *Law and Crisis in the Third World*, London, Melbourne, Munich & New Jersey: Hans Zell Publishers.

Fontana, Andrea and James Frey. (1994). "Interviewing: the art of science," Norman Denzin and Yvonna Lincoln (eds.), *Handbook of Qualitative Research*, Thousand Oaks, London & New Dehli: Sage Publications.

Foucault, Michel. (1984). "The Juridical Apparatus," William Connolly (ed.), *Legitimacy and the State*, New York: New York University Press.

Foucault, Michel. (1977). *Discipline and Punish: The Birth of the Prison*, (trans. Alan Sheridan), New York: Pantheon Books.

Fowler, Robert (1997). *Striking a Balance: a guide to enhancing the effectiveness of non-governmental organizations in international development*, London: Earthscan.

Friedrich Ebert Stiftung (2001). *Political and Electoral Violence in East Africa*, Nairobi: Friedrich Ebert Stiftung.

Fukuyama, Francis. (1992). *The End of History and the Last Man*, New York: Free Press.

Gallarotti, Guilio M. (2001). "The Limits of International Organization," Lisa L. Martin and Beth A. Simmons (eds.), *International Institutions*, Cambridge, MA. & London: The MIT Press.

Galtung, Johan. (1986). "On the Anthropology of the United Nations System," David Pitt and Thomas G. Weiss (eds.), *The Nature of United Nations Bureaucracies*, London & Sydney: Croom Helm.

Gaskell, George. (2002). "Individual and Group Interviewing," Norman Denzin and Yvonna Lincoln (eds.), *Handbook of Qualitative Research*, Thousand Oaks, London & New Dehli: Sage Publications.

Ghai, Yash. (1993). "Constitutions and Governance in Africa: A Prolegomenon," Sammy Adelman and Adbul Paliwala (eds.), *Law and Crisis in the Third World*, London, Melbourne, Munich & New Jersey: Hans Zell Publishers.

Gill, Rosalind. (2002). "Discourse Analysis," Martin W. Bauer and George Gaskell (eds.), *Qualitative Researching with Text, Image and Sound*, London, Thousand Oaks & New Dehli: Sage Publications.

Gills, Barry and Joel Rocamora and Richard Wilson (eds.). (1993). *Low Intensity Democracy*, London & Boulder: Pluto Press.

Global Witness. (2002). *All the President's Men: The Devastating Story of Oil and Banking in Angola's Privatised War*, London: Global Witness Ltd.

Good, Kenneth. (2002). "Rethinking Corruption and Non-Accountability in Botswana," *Africa Insight*, 32:3.

Good, Kenneth. (1999). "Enduring Elite Democracy in Botswana," *Democratization*, 6:1.

Gordon, Robert J. (2002). "Unsettled Settlers: Internal Pacification and Vagrancy in Namibia," in Carol J. Greenhouse, Elizabeth Mertz and Kay B. Warren (eds.), *Ethnography in Unstable Places: Everyday Lives in the Context of Dramatic Political Change*, Durham & London: Duke University Press.

Gourevitch, Philip. (1998). *We wish to inform you that tomorrow we will be killed with our families: stories from Rwanda*, New York: Farrar, Straus, and Giroux.

Graf, William. (1996). "Democratization for the Third World," *Canadian Journal of Development Studies*.

Gregory, Donna U. (1989). "Foreward," James Der Derian and Michael J. Shapiro (eds.), *International and Intertexual Relations: Postmodern Readings of World Politics*. New York: Lexington Books: Toronto: Maxwell Macmillan

Canada: New York: Oxford: Singapore: Sydney: Maxwell MacMillan International.

Greenhouse, Carol J., Elizabeth Mertz and Kay B. Warren (eds.) (1999). *Ethnography in Unstable Places: Everyday Lives in the Context of Dramatic Political Change*, Durham & London: Duke University Press.

Grovogui, Siba N'Zatioula. (1996). *Sovereigns, Quasi Sovereigns and Africans*, Borderlines, Vol. 3. Minneapolis: University of Minnesota Press.

Guba, Egon and Yvonna Lincoln. (1994). "Competing Paradigms in Qualitative Research," Norman Denzin and Yvonna Lincoln (eds.), *Handbook of Qualitative Research*, Thousand Oaks, London & New Dehli: Sage Publications.

Gulbrandsen, Ornulf. (1996). "Living in their courts: the counter-hegemonic force of the Tswana *kgotla* in a colonial context," Olivia Harris (ed.), *Inside and Outside the Law*, New York: Routledge.

Habermas, Jurgen. (1984). "What does a legitimation crisis mean today? Legitimation Problems in Late Capitalism," William Connelly (ed.), *Legitimacy and the State*, New York: New York University Press.

Habermas, Jurgen. (2000). *The Post National Constellation*, (trans. by Max Pensky), Cambridge: Polity Press.

Halisi, C.R.D. *et al.* (1998). "Rethinking Citizenship in Africa: Guest editor's introduction: The multiple meanings of Citizenship—rights, identity, and social justice in Africa." *Africa Today*. July-December, 45:3–4.

Hall, Stephen S. (2004). "I Mercator," Harmon, Katherine. (ed.). *You Are Here: Personal Geographies and Other Maps of the Imagination*. New York: Princeton Architectural Press.

Hall, Stuart. (1992). "The Question of Cultural Identity," Stuart Hall, David Held and Tony McGrew (eds.), *Modernity and its Futures*, Oxford: Polity Press.

Halpern, Diane. (1997). *Critical Thinking Across the Curriculum*, London: Lawrence Erlbaum Associates Publishers.

Hancock, Graham (1989). *Lords of Poverty: The Free-Wheeling Lifestyles, Power, Prestige and Corruption of the Multi-Billon Dollar Aid Industry*, London: Macmillan.

Harmon, Katherine. (ed.) (2004). *You Are Here: Personal Geographies and Other Maps of the Imagination*. New York: Princeton Architectural Press.

Harris, Olivia. (1996). "Inside and Outside the Law" Olivia Harris (ed.), *Inside and Outside the Law*, London: Routledge.

Havel, Vaclav. (1992). "The End of the Modern Era," *The New York Times*, March 9, E15.

Hatch, Mary Jo. (1997). *Organization Theory*, Oxford: Oxford University Press.

Haugaard, Mark. (1997). *The Constitution of Power*, Manchester: New York: Manchester University Press.

Held, David. (1993). "Democracy: From City-States to a Cosmopolitan Order?" David Held (ed.), *Prospects for Democracy: North, South, East and West*, Standford: Standford University Press.

Held, David. (2000). "The Changing Contours of Political Community: Rethinking Democracy in the Context of Globalization," in Barry Holden (ed.), *Global Democracy: Key Debates*, London & New York: Routledge.

Hellsten, Sikku. (2002). 'The State of the Rule of Law and Human Rights in East Africa-Political, Legal and social Development in Tanzania,' Sikku Hellsten (ed.), *Politics, Governance, and Cooperation in East Africa*, Dar es Salaam: Mkuki na Nyota Publishers & REDET.

Herod, Andrew, Gearóid Ó Tuathail, and Susan M. Roberts (eds.) (1998). *An Unruly World? Globalization, Governance and Geography*, London: Routledge.

Herman, Edward S. and Noam Chomsky (2002). *Manufacturing Consent: The Political Economy of Mass Media*, New York: Pantheon.

Heywood, Linda. (2000). *Contested Power in Angola: 1840s to the Present*, Suffolk: University of Rochester Press.

Hirst, Paul. (2000). "Democracy and Governance," Jon Pierre (ed.), *Debating Governance*, Oxford: Oxford University Press.

Hodges, Tony. (2000). *Angola from Afro-Stalinism to Petro-Diamond Capitalism*, Oxford: James Curry.

Hollis, Martin. (1994). *Philosophy of Social Science*, Cambridge: Cambridge University Press

Holm, John. D. (1993). "Political Culture and Democracy: a study of mass participation in Botswana," *Botswana: The Political Economy of Democratic Development*, Boulder: Lynne Reinner Publishers.

Hoogvelt, Ankie. (2001). *Globalization and the Postcolonial World: The Political Economy of Development*, Baltimore: Palgrave.

HRW—Human Rights Watch. (1999). *Angolan Civil Society and Human Rights*, available at: http://www.hrw.org/reports/1999/angola/ang1998–11.htm, accessed on 19 March 2001.

Huntington, Samuel. (1991). *The Third Wave: Democratisation in the Late Twentieth Century*, New York: Columbia University Press.

Hyden, Goran and Michael Bratton (eds). (1992). *Governance and Politics in Africa*, Boulder: Lynne Reinner Publishers.

Hyden, Goran. (1999). "Top-Down Democratization in Tanzania," *Journal of Democracy*, 10:4.

International Commission on Intervention and State Sovereignty. (2002). *The Responsibility to Protect*, Ottawa: IDRC

Information Sheet—Media Council of Tanzania. (July 2002). *Non Legal Barriers to Media Development in Tanzania*.

Jackson, Robert. (2000). *The Global Covenant: Human Conduct in a World of States*, Oxford: Oxford University Press.

Jackson, Robert and Carl Rosberg. (1986). "Why Africa's Weak States Persist?" in Marion E. Doro and Newell M. Stultz (eds.), *Governing in Black Africa*, New York & London: Africana Publishing Company.

Jenkins, Rob. (2002). "The emergence of the governance agenda: sovereignty, neoliberal bias and the politics of development," Vandana Desai and Robert Potter (eds.), *The Companion to Development Studies*, London & New York: Oxford University Press.

Jett, Dennis. (1999). *Why Peacekeeping Fails*, New York: Palgrave.

Jocknick, Chris. (2001). "The Human Rights Challenge to Global Poverty," Willem van Genugten and Camilo Perez-Bustello (eds.), *The Poverty of Rights:*

Human Rights and the Eradication of Poverty, London & New York: Zed Books.

Kaldor, Mary. (1999). "Transnational Civil Society," Tim Dunne and Nicholas Wheeler (eds), *Human Rights in Global Politics*, Cambridge: Cambridge University Press.

Karashani, Fili. (2001, February). "How information-starved rural women were exploited in Election 2000," *The Journalist*. Dar es Salaam: Association of Journalist and Media Workers.

Keating, Michael. (2001). *Plurinational Democracy*, Oxford: Oxford University Press.

Keck, Margaret and Katherine Sikkink. (1999). *Activists Beyond Borders: Advocacy Networks in International Politics*, Ithaca, NY: Cornell University Press.

Keulder, Christiaan, and Dirk Spilker. (2002). *In Search of Democrats: Youth Attitudes Towards Democracy and Non-democratic Alternatives*, IPPR Briefing Paper, No. 10, May.

Keulder, Christiaan. (2002). *Perception of Human Rights and Rights-related Issues Among Namibian Youth: Results from Focus Group Discussions*, IPPR Research Report No. 3.

Kincheloe, Joe and Peter McLaren. (1994). "Rethinking Critical Theory and Qualitative Research," Norman Denzin and Yvonna Lincoln (eds.), *Handbook of Qualitative Research*, Thousand Oaks, London, New Dehli: Sage Publications.

Kobb, Daniel. (2000). *Corruption in Tanzania: Counting and Franchise Bidding*, available at: http://www.esrftz.org/anticorruption/corruption_in_tz.htm; accessed 3 February 2003.

Kratochwil, Friedrich and John Gerald Ruggie. (2001). "A State of the Art on the Art of the State," Lisa L. Martin and Beth A. Simmons (eds.), *International Institutions*, Cambridge, MA & London: The MIT Press.

Leach, Joan. (2002). "Rhetorical Analysis," in Martin W. Bauer and George Gaskell (eds.), *Qualitative Researching with Text, Image and Sound*, London, Thousand Oaks & New Dehli: Sage Publications.

Lindholt, Lone. (1997). *Questioning the Universality of Human Rights*, Brookfield, Singapore & Sydney: Ashgate.

Linz, Juan L. and Alfred Stepan. (1996). *Problems of Democratic Transition and Consolidation. Southern Europe, South America, and post-Communist Europe*, Baltimore: John Hopkins University Press.

Lipschutz, Ronnie. (2000). *After Authority*, Albany: State University of New York Press.

Lodge, Tom. (1999). *The Namibian Elections*, South Africa: The Electoral Commissions Forum of SADC Countries.

MacKinnon, Catharine. (1989). *Toward a Feminist Theory of the State*, Boston: Harvard University Publishers.

MacLean, Sandra. (2001). "Issues of Sovereignty and Identity in Southern Africa," Kevin C. Dunn and Timothy M. Shaw (eds.), *Africa's Challenge to International Relations Theory*, London: Palgrave.

Maliyamkono, T.L. (1995). *Who Votes in Tanzania and Why*, Dar es Salaam: Temo Publishers Company Ltd.

Mamdani, Mahmood. (2001), *When Victims Become Killers: Colonialism, Nativism, and the Genocide in Rwanda*, Kampala: Fountain Publishers.

Mamdani, Mahmood. (1995). "Democratization and Marketization," K. Mengisteab and I. Logan (eds.), *Beyond Economic Liberalization in Africa*, London: Zed Books.

Mandelbaum, Michael. (1994). "The reluctance to intervene," *Foreign Policy*, Summer.

Mann, Michael. (1986). *The Sources of Social Power, Volume I*, Cambridge: Cambridge University Press.

Manning, Carrie. (1999). "Citizen View of Peace Building and Political Transition in Angola, 1997," Padraig O'Malley. (ed), *Southern Africa*, National Democratic Institute for International Affairs: University of the Western Cape Press.

Marks, S. (1991). *Southern History in Black and White*, Princeton: Princeton University Press.

Marks, Susan (2000). *The Riddle of All Constitutions*, Oxford: Oxford University Press.

Martin, Lisa and Beth Simmons (eds.) (1995). *International Institutions: An International Organization Reader*, Cambridge, MA & London: The MIT Press.

McGee, R. (2002). *Assessing Participation in Poverty Reduction Strategy Papers: A Desk-Based Synthesis of Experience in sub-Saharan Africa*, Sussex: University of Sussex Institute for Development Studies.

McIntosh, Susan Keech (ed.). (1999). *Beyond Chiefdoms: Pathways to Complexity in Africa*, Cambridge: Cambridge University Press.

Melber, Henning. (2000). "The Culture of Politics," Henning Melber (ed.), *Namibia: A Decade of Independence*, Windhoek: NEPRU.

Mills, Albert J. and Tony Simmons. (1999). *Reading Organization Theory*, Toronto: Garamond Press.

Mills, Sara. (1997). *Discourse,* London & New York: Routledge.

Media Institute for Southern Africa (MISA). (2001). *So This is Democracy: State of the Media in Southern Africa*, Windhoek: Solitaire Press.

Media Institute for Southern Africa (MISA). (2002). *Media Monitoring Project Namibia (MMPN): Pilot Phase Report*, MISA: Open Society Initiative for Southern Africa.

Mohamed Salih, M.A. (2001). *African Democracies and African Politics*, London: Virginia: Pluto Press.

Monga, Celestin. (1997). "Eight Problems with African Politics," *Journal of Democracy*. 8:3.

Moore, David and Gerald Schmitz (eds). (1995). *Debating Development Discourse: Institutional and Popular Perspectives*, Basingstoke: Macmillan.

Moore, Donald. (1993). "Contesting Terrain in Zimbabwe's eastern Highlands: Political Ecology, Ethnography and Peasant Resource Struggles," *Economic Geography*, 69: 4.

Mukandala, Rwekaza, and Charles Gasarasi (eds.). (2000). *Governance and Development at the Grassroots in Tanzania*, Dar es Salaam: DUP Ltd.

Mushi, Samual, *et al.* (eds.) (2001). *Tanzania's Political Culture: A baseline survey,* Dar es Salaam: University Department of Political Science and Public Administration.

Mutakyahwa, R.G. (2002). "The Impact of Non Governmental Organizations in Development," *Political Handbook NGO Calendar 2002*, Nairobi: Freidrich Ebert Stiftung Foundation.

Navarro, Luiz Hernandez. (2001). "Indigenous Poverty and Social Mobilization," Willem van Genugten and Camilo Perez-Bustello (eds.), *The Poverty of Rights,* London & New York: Zed Books.

Ncube, Welshman. (1993). "Constitualism and Human Rights: Challenges of Democracy," Pearson Nherere and Marina d'Engelbronner-Kolff, *The Institutionalisation of Human Rights in Southern Africa*, Copenhagen : Nordic Human Rights Publications.

Nkiwane, Tandeka. (2001). "African Challenges to Liberalism," Kevin C. Dunn and Timothy M. Shaw (eds.). (2003). *Africa's Challenge to International Relations Theory*, London: Palgrave.

Namibian Society for Human Rights (NSHR). (2002). *Namibia: Human Rights Report 2002*, Windhoek: NSHR

Nyang'oro, Julius and Timothy M. Shaw. (1998). "The African State in the Global Economic Context," Leonardo Villalon and Phillip A. Huxtable (eds.), *The African State at a Critical Juncture*, Boulder: Lynne Rienner Publishers.

Obeng, Kenneth. (2001). *Botswana: Institutions of Democracy and Government of Botswana*, Gaborone, Botswana: Associated Printers.

Ochoa, Marco Aurelio Ugarte. (2000). "Poverty and Human Rights in the Light of the Philosophy and Contributions of Father Joseph Wresinski," Willem van Genugten and Camilo Perez-Bustello (eds.), *The Poverty of Rights: Human Rights and the Eradication of Poverty*, London & New York: Zed Books.

Overseas Development Institute. (1992). *Democracy, Governance and Economic Policy: Sub-Saharan African in Comparative Perspective*, London: Overseas Development Institute.

Off, Carole. (2001). *The Lion, The Fox and The Eagle*, Toronto: Random House of Canada.

O'Hara, Maureen. (1995). "Constructing Emancipatory Realities," Walter Truett Aanderson (ed.), *The Truth about the Truth*, New York: Penguin Putnam Inc.

Okafor, Obiora Chinedy. (2000). *Re-Defining Legitimate Statehood*, The Hague, Boston & London: Martinus Nijhoff Publishers.

Oppenheimer, Franz. (1975). *The State*, Quebec: Black Rose Books.

Orwell, George. (2003). *1984*, available at: http://www.online-literature.com/orwell/1984/, accessed 7 August 2003.

Parpart Jane L., Shirin M. Rai and Kathleen Staudt (eds.) (2002). *Rethinking Empowerment: gender and development in a global/local world,* London & New York: Routledge.

Parpart, Jane. (1995). "Deconstructing the Development Expert: Gender Development and the Vulnerable Groups, Marianne Marchand and Jane Parpart (eds.), *Feminism Postmodernism Development*, London & New York: Routledge.

Peterson, Spike. (ed.). (1992). *Gendered States: Feminist (Re) Visions of International Relations Theory*, Boulder & London: Lynne Rienner Publishers.

Pettman, Jan Jindy. (1996). *Worlding Women*, London & New York: Routledge.

Pierre, Jon. 2000. *Debating Governance*, Oxford: Oxford University Press.

Pierson, Christopher. (1996). *The Modern State*, London: Routledge.

Pieterse, Jan Nederveen. (2002). *Development Theory: Deconstructions/Reconstructions*, London, Thousand Oaks & New Dehli: Sage Publications.

Powers, Samantha. (2001, September). *Bystanders to Genocide: America in the Age of Genocide*, The Atlantic Monthly On-line, available at: http://www.mtholyoke.edu/acad/intrel/power.htm, accessed 12 December 2001.

Reason, Peter. (1994). "Three Approaches to Participative Inquiry," Norman Denzin and Yvonna Lincoln (eds.), *Handbook of Qualitative Research*, Thousand Oaks, London & New Dehli: Sage Publications.

Reno, William. (1998). *Warlord Politics and African States*, Boulder: Lynne Rienner Publishers.

Rhodes, R.A.W. (2000). "Governance and Public Administration," Jon Pierre (ed.), *Debating Governance*, Oxford: Oxford University Press.

Righter, Rosemary. (1995). *Utopia Lost: The United Nations and World Order*, New York: The Twentieth Century Fund Press.

Risse-Kappen, Thomas. (1997). "Between a New World Order and None: Explaining the Reemergence of the United Nations in World Politics," Michael C. Williams and Keith Krause (eds.), *Critical Security Studies*, Minneapolis: University of Minnesota Press.

Robbins, Richard H. (1999). *Global Problems and the Culture of Capitalism*, SUNY at Plattsburg: Allyn and Bacon Publishing, Inc.

Rosenau, James. (1992). *The United Nations in a Turbulent World*, Boulder: Lynne Reinner Publishers.

Ruggie, John Gerard. (2003, July-September). "The United Nations and Globalization: Patterns and Limits of Institutional Adaptation," *Global Governance*, 9:3.

Ruggie, John Gerald. (1998). "What Makes the World Hang Together? Neo-utilitarianism and the Social Constructivist Challenge," *International Organisation*, 52:4.

Rugumamu, S. (1999). *Foreign Aid, Grassroots Participation and Poverty Alleviation in Tanzania: The HESAWA Fiasco*, Dar es Salaam: REPOA.

Rummel, R.J. (1997). *Death By Government*, New Brunswick, NJ: Transaction Publishers.

SARDC. (1999). *Democracy: factfile—Tanzania*, Harare: SARDC.

Schmitz. Gerald. (1995). "Democratization and Demystification: Deconstructing 'Governance as Development Paradigm," David Moore and Gerald Schmitz (eds), *Debating Development Discourse: International and Popular Perspectives*, Basingstoke: Macmillan.

Schwandt, Thomas. (1994). "Constructvist, Interpretivist Approaches to Human Inquiry," Norman Denzin and Yvonna Lincoln (eds.), *Handbook of Qualitative Research*, Thousand Oaks, London, New Dehli: Sage Publications.

Scott, James C. (1998). *Seeing Like a State: how certain schemes to improve the human condition have failed*, New Haven: Yale University Press.

Scott, Bruce. (2003; 2001). "The Great Divide in the Global Village," Robert Griffiths (ed.), *The Developing World 03/04*, Connecticut: McGraw-Hill.

Selolwane, Onalenna Doo. (1998). "Gender and Democracy in Botswana: Women's Strugge for Equality and Political Participation," Georges Nzongola-Ntalaja and Margaret Lee (eds.), *The State and Democracy in Africa*, Trenton, Eritrea: Africa World Press.

Sen, Amartya. (2000). *Development as Freedom*, New York: Anchor Books.

Shaw, Martin. (1999). "Global Voices: civil society and the media in global crisis," Tim Dunne and Nicholas Wheeler (eds.), *Human Rights in Global Politics*, Cambridge: Cambridge University Press.

Shaw, Timothy M. (1984). "The Political Economy of Self-Determination: A World Systems Approach to Human Rights in Africa," Clause E. Welsh, Jr. and Donald I. Meltzer (eds.), *Human Rights and Development in Africa*, Albany: State University of New York Press.

Shaw, Timothy M. (2001). "African Foreign Policy in the New Millennium: From Coming Anarchies to Security Communities? From New regionalisms to New Realisms?" Kevin C. Dunn and Timothy M. Shaw (eds.), *Africa's Challenge to International Relations Theory*, London: Palgrave.

Shaw, Timothy M. (2002). "Peace-building Partnerships and Human Security," Vandana Desai and Robert Potter (eds.), *The Companion to Development*, London: Arnold.

Shawcross, William. (2000). *Deliver Us from Evil: Peacekeepers, Warlords and a World of Endless Conflict*, London: Bloomsbury.

Sheikh, Leila. (2001, February). "The Place of A Woman in the Media," *The Journalist*, Dar es Salaam: Association of Journalists and Media Workers.

Shore, Cris and Susan Wright. (1997). "Policy: a new field for anthropology," Cris Shore and Susan Wright (eds.), *Anthropology of Policy: Critical Perspectives on Governance and Power*, London: Routledge.

Smith, Steve. (1991). "Reflectivist and Constructivist Approaches to International Theory," John Baylis and Steve Smith (eds), *The Globalisation of World Politics*, Oxford: Oxford University Press.

Snyder, Jack. (2000). *From Voting to Violence: Democratisation and Nationalist Conflict*, New York: W.W. Norton and Company.

Sorensen, Georg. (1996). "Development as Hobbesian Dilemma," *Third World Quarterly*, 17:5.

Steiner, Henry and Philip Alston. (2001). *International Human Rights in Context*, Oxford: Oxford University Press.

Strauss, Anselm and Juliet Corbin. (1994). "Grounded Theory Methodology: An Overview," Norman Denzin and Yvonna Lincoln (eds.), *Handbook of Qualitative Research*, Thousand Oaks, London, New Dehli: Sage Publications.

Stromberg, Roland. (1996). *Democracy: a short, analytical history*, New York: M.E. Sharpe.

Swatuk, Larry. (1999). *What Clinton Didn't See: Botswana as Paragon of Democracy and Stability*, unpublished manuscript.

Thérien, Jean-Philippe. (1999). "Beyond the North-South divide: the two tales of world poverty," *Third World Quarterly*, 20: 4.

Tilly, Charles. (1987). *From Mobilization to Revolution*, Reading, MA: Addison-Wesley.

Turok, Ben. (1987). *Africa: what can be done?* London: Zed Books.

Twangiramariya, Clotilde and Meredith Turshen. (1999). "What Women do in Wartime," Meredeth Turshen and Clotilde Twagiramariya (eds.), *What Women do in Wartime*, London & New York: Zed Books.

United States Department of State. (2002). *Country Reports on Human Rights Practices*, released by the Bureau of Democracy, Human Rights and Labour, March 4, 2002.

Vale, Peter. (2003). *Security and Politics in South Africa: the regional dimension*, Boulder & London: Lynne Rienner Publishers.

van Cranenburg, Hans. (1999). "International Policies to Promote African Democratization," Jean Grugel (ed.), *Democracy Without Borders: Transnationalisation and Conditionality in New Democracies*, London & New York: Routledge.

Van Creveld, Martin. (2000). *The Rise and Decline of the State*, Cambridge: Cambridge University Press.

van der Waals, W.S. (1993). *Portugal's War in Angola 1961–1974*, Gaborone: Ashanti Publishing.

Ufford, Phillippe Quarles. (1988). "The Hidden Crisis in Development: Development Bureaucracies," Philip Quarles van Ufford, Dirk Kruijt, Theodore Downing (eds.), *The Hidden Crisis in Development: Development Bureaucracies*, Amsterdam: Free University Press.

Weiss, Thomas. (2000). "Governance, good governance and global governance: conceptual and actual challenges," *Third World Quarterly*, 21:5.

Weiss, Thomas and David Pitt (eds.). (1986). *The Nature of United Nations Bureaucracies*, London & Sydney: Croom Helm.

Welsh, Scott. (2002). "Deliberative Democracy and the Rhetorical Production of Political Culture," *Rhetoric and Public Affairs*, 5:4.

Wilson, J. Zoë. (2005a). 'Truth, Certainty and Subjectivity: the ethics of war-time research in contested spaces.' Researching Violently Divided Societies. Elisabeth Porter *et al.* (eds.). Tokyo: United Nation University Press.

Wilson, J. Zoë. (2005b). 'State-making, Peacemaking and the Inscription of Gendered Politics into Peace: lessons from Angola.' *Gender, Complex Emergencies, and Peacekeeping: National and International Feminist Perspectives.* Jane Parpart, Angela Raven-Roberts and Dyan Mazurana (eds.), Rowman & Littlefield Publishers, Inc.

Wilson, J. Zoë. (2004). 'Paradoxes and Dilemmas of Institutional Change: human rights and livelihoods in rural Angola.' *Journal of Peacebuilding and Development*. Vol. 2, No.1. Dec.

Wilson, J. Zoë and David Black. (2004). "Foreign Policy and the Politics of Identity: Human Rights, Zimbabwe's 'land crisis' and South Africa's 'quiet diplomacy," Patricia M. Goff and Kevin C. Dunn (eds.), *Identity and Global Politics: Theoretical and Empirical Elaborations*, New York: Palgrave.

Wilson, J. Zoë and Arsene Mwaka. (2003). "Angola after Savimbi: is there new hope for the region?" Frederick Soderbaum and Andrew Grant (eds), *New Regionalisms in Africa*, Burlington, VT: Ashgate.

Wilson, J. Zoë. (2002). 'International Citizen and Subject: constructive engagement post-Savimbi," Sandra J. Maclean, Timothy M. Shaw and John Harker (eds), *Advancing Human Security and Development in Africa*, Halifax: Centre for Foreign Policy Studies.

Wilson, J. Zoë. (1998). "Gender Discrimination Re-conceptualized as Market Distortion: A Critique of World Bank Structural Adjustment Theory for Sub-Saharan Africa," *Scandinavian Journal of Development Alternatives*, 17:2&3. June-September.

Woo-Cummings, Meredith (ed.). (1999). *The Developmental State*, Ithaca & London: Cornell University Press.

World Bank (2005). 'Meeting the Challenge of Africa's Development: A World Bank Group Action Plan,' Washington: *Africa Region*, 7 September.

World Bank. (2002). *World Development Report: Building Institutions for Markets*, Oxford: Oxford University Press.

World Bank. (2001). *Enhancing Human Development in the HIPC/PRSP Context: Progress in the African Region 2000*, Washington: The World Bank.

Young, Iris Marion. (1997). "Difference as a Resource for Democratic Communication," James Bohman and William Rehg (eds.), *Deliberative Democracy: Essays on Reason and Politics*, Cambridge, MA & London: The MIT Press.

Zolo, Danilo. (2000). "The Lords of Peace: from the holy alliance to the new international criminal tribunals," in Barry Holden (ed.), *Global Democracy: Key Debates*, London: Routledge.

UN Texts Examined

CCF-Common Country Framework. (2001). *Second country cooperation framework for the United Republic of Tanzania*, DP/CCF/URT/2

CCF—Common Country Framework. (1997). *UNDP: Country cooperation frameworks and related matters: first country cooperation framework for Botswana (1997–2002)*, DP/CCF/BOT/1.

ECA—Economic Commission for Africa. (2001). *Second Regional Cooperation Framework for Africa*, available at: http://www.uneca.org/cfm/25/Position%20paper%20on%20%20UNDP%202%20Regional%20cooperationframework.htm; accessed 19 December 2001.

OCHA—Office for the Coordination of Humanitarian Affairs. (2000). *OCHA Provincial Profile: Uige Province*, Angola Country Office, United Nations Office for the Coordination of Humanitarian Affairs.

UNDP—United Nations Development Program. (2002). *Local Governance and Poverty Reduction in Africa: UN-AGF-V Concept Paper*, Angola Country Office, United Nations Office for the Coordination of Humanitarian Affairs.

Republic of Angola. (2001). *Internal Regulations of the Provincial Comitee [sic] on Human Rights: Uige Province*, Angola Country Office, United Nations Office for the Coordination of Humanitarian Affairs.

UNDP—United Nations Development Program. (2000). *Human Development Report*, United Nations Development Program: Oxford University Press.

UNDP—United Nations Development Program. *Human Development Report*, United Nations Development Program: Oxford University Press.

UNDP—United Nations Development Program. (2002). *United Nations Development Assistance Framework for Namibia*, Windhoek: UNDP.

United Nations General Assembly (2001a). *United Nations Millennium Declaration*, available http://www.un.org/millennium/declaration/ares552e.htm; accessed April 26, 2002.

United Nations General Assembly (2001b*). Road map towards the implementation of the United Nations Millennium Declaration*, A/56/326

United Nations General Assembly (1998). *The causes of conflict and the promotion of durable peace and sustainable development in Africa*, available at http://www.un.org/ecosocdev/geninfo/afrec/sgreport/report.htm; accessed April 26, 2002.

United Nations General Assembly. (1996). *Implementation of the United Nations New Agenda for the Development of Africa*, A/51/228.

United Nations General Assembly. (1993). *United Nation New Agenda for the Development of Africa in the 1990s*, A/48/334.

United Nations General Assembly and Economic and Social Council. (1999). *Development of Africa: implementation of the recommendations in the report of the Secretary-General to the Security Council and the General Assembly*, A/54/133.

United Nations Inter-Agency consolidated Appeal for Angola. (2001). *Summary of Requirements and Contributions—By Appealing Organization as of 01-April-2004, available at:* http://www.reliefweb.int/fts/reports/pdf/OCHA_1_503.pdf; accessed 17 May 2004.

UNHCR—United Nations High Commission for Refugees. (July 2000—December 2001). *Angola: IDP Protection Programme*, Angola Country Office, United Nations Office for the Coordination of Humanitarian Affairs.

United Nations Security Council. (2000). *Report of the Secretary-General in the United Nations Office in Angola.* S/2000/304.

Index

www.ingramcontent.com/pod-product-compliance
Ingram Content Group UK Ltd.
Pitfield, Milton Keynes, MK11 3LW, UK
UKHW020432010325
455677UK00029B/1124